37859   nd

F   Hafen, Le Roy
592   Reuben, 1893-
.F58
H33   Broken Hand, the
1981   life of Thomas
            Fitzpatrick,
            mountain man, guide
            and Indian agent

DATE	BORROWER'S NAME	

Broker

University of Nebraska Press / Lincoln and London

The Life of Thomas Fitzpatrick:
Mountain Man, Guide
and Indian Agent

BY LEROY R. HAFEN

)and

First Bison Book printing: 1981
Most recent printing indicated by first digit below:
1   2   3   4   5   6   7   8   9   10

Library of Congress Cataloging in Publication Data

Hafen, LeRoy Reuben, 1893–
    Broken Hand, the life of Thomas Fitzpatrick, mountain man, guide and Indian agent.

    Reprint of the ed. published by Old West Pub. Co., Denver.
    Includes bibliographical references and index.
    1. Fitzpatrick, Thomas, 1799–1854. 2. Frontier and pioneer life—The West. 3. The West—History—To 1848. 4. Pioneers—The West—Biography.
    I. Title.
[F592.F58H33 1981]   978′.02′092′4 [B]   80–23451
    ISBN 0–8032–7208–1 (pbk.)

Published by arrangement with LeRoy R. Hafen
Manufactured in the United States of America

To my wife
Mary Woodbury Hafen

Contents

Illustrations

Thomas Fitzpatrick

Preface

MY OWN CONNECTION with the biography of Thomas
Fitzpatrick and the publishing house that produced it, may
be of some interest. The Fur Trade of the West intrigued
me from the first days of my graduate study. Upon receiv-
ing the appointment as State Historian of Colorado in 1924,
I hustled my wife and two children into the four-year-old
model T and drove from Berkeley to Denver.

With a good position and a great challenge, I plunged
into the study and writing of Colorado history, not neglect-
ing the transportation and fur trade phases of the story.
I amplified somewhat my doctoral dissertation of 1924 and
it was published as the *Overland Mail to California*, in 1926.
I unearthed foundations of fur trade posts on the banks of
the South Platte and revelled in the search for fugitive material on the trappers and their business. An outstanding
figure in the trade emerged as Thomas Fitzpatrick, whom
I soon selected for a biography.

After I had finished the first draft of the complete story
I learned that W. J. Ghent, of Washington, D.C., a good
popular writer, was working on the same subject. Through
correspondence we agreed to pool our resources, especially
upon Ghent's assurance that he could produce a popular
account and sell it to a leading magazine for serialization.

With the Depression which followed the financial col-
lapse of 1929, the publication market slumped and Ghent

failed to get an acceptance of the manuscript. Being eager for early publication, I dreamed up a scheme to achieve the goal. To my friend John Van Male, endeavoring to develop a book selling business, I suggested that we start a publication venture. Inasmuch as I was to teach a summer session at the University of Colorado and would be getting some extra money, we could start the project. We would give the printer a down payment, and promise most of the rest in sixty days. I would see copy through the press and Van Male would circularize his customers and handle the sales and bookkeeping. Mr. Ghent, somewhat discouraged at his failure to sell the story, agreed to accept $100 as advance on his half of the royalties and release the manuscript to us.

We proceeded with dispatch, and the book came out in 1931 under our new imprint, "The Old West Publishing Company." The printing order was for a 500 regular and a 100 special edition; the first priced at $5.00 and the second at $7.50. We had the printer hold the type for a possible second run. The sales went pretty well; within two years the books were sold; but the demand was satisfied. We had paid all bills and gave a ten per cent royalty to the authors; but there was very little left for division between the two business partners.

Finally we released the type and gave up the hope for a reissue. Continuation of the Depression dulled and eventually destroyed hope of continuing the publication venture.

After Mr. Van Male's early and lamented death, my very good friend, Fred Rosenstock, was about to launch a publishing venture. His first book was to be Melvin Schoberlin's *From Candles to Footlights,* and the second was to be a Colorado school history by my wife and me. He was pleased to accept the suggestion that he take over and publish under the name, "The Old West Publishing Company." He has continued to use the name, giving luster to it with the outstanding volumes he has issued under the imprint.

Through the successive years the demand for copies of *Broken Hand; The Life Story of Thomas Fitzpatrick, Chief of the Mountain Men,* has persisted, with the price in the rare book market running in recent years well above $100.

Mr. Rosenstock has for some years urged the preparation of a new, revised edition; and I have continued to search out new material. Finally my desk was cleared sufficiently for me to undertake a revision.

In the forty-two years since the first publication, competent and dedicated scholars have unearthed substantial new facts and much additional information. This has necessitated a complete rewriting of the first half of the book and considerable revision of the remainder. We trust that the new biography will serve its intended purpose and have general acceptance.

LEROY R. HAFEN

Provo, Utah

Introduction

THE LIFE STORY OF THOMAS FITZPATRICK is an epitome of the early history of the Far West. The whole region north of the Spanish settlements was his theater of action. His career covered the thirty-year period from the opening of the rich fur country west of the Rockies to the beginning of settlements beyond the Great Bend of the Missouri.

No other man is so representative of this epoch. He was with Ashley on the second voyage up the Missouri. He was one of the little party that in March 1824, made the effective discovery of South Pass, the future gateway to Oregon. He was a leader of trapper bands, an explorer of the wilderness, an Indian fighter, the head of the Rocky Mountain Fur Company. He guided the first two emigrant trains that set out for the Western Coast by the Oregon Trail, and he took Father De Smet and his fellow missionaries all the way into the remote country of the Flatheads. He was at once guide and adjutant to Frémont on the expedition that crossed the High Sierras in midwinter. He showed Kearny, with the Dragoons, the way to South Pass; he led Abert safely through the hostile country from Bent's Fort along the Purgatory and the Canadian to Fort Gibson; he guided the Army of the West, under Kearny, to Santa Fe, and the California expedition as far as Socorro. He was the first agent appointed for the wild tribes of the plains — a post that he held until his death; and he passed away in the year that white men were first permitted to settle in Kansas and Nebraska (1854).

No man of his time and place was more widely and favorably known. The testimony that comes down to us from those who knew him portrays a man of dauntless courage and tireless activity, skillful and persevering in every task that he undertook. His reports and letters reveal a man of broad sympathies, of keen intelligence and close observation — a reading and thinking man, well schooled, and gifted with a turn for accurate and telling expression.

He died at the height of his fame; yet by some caprice of history he was gradually forgotten. Then some scholars noted the infrequent references to him in early newspapers and government documents, and became conscious of his importance. But by 1902 the great historian of the fur trade, H. M. Chittenden, wrote of Fitzpatrick: "His comings and goings are lost behind the scenes, and all that is known of him is from transient glimpses while he is passing across the stage before us."

When work on a full-length biography of him was begun in the 1920s, no one could say, from any current print, where and when he was born, or when and how he died; nor was much available in accessible sources to fill out his life story.

The biography by Hafen and Ghent, published in 1931, was issued in a small edition that soon went out of print and became difficult and expensive to obtain. It is hoped that this new edition will fill the need for an available full-length biography of Thomas Fitzpatrick, and will help to give him the high place he deserves among the early pioneers of Western America.

Chapter 1

Up the Missouri and the
Arikara Fight

IN THE FRONTIER CAPITAL OF ST. LOUIS excitement
mounted as March 10 approached. In this spring of 1823
two keelboats lay at the wharf ready for a great venture:
to carry a large trapping expedition up the Missouri River
to the fabulous Yellowstone country. The departure would
be no ordinary event. This was a William Henry Ashley
expedition, and the distinguished man, General of the
Militia and Lieutenant Governor of the newly-created
State, would himself be its leader.

A year before he had given a fresh impetus to the fur
trade by breaking into a field of competitors and taking
trappers to the upper Missouri. Three boats he had dispatched from St. Louis in 1822. The first, under his experienced partner Andrew Henry, had reached its destination;
the second had floundered, and $10,000 in boat and goods
was swallowed by the hungry river. The third boat Ashley
had himself captained, successfully taking it to the mouth

3

of the Yellowstone.[1] After directing his men to trapping fields, he had returned to St. Louis, here to prepare re-enforcements for the following spring.

It was a thriving and confident little city in which Ashley formed his new company in early 1823. St. Louis faced the West. Already the emporium of the western fur trade and center of river commerce, she kept a jealous eye on the traffic from the upper Missouri, where British forces intruded, and peered covetously across the plains at the Mexican trade in the Southwest.

The census of 1820, as *Missouri Gazette & Illinois Advertiser* somewhat proudly announced about the end of the year, had shown a growth in population from the meager 1,400 of 1810 to the proud total of 4,598. There were fifteen physicians, twenty-three lawyers, and forty-nine grocers and tavernkeepers; there were two printing offices, a bank, at least one hotel "of consequence," and within or near its boundaries two sawmills and a gristmill.[2] Perhaps a thousand more inhabitants had been added

---

[1] For firsthand accounts of the adventures and adventurers of 1822 see Jedediah Smith's report in Maurice S. Sullivan, *The Travels of Jedediah Smith* (Santa Ana, Calif., 1934), 1–10; Daniel T. Potts' story and contemporary newspaper accounts in Donald M. Frost, *Notes on General Ashley, the Overland Trail, and South Pass* (Worcester, Mass., 1945); and Dale L. Morgan, *The West of William H. Ashley* (Denver, 1964), 59–70. Excellent summary narratives with discussion of settings and events, and with quotations and citation of sources are: Dale L. Morgan, *Jedediah Smith and the Opening of the West* (Indianapolis, 1953); John Sunder, *Bill Sublette, Mountain Man* (Norman, Okla., 1959); J. Cecil Alter, *James Bridger, Frontiersman, Scout and Guide* (Salt Lake City, 1925); and Don Berry, *A Majority of Scoundrels; an Informal History of the Rocky Mountain Fur Company* (New York, 1961).

[2] *Missouri Historical Society Collections*, V, no. 2 (Feb. 1928), 166. The description of St. Louis is based on this publication and on a number of other sources, such as F. L. Billon, *Annals of St. Louis in its Territorial Days from 1804 to 1821* (St. Louis, 1888), *Edwards' Great West* (St. Louis, 1860); and contemporary newspapers.

during the last two years. Surely the village was becoming a metropolis.

True enough, it was a primitive sort of city. A few of the great traders had what were then considered palatial homes, but most of the houses were small and mean, and widely scattered, for only part of one of the streets was closely built. The city had little of the order and cleanliness of some of the cities farther east. Except for a few short stretches here and there it was unpaved, and it had no sidewalks to speak of. In rainy spells its inhabitants waded ankle deep in mud; and in dry spells they walked through whirling dust. At night they made their way by the dim light of lanterns.

But despite its crudities and discomforts it bore a cosmopolitan air. All sorts and conditions of men and women thronged its streets. Buckskin-clad trappers and hunters, back from the wilderness, wandered about or gathered in the grogshops. Bands of gaily dressed Indian warriors, with their women and children, came in to talk with the Redhead Father, General William Clark, and pitching their tepees on the vacant lots, passed up and down, staring at all the wonders of this settlement of the incomprehensible palefaces. Boatmen, emigrants from across the Mississippi, visitors from foreign lands to see this famed outpost of civilzation, merchants, mechanics, jobless wanderers, women of all ranks from the slave negress to the richly dressed trader's wife, passed back and forth in shifting procession.

It was neither a quiet nor a peaceful city. Political feeling ran high, and there was free indulgence in bitter personalities. The cruder sort of men settled their differences on the spur of the moment with fists or weapons, the more

5

dignified by the duel; and the favorite ground for affairs of honor, Bloody Island, in the Mississippi, saw victims brought to their death. Brawls on the streets or in the taverns were common, and murder was not infrequent.

It was a city of many extremes. Of the resident population probably a half was by now white Americans. Though the recent influx represented in large part the rougher element of the frontier, it included men and women of the best types — an element that, joining with the old French families, formed a society of exceptional refinement and cultivation. The steamboat had broken the former isolation, placing the city within easy distance of the cities to the east and bringing arts and creature comforts to which it had been unaccustomed. From the old French village days the people had retained their love of social gatherings — of music, dancing and card playing. In spite of a long struggle against clerical condemnation they had now firmly established a theater.

The fame of the dancing entertainments of the city had spread to the East, and so also that of the beauty, grace, and rich garmenting of its women. "I never saw anywhere," wrote the young Philadelphian, Henry Marie Brackenridge, "greater elegance of dress than at the balls of St. Louis." Though it was not at this time the capital of the new State — the legislature having fixed the seat of government at the insignificant village of St. Charles — it remained, nevertheless, the commercial and social capital of a great empire — the Rome of all that vast region from the Mississippi to the Spanish settlements in the Southwest and on the Pacific.

Into this city, in the winter of 1822–23, came a young man eager to see the Great West. Thomas Fitzpatrick was his name — though in later times he was to be widely known as "Broken Hand" and "White Hair." He was born in County Cavan, of the "Ould Sod," in 1799. We know little about his youth except that he came of what is called a "good family," with some pretensions to gentility; that it was a Catholic family, and that he received the fundamentals of a sound education.[3] From what we know of him in later years we may picture him as of about medium height, of somewhat slender frame, though well knit and muscular; alert, active, keen-sighted, and with good Irish color in his cheeks. A restless fever in his blood caused him to leave home before he was seventeen and to come to the United States. He sought the Middle West, doubtless knocked about in various capacities, and before long found himself in the Indian trade, probably as a clerk somewhere along the upper Mississippi. He was of the authentic stuff of which the pioneer explorers were made, and he longed to penetrate the wilderness of the Far West. The Ashley expedition was his opportunity, and he signed up for the voyage.

He must, while waiting for the day of departure, have come to know many of those who were to be his companions on that historic voyage. Already at the Yellowstone were Major Andrew Henry, Jedediah Smith, Etienne Provost, Daniel Potts, and young James Bridger, who had

---

[3] Most of the family data — distressingly scant — came in letters to LeRoy R. Hafen from Fitzpatrick's daughter Virginia, dated June 7 and Sept. 24, 1928, from El Reno, Oklahoma; from his grandniece, Mrs. M. G. McCarthy of Washington, D.C., Mar. 14, 1929; and from W. J. Ghent's interview with Mrs. McCarthy in September 1928. Fitzpatrick's mother's maiden name was Mary Kiernan; his father's given name not known. Thomas Fitzpatrick had two brothers, Francis and Patrick; and four sisters, Mary, Katherine, Elizabeth, and Bridget. Mary, who married Bartholomew Leonard, was Mrs. McCarthy's grandmother. This Mrs. Leonard told her granddaughter that some of her ancestors owned a castle in Ireland, called Castle Hamilton, and that they lost it during the Cromwell invasion.

made the voyage the previous year. In this new company
was a Virginian frontiersman seven years older than Fitzpatrick — James Clyman, whose diaries and recollections
were to reveal to us so much of the history of that early
time; William L. Sublette, a Kentuckian of the same age
as Fitzpatrick, later to attain a leading place in the fur
trade; Louis Vasquez, to be Bridger's partner in the celebrated trading post of Fort Bridger; Thomas Eddie, who
was to outlive most, if not all of his companions; and that
strange half-savage mulatto, Edward Rose, whose incredible career makes the most adventurous fiction seem tame
and pallid.[4] With most of these men Tom Fitzpatrick was
to be closely associated in after years; with some he was
to enjoy a lifelong friendship.

At the wharf on March 10 lay the two large keelboats,
the *Rocky Mountains* and the *Yellow Stone Packet*. Each
was about fifty feet long by fifteen feet beam, with sharp
bow and stern, a mast and sails. The hull was decked over,
forming a compartment about five or six feet deep, where
supplies were stored. At the bow was a small cannon.
Amidships was the cabin, and on each side, extending the
length of the boat, was a narrow walk, or *passeavant*, along
which the men could walk while poling the vessel through
shallow water.

On or about the boats was a force of about a hundred

[4] The careers of J. S. Smith, W. L. Sublette, and James Bridger are detailed in
the excellent biographies cited above. The experiences of James Clyman, as reported in his "reminiscences and diaries," were presented by Charles L. Camp
in 1928 and then in a "Definitive Edition" by the same editor in 1960. The
others named have not been honored by full-length biographies but Edward
Rose's adventures are recounted in Reuben Holmes, "The Five Scalps," first
appearing in a St. Louis newspaper and later in *Glimpses of the Past* (Missouri
Historical Society Publications), V, 12–18.

8

trappers, hunters, and boatmen, who had responded to the Ashley and Henry advertisement offering $200 per year for trapper service.[5] Despite the presence among them of a number of sterling men, later to become noted, the crew as a whole was an uncouth, ragamuffin body, composed of the odds and ends of humanity, picked up on the streets, in taverns, and wherever and however man could be induced to join.

A crowd gathered to witness the departure. It was an adventuresome journey on which these men were to set out. The voyagers would face the constant perils of the river; they would traverse the country of the arrogant Sioux and of the treacherous Arikaras and might even invade the strongholds of the implacable Blackfeet. By hard labor and favored by lucky circumstance, they might reach the Yellowstone in four or five months. The hazards of the voyage were well known, and fathers and mothers, wives and children and friends of the voyagers would wait the long months in suspense for news.

The last orders were given, the last farewells were said; the boats slipped from their moorings and with spread sails started up the Mississippi toward the mouth of the Missouri, some fifteen miles away. What Fitzpatrick thought or felt on thus setting out into the unknown we cannot say. In later days he was to write long reports of his dealings with the Indians — reports which showed a mind richly stored, a faculty of close observations and a rare force and exactness of expression. But of his entrance into this strange new world and of his many adventures in the years immediately

---

[5] The advertisements appeared in the *Missouri Republican* of Jan. 16, 1823 and subsequent issues, and in the *St. Louis Enquirer* of February 1.

following, he left so far as we are aware, no record. If he wrote letters to his people at home, they have perished. We know this part of his life only through the words of others, and sometimes the record is scant to the point of barrenness.

The boats entered the Missouri. From now on the men would have an unceasing struggle with the mighty and capricious stream. When the wind was fresh and the channel clear they would proceed by sail; when they came to shallows, they could move only by thrusting long poles into the oozy bottom and pushing the boat forward; at times they resorted to oars. But a main reliance for progress was the towline, or *cordelle,* attached on the mast and pulled by a squad of men walking along the bank. Trudging through water, mud, nettles, and brush, with hundreds of mosquitoes on their backs, the singing, shouting, swearing chorus would drag the boats forward at perhaps two miles an hour. The vigilance of pilot and helmsman must never be relaxed. The channel would be thickly sown with uprooted trees. There was the snag, often invisible, but nonetheless to be avoided; the "sawyer," or tree with roots embedded in the sand and with branches, under the influence of the currents, whipping the stream like a flail; there were sandbars, shallows, and falling banks.

Slowly the boats passed the little towns that had sprung up along the river. At St. Charles three men were conveying 300 pounds of powder in a cart to the boats when fire from a pipe ignited the powder. "The men were blown into the air to the height of several hundred feet, and the cart shivered to pieces," ran the report in the *Enquirer.*[6]

---

[6] Quoted in D. M. Frost, *op. cit.,* 71.

Upper: BULLBOATS AT MANDAN VILLAGE

Lower: KEELBOATS AND GROSVENTRE CAMP ON UPPER MISSOURI

(Drawings by Charles Bodmer for Maxmilian's *Travels*)

They reached Franklin, now enjoying its brief season of prosperity from the opening of the Santa Fe trade, but soon to be washed away; and farther on, Lexington, founded a year before. Here the settlements ended. It would be four years before the founding of Independence. At long intervals the boats would pass a lonely trading post, where a factor, or *bourgeois,* and a few trappers held a perilous position among the savages, who might at any time, in a fit of murderous caprice, wipe them out.

On and on they forced their way until, early in May, they came to the region of the old Council Bluffs, so named by Lewis and Clark; and here, about sixteen miles north of the present Omaha, they saw with delight the Stars and Stripes flying from a tall mast above the ramparts of a fortress. This was Fort Atkinson, the most western outpost of the Government, established as Camp Missouri late in 1819 by the Stephen H. Long Expedition, and now garrisoned by about 350 soldiers. It was at once a stronghold set up in the heart of the Indian country; a council place for the savages (for it had an Indian agent whose business it was to keep the Great Father's unruly red children from fighting one another); a recruiting point for trapping expeditions setting off into the interior; a resting place for wanderers, and a refuge from Indian attacks. Remote as it was, it kept in close communication with the settlements, for keelboats came to it often, steamboats occasionally, and mounted couriers, with private mail and Government messages, sped swiftly along the way to and from St. Louis. What this tower of refuge meant to the wanderers in that great wilderness can hardly, in these settled days, be imagined. Clyman, a year later, after losing his companions on the upper Platte, stoically started afoot over the six hundred miles of unknown country to the Missouri; and after eighty days of painful travel, half dead from fatigue and hunger, and not knowing where he was, suddenly looked up to the northeast, saw the flag flying and swooned for joy.[7]

Here the men landed, to be greeted with a hearty welcome and to be furnished with what they most craved, fresh vegetables. Eight or ten of the men, their courage having oozed out as they penetrated into the Indian country, chose the greater security of garrison life and therefore withdrew and enlisted as soldiers; while two or three enlisted men whose terms were expiring joined the party.

About ninety strong, they started forward again. Game became more plentiful. They passed the sites of the present Sioux City, Yankton, Chamberlain (near which the American Fur Company had recently set up a trading post, Fort Kiowa), and on past Pierre, to beyond the mouth of the Grand River. Here at last they were in the country of the dreaded Arikaras, and what they had heard on the voyage was not likely to allay their apprehensions. There had been brushes with these Indians recently. They had robbed some Missouri Fur Company men, and some trappers later killed two Arikaras; now the tribe was said to have declared war on all Americans.

Ashley's partner, Andrew Henry, who had wintered on the upper Missouri, 1822–23, was in need of horses and had sent Jedediah Smith down river to apprise Ashley of his requirements. So Ashley was eager to engage in trade and procure horses.

On the west bank of the Missouri, somewhat back from

---

[7] Camp's Clyman, *op. cit.*, 28.

a long crescent of sandy beach, were their two villages, the lower one being the smaller. Their dwellings were not the familiar tepees, but rounded structures looking for all the world like covered giant potato pits — eight or ten feet high in the center, dome topped, and ten or fifteen feet in diameter. Both villages were palisaded with good stout timbers, six to eight inches thick and twelve to fifteen feet high. The arrival of the whites was known at once, for the beach was seen to be lined with women scooping up water in pans and kettles. This labor was an ominous sign, for it meant that the Indians expected to withstand a siege.

Ashley, arrived at the Arikara villages on May 30, was at first cautious; and it would have been far better for him and his men if he had not later allowed his caution to be overcome by the fair words of the Arikara warriors. On May 31 he anchored his two boats, some distance apart, on a line about ninety feet from the beach, and with two men went ashore in a skiff. A party of warriors, including the chiefs, greeted him pleasantly and suggested that trading be opened. The General "sounded" them regarding their attitude, and they avowed the utmost friendliness. He accordingly agreed to trade on the following day, stipulating only that the market should be held on the beach instead of in the village, the place favored by the warriors. With all matters amicably settled, he returned to his boat; but later in the afternoon, on the invitation of Chief Bear, paid a brief visit to the village.

On the morning of the following day trade began. Ashley wanted horses, for he meant to divide his party and send one section to the Yellowstone by land. The Indians wanted only muskets and ammunition. When about forty horses had been obtained, trading ceased, and the General, leaving some forty men on the beach, returned to his boat. The white men's fears had been allayed, and on the morrow the expedition would be ready to move forward. The men on the shore continued their friendly relations with the warriors, and a few accepted without permission the invitation of the Arikaras to spend the night in the villages.

Darkness settled upon a scene of tranquility. But sometime after midnight Edward Rose burst into camp with the news that one of the whites who had gone to the villages had been killed and that the Arikaras were planning a general attack.[8] The other whites later came straggling in. Word was carried to Ashley. But the General, still serene in his belief that the Arikaras were well disposed, decided to wait till morning, when he would see the chiefs and demand the murderer.

About sunrise a shot was fired from the nearer village into the group of men and horses on the beach. It was evidently a signal, for at once firing became general. The land party of whites returned the fire, but with no effect, while their own unprotected position made them easy targets. Man and horse alike went down before the hail of lead. Ashley ordered his men with the boats to move inshore so as to combine forces for repelling the attack, but they were paralyzed with fear and broke out in open mutiny. Finally he succeeded in getting the two skiffs to the beach, and several of the land party climbed aboard; but the remainder, maddened by fury, determined to keep up the unequal

---

[8] The story of the contact and subsequent fight with the Arikaras is told in letters of General Ashley written immediately after the battle and published in Missouri newspapers (reprinted in Frost, *op. cit.*, 78–81); in Morgan, *West of General Ashley*, 25–31; in Clyman, 8–12; and in other sources.

contest. Under a withering fire they held their ground until they saw the hopelessness of further defense. The survivors, many of them wounded, then jumped into the river and swam for the boats, which immediately dropped downstream. Twelve men were killed outright; one or more mortally and about ten more or less seriously wounded. Over the bodies of John S. Gardner and Reed Gibson, two of the slain, Smith delivered what was called a "powerful prayer," and by some called the first act of public worship in South Dakota.

So ended the battle of June 2, 1823. At the first patch of downstream timber, in the vicinity of Ashley Island, the boats were halted and the men landed. Ashley pleaded and argued with his men to renew the voyage by running the gauntlet of the villages, but most of them refused. On the following morning he repeated his plea, but in vain. He called for volunteers, and thirty responded, but as for the rest they had enough of Indian warfare and wanted to go home. He then resolved to ask help of Colonel Henry Leavenworth, at Fort Atkinson, and accordingly sent downstream one of his boats, the *Yellow Stone Packet*, with five of the wounded and such of the others as refused to stay, along with a message to Leavenworth. He also sent two messengers across country to Major Henry, at the mouth of the Yellowstone, urging him to come and bring with him such men as he could spare. Soon afterward Ashley moved down some seventy miles to the mouth of the Cheyenne River, to await reinforcements.

What part Fitzpatrick had in this tragic encounter we do not know. There were brave deeds that went unrecorded and brave men unnamed. We may be sure that he bore his part, whatever it was, manfully; that he was among the last to leave the death-strewn beach, and that he was one of the thirty who volunteered to run the gauntlet of the Indian villages. We shall see a little later that he was placed second in command of a daring enterprise of the first importance — a post for which he would not have been chosen had he here failed in duty. He was, so far as we know, a novice, and this was his baptism of fire. He was to have many thrilling encounters with savages, and we cannot doubt that in this first shock of arms he displayed the resolute courage he is known to have borne in later days.

The messengers to Henry reached him soon after he himself had suffered a disaster at the hands of Indians, for attempting to invade the Missouri River region in the vicinity of the Great Falls. Four of his men had been killed by Blackfeet and the remainder were driven down the river to his post near the mouth of the Yellowstone. Leaving twenty men at this post he at once started downstream by boat with the remainder of his men, and before the end of June was at Ashley's camp.

The news of the Arikara disaster reached Colonel Leavenworth on June 18. On June 22, with about 250 soldiers and two six-pound cannon, he started north by land and water. On June 27 he was overtaken by Joshua Pilcher, head of the Missouri Fur Company, with some sixty men and a howitzer, and later on was joined by several bands of Sioux, eager to take part in a campaign against their ancient enemies. The various commands, totaling some 400 whites and 700 Indians, were united about August 1.

Ashley's force, now about eighty men, had been divided

into two companies, captained by Jedediah Smith and Hiram Scott, with William Sublette as sergeant-major and Fitzpatrick as quartermaster. On August 9 the little army reached the vicinity of the villages. Mounted Sioux attacked an advance party of Arikaras, and when the soldiers and traders came up the Arikaras retreated to their picket enclosure, leaving a number of dead behind. Thereupon the Sioux amused themselves by mangling and dissevering the bodies of the slain and strewing the fragments about the field. Within a few hundred yards of the village Colonel Leavenworth halted to await the bringing up of the artillery in the keelboats.

What followed has been frequently told and retold, and need not be repeated in detail.[9] There was mismanagement, indecision, delay. The Sioux, who could not be controlled, soon tired of the conflict, and after plundering the Arikara cornfield, stole some horses and mules and left the scene. During the next two days there was some desultory fighting. Then came a conference with some of the Arikaras and the signing of a treaty of peace, in which the warriors promised good behavior and the restoration of Ashley's property. They had no intention of keeping either promise, and at night they abandoned their villages and fled. Nothing of benefit had been accomplished, but only harm. The Sioux had left in disgust, contemptuous of the white man's military prowess; and the Arikaras, unpunished, were to continue for many years their wanton attacks.[10]

---

[9] A good general account is that of Dale Morgan in his *Jedediah Smith*, 67–77.
[10] A first report of the brush with the Arikaras was published in an extra in the Franklin *Missouri Intelligencer* of Sept. 9, 1823, and then in the regular edition of September 16. The official reports of Col. Leavenworth said the objects of the expedition were effected and that "the blood of our countrymen

Leavenworth, waiting in the evident belief that the Arikaras would return and give proof of their repentance, lost hope on August 15 and started with his troops downstream. So, about the same time, did Pilcher and his trappers. To Pilcher the whole episode was a crushing disaster. He had but recently suffered the defeat of a band of his trappers (the Jones-Immel party), with the loss of its furs, by the Blackfeet,[11] and he now found this nearer region rendered unsafe by the failure to teach the Arikaras a lesson. The disaster was wholly due, in his opinion, to the bad judgment and vacillation of Leavenworth. "You came (to use your own language)," he wrathfully wrote to the Colonel, "to 'open and make good this great road'; instead of which you have, by the imbecility of your conduct and operations, created and left impassable barriers."[12]

It was no less a disaster to Ashley. Frustrated in all his plans, he prepared to return to St. Louis. But he had with him an incomparable body of frontiersmen, many of whom were later to become famous in the annals of the West — "the most significant group of continental explorers," writes Harrison C. Dale, "ever brought together."[13] The problem of what to do with them now engaged his attention. He still had, at the mouth of the Yellowstone, a force of twenty

has been honorably avenged, the Aurickarees humbled." Others took a less rosy view. Joshua Pilcher was especially bitter in denouncing the Colonel. The controversy, as carried on in the press, is reprinted in Frost, *op. cit.*, 87–127. Leavenworth's official report was printed in *Sen. Ex. Doc. 1*, 18th Cong., 1st Sess. (Ser. 89), 55-108.

[11] For accounts of this affair see A. P. Nasatir, "The International Significance of the Jones and Immell Massacre and of the Aricara Outbreak in 1823," in *Pacific Northwest Quarterly*, XXX, 77–108; and Morgan's *Jedediah Smith*, 63–64 and 383.

[12] Reprinted in Frost, 114.

[13] H. C. Dale, *The Ashley-Smith Explorations and the Discovery of a Central Route to the Pacific* (Glendale, Calif., 1941), 84.

men, who might, if reinforced, accomplish something; and so he sent Henry, with perhaps twenty-five followers, to join them. Doubtless he also instructed Henry to move farther into the interior — even as far as the mouth of the Bighorn. With the remnant of his command he then dropped down to the trading post of Fort Kiowa.

His losses in men and property during this two years had been enormous. He was heavily in debt, and his credit was impaired. The Missouri River, by everyone regarded as the one road to the fur country, was now obstructed to a degree that made its further use hazardous. He was faced with ruin, and only some bold counter-stroke against fate might extricate him from his difficulties; this he was to take.

Chapter 2

Over South Pass
and in Green River Valley

NEWS OF THE RICH GLEANINGS made by the North West
Company and later by the Hudson's Bay Company west of
the Rockies fired the eagerness of American traders and
trappers to invade this ground. To one particular region
rumor had given a fabulous wealth of beaver. This was the
valley of the Spanish River, or Rio Colorado, now coming
to be known as the Rio Verde or the Green, in the western
part of what we now call Wyoming. No doubt Ashley had
meant to reach it, if possible, by the long and roundabout
course of the Missouri, the Yellowstone, and the Bighorn.
Now that he found the river route obstructed, he made the
bold decision to attempt to reach it overland. He would
send a party directly west to the country of the Crows and
thence across the continental divide to the Spanish River.

An inestimable advantage was his in having with him
the daredevil adventurer, Edward Rose. This man had voyaged with Manuel Lisa's party to the Bighorn in 1807,

had lived with the Crows, had been made by them a chief, and though he had deceived and deserted them, was still supposed to be held by them in some degree of favor.[1] In such an enterprise as Ashley's an intermediary would be of prime importance. For the Crows, though in later times almost uniformly friendly with the whites, were then a tribe of freebooters, given to the plundering of white and red alike. Although reached in 1743 by Verendrye, and probably by other Frenchmen subsequently, one of their first known contacts with American whites was in the summer of 1806, when they saw Clark's section of the Lewis and Clark company on its return down the Yellowstone, and stole the party's horses.

With Lisa's expedition to the Bighorn in the following year they had been friendly, and to the westbound Astorians of 1811, who had Rose as guide and interpreter, at least civil. But in the following year one of their bands had robbed Stuart's eastbound Astorians of their horses, compelling that heroic little party to make the rest of its long and painful journey to the Missouri afoot. They had since then distinguished themselves by various acts of plundering and pilfering among such trappers as they encountered. Rose, it was felt, could assure the party some protection.

This mid-region was, in the main, unknown. To the north it had been crossed by Wilson Price Hunt moving westward; somewhat to the south by Robert Stuart traveling east. Parts of it had been traversed by small parties from Lisa's Fort Raymond, on the Bighorn; by Henry's men from the stockade on Henry's Fork of the Snake; and by

---

[1] See Holmes, "The Five Scalps," *op. cit.*

Ezekiel Williams' party of wanderers from Lisa's Fort Mandan. Hudson's Bay Company brigades had ascended the Snake River branch of the Columbia and had pushed eastward to the Bear River and probably to the Green. From the east the region had been penetrated by Jacques Laramie and a few others into the southeastern quarter of what is now Wyoming. But of the hardy pioneers who ventured so far some never returned; and for lack of definite information about the region men satisfied themselves with vague guesses.

Ashley's enterprise was to find and utilize an easy pass over the continental divide, to change the westward route from the roundabout river course to a direct one from St. Louis, to create a highway to the Pacific, and incidentally to bring him, within three years, a comfortable fortune.

This historic little company, as Clyman remembered it some fifty years after, consisted of eleven men. Very likely the number was four or five more than that.[2] It was captained by Jedediah Smith, with Thomas Fitzpatrick as second in command, and it included William Sublette, James Clyman, Thomas Eddie, and Edward Rose. There was also a man named Stone and another named Branch, but the names of the others are not definitely known.[3] About the end of September, with a guide and horses borrowed from the "French company" of Berthold, Chouteau, and Pratte, the party left Fort Kiowa. Eagerly the men set forth, for

---

[2] Solitaire [John S. Robb], "Major Fitzpatrick, the Discoverer of the South Pass," in the *St. Louis Weekly Reveille,* Mar. 1, 1847, and reprinted in the present volume as Appendix B. This source is hereafter cited as Solitaire. This article says sixteen men.

[3] Frank Triplett, who interviewed Eddie about 1883, says in his *Conquering the Wilderness* (Chicago, 1883), 443, that "Old Bill" Williams and "Pegleg" Smith were in the party, but this statement has not been verified.

they knew that they were on no common quest. But the novices among them were soon to learn that the adventurous life they were so ardently seeking had perils and sufferings they had not contemplated.

After proceeding "westward over a dry rolling highland,"[4] they reached what was probably Medicine Creek, and followed it better than a day. Now the guide warned of a long dry stretch that would require twenty-four hours to cross. Facilities for carrying water were small and few. After a hard march they made a dry camp, and on the following day continued the journey, the men and animals suffering greatly from exhaustion and thirst. They reached the supposed waterhole only to find it dry. There was nothing to do but to keep on another fifteen miles to the next hole. The guide went ahead, and the half-crazed men began to scatter in the hope of finding water near at hand. Some of them, as their horses failed, gave up in despair and sank to the ground. Clyman, still going ahead in an attempt to follow the guide, stumbled onto a waterhole, fired his gun as a signal and then in a transport of joy "ran into the pool arm deep my horse foloing me." One after another the men with their mounts straggled up. Two of them who had been trailing behind, were left lying where they dropped; but Smith carried water back to them and brought them in.[5]

---

[4] Camp's *Clyman, op. cit.,* 15. Clyman's reminiscent account is the chief source for our story of this trip to the Crow country and into the Green River region, and where not otherwise credited, the information and quotations are taken from this narrative. Clyman's account is remarkable, the more so when we realize that it was written when he was 79 and 87 years of age (see the volume, edited by Charles Camp, pp. 7 and 25).

[5] The route from Fort Kiowa westward is difficult to determine. As Dr. Charles Camp states in his excellent edition of the Clyman narrative (p. 308), "Clyman's recollections are not wholly accurate and have been the source of speculation as to the route in this area." "There is no large bend on this part of White

The next day they came to the running water of White River, a clear stream with a gravelly bottom. Proceeding up the river they came to a camp of Sioux, from whom they were able to purchase enough horses to give each man a mount and a pack animal, with several horses in reserve. A guide, with the borrowed horses, now left them to return to the Missouri.

After ascending White River some distance they "proceeded north westerly over a dry roling Country for several days meting with Buffaloe now and then which furnished us with provision for at least one meal each day our luck was to fall in with the Oglela tiribe of Siouxs whare [we] traded a few more horses and swaped of[f] some of our more ordina[r]y.

"Country nearly the same short grass and plenty of cactus untill we crossed the [South Fork of] Chienne River a few miles below whare it leaves the Black Hill range of Mountains" (p. 17).

Upon entering the Black Hills, the country improved greatly, with pine and juniper covering a handsome region. As they descended the western slope of the Hills they thought the creeks encountered were waters of Powder River.[6] If so, the party was approaching Absaraka, the land of the Crows, whom they were seeking. So Edward Rose,

---

River," he admits, to account for about two days without water. Also, Clyman says they "proceded westward" from Fort Kiowa, which would bring them to Medicine Creek, instead of along a southwest course to White River. After following Medicine Creek for a day, a westward course would lead them over the dry region described, before they intercepted White River.

[6] They were not. The Cheyenne River with its two branches encircle the Black Hills, draining all slopes. The south branch, usually called the Cheyenne, flows around the south end and has such branches as Stockade and Beaver creeks that drain western slopes of the Hills. Similarly the Belle Fourche, northern branch of the Cheyenne, circles the north end of the Black Hills and drains the western portion of the northern section of the Hills.

who spoke the Crow language, was sent ahead to contact his Indian friends, the remainder of the party to follow "directly west as near as circumstances would permit."[7]

About five days later the party had its first experience with that most dreaded of wilderness animals, the grizzly bear. Winding in single file through a brushy bottomland, with Smith walking at the head, the little company made its way, no one dreaming of danger. Just as the leader reached the end of the thicket and emerged into an open glade, he was pounced upon by a gigantic bear, which felled him to the earth and grasped his head in its jaws. Before he could be rescued and the bear killed he had received frightful injuries. Several ribs were broken, and his head was badly lacerated. Though none of his companions knew anything about surgery, Smith, with iron will and perfect composure, directed a course of treatment. Some were sent for water to wash the wounds, while Clyman undertook repairs. He writes:

I got a pair of scissors and cut off his hair and then began my first job of d[r]essing wounds   upon examination I [found] the bear had taken nearly all of his head in his capcious mouth close to his left eye on one side and clos to his right ear on the other and laid the skull bare to near the crown of the head leaving a white streak whare his teeth passed   one of his ears was torn fom his head out to the outer rim   after stitching all the other wounds in the best way I was capabl and according to the capains directions the ear being the last I told him I could do nothing for his

---

[7] Their route over the Black Hills cannot be verified with certainty. It has been generally assumed that the party crossed the southern end of the Black Hills, and Clyman's description of the country appears to bear this out. But Clyman's statement that they took a "north westernly" course from the White to the Cheyenne River would suggest a crossing farther north. Also, after crossing the Black Hills, Clyman says they took as nearly as possible a directly westward course. And that took them to the upper Tongue River, a little north of modern Sheridan, Wyoming. This also would suggest a more northern crossing of the Black Hills.

Eare. O you must try to stich up some way or other said he   then
I put in my needle stiching it through and through and over and
over laying the lacerated parts togather as nice as I could with
my hands   water was found in about ame mille when we all moved
down and encamped the captain being able to mount his horse
and ride to camp whare we pitched a tent the onley one we had
and made him as comfortable as circumstances would permit (p. 18).

Near the scene of the accident the company encamped
a few days. Then it appears that Fitzpatrick pushed ahead
with most of the party, leaving two men to stay with Smith
while his wounds healed. Shortly afterward a party of
Missouri Fur Company men, under Charles Keemle and
William Gordon reached Smith, and together they followed
Fitzpatrick's trail and caught up with him at a Cheyenne
Indian camp.[8]

A day or two later the combined parties met Rose with
a party of Crows, from whom the whites obtained some
fresh horses. As they moved westward the Crows insisted
on moving too fast for the whites, who wanted to do some
trapping. So Rose and his Indians took their own gait, and
the Smith-Fitzpatrick party followed more leisurely. With
the finding of beaver Fitzpatrick had his first lessons in
trapping. There are many descriptions of the art as then
practiced, of which one of the best is that by Joseph L.
Meek in his reminiscences given to Mrs. Victor:

[The trapper] has an ordinary steel trap weighing five pounds,
attached to a chain five feet long, with a swivel and ring at the end,
which plays round what is called the *float,* a dry stick of wood,
about six feet long. The trapper wades out into the stream, which

---

[8] This version is from the Solitaire account, reprinted below, in Appendix B.
The information there is from Keemle, who became senior editor of *The
Reveille,* in which this story was printed in 1847. Keemle says the bear attack
on Smith occurred on waters of the Powder River; Clyman says on a branch
of the Cheyenne.

is shallow, and cuts with his knife a bed for the trap, five or six inches under water. He then takes the float out the whole length of the chain in the direction of the centre of the stream, and drives it into the mud, so fast that the beaver cannot draw it out; at the same time tying the other end by a thong to the bank. A small stick or twig, dipped in musk or castor [taken from the long glands just beneath a beaver's skin in front of the genital organs] serves for bait, and is placed so as to hang directly above the trap, which is now set. The trapper then throws water plentifully over the adjacent bank to conceal any foot prints or scent by which the beaver would be alarmed, and going to some distance wades out of the stream.

In setting a trap, several things are to be observed with care: — first, that the trap is firmly fixed, and the proper distance from the bank — for if the beaver can get on shore with the trap, he will cut off his foot to escape: secondly, that the float is of dry wood, for should it not be, the little animal will cut it off at a stroke, and swimming with the trap to the middle of the dam, be drowned by its weight. In the latter case, when the hunter visits his traps in the morning, he is under the necessity of plunging into the water and swimming out to dive for the missing trap, and his game.[9]

Usually the beaver were skinned at the place where they were trapped, and only the pelt, castor glands, and tail were taken. The tail was considered a delicacy, but only when meat was extremely scarce would the trappers eat any other part of the body.

As the party moved westward toward the high and handsome Bighorn Mountains it reached beautiful country, abounding with game. Crazy Woman Creek and Clear Creek, west branches of Powder River, were good beaver streams, as also were Goose Creek and other upper waters of Tongue River.[10]

---

[9] F. F. Victor, *The River of the West,* etc. (Hartford, Conn., 1870), 64–65.

[10] In September 1959, when identifying the routes of the Powder River and the Sawyers expeditions of 1865, we drove or walked over this interesting country. See L. R. and A. W. Hafen, *Powder River Campaigns and Sawyers Expedition of 1865* (Glendale, 1961).

After trapping this region, which Clyman pronounced "the Best Supplied with game of any we passe through in all our Travels," they were warned by the frosty nights of late November to be on their way to a winter camp. Following the Crow trail, they ascended the Powder River, reached the top plateau of the Bighorns and made the steep descent by Shell Creek to Bighorn River.[11]

Journeying southward, up the valley of the Bighorn, they had a near starving time. The country was barren, and what game there may have been had been killed or frightened away by the Crow band that preceded the trappers. The whites continued upstream to the sharp turn of the river, above where it changes name from Bighorn to Wind River. Farther ascending, now in a northwest course, they came to the winter camp of the Crows. This was north of what was later named Fremont Peak and in the narrow Wind River Valley in the vicinity of the present town of Crowheart.

Buffalo were abundant and the whites joined the Indians in the chase. On the second grand hunt Clyman reports: "As to how many were slaughtered that day every one said a thousand or upwards thi[s] I did not dispute thinking it fell near the fact myself and about 20 Indians who stood on the rocks of [the] Kenyon Killed Seventy by my own count" (p. 21).

It appears that this winter camp of the Crows was found and joined by a trapping brigade sent out by Andrew Henry and captained by John Weber. Daniel Potts, prob-

---

11 We first traversed this route with the Pioneer Trails Association party in the summer of 1940. The precipitous highway descent of the west slope of the Bighorns, with its numerous sharp hairpin curves, is one to remember.

ably a member of the party, gives additional information on the camp and region.[12]

From the Crows the trappers learned that the Green River would be good trapping country; indeed the Chief said that "beaver were so abundant upon these rivers that traps were unnecessary to catch them — they could club as many as they desired.[13] So the Smith-Fitzpatrick men, eager to get to the region of easy fur harvest, attempted a crossing of the range in February (1824). This was probably west of Dubois, at Union Pass, which they found too clogged with snow to permit a passage. So they returned and decided to take a longer but more feasible course, around the southern reaches of the Wind River Range.

From the bend of the river in the vicinity of present Riverton, the party turned south, up the Popo Agie branch. About eight miles south of present Lander they noted a strange thing — an oil spring — which they passed unconcernedly, with no thought that its black and oozy product would prove a source of greater wealth than all the beaver in the Rockies.

Game was now scarce, the men became weak from hunger, and the high winds and intense cold proved almost unbearable. But trapping was not a trade for the weak. Clyman and Sublette, riding off in search of game, saw at a distance, about sundown, three buffalo bulls. The horses

---

[12] For the fullest biographical sketch of John H. Weber, see LeRoy R. Hafen, Editor, *The Mountain Men and the Fur Trade of the Far West* (Glendale, Calif., 1965-72), IX, 379-84. This series of ten volumes, completed in 1972, contains 292 biographical sketches, signed by the 84 writers. These sketches include most of the more important men involved in the fur thade. The specific biographies supply much valuable information, so we make a general reference to them here, but shall not hereafter cite them individually in this work. *See also*, Pott's letter, of July 16, 1826, as reprinted in Frost, *op. cit.*, 59-63.

[13] The Solitaire account, in Appendix B.

were too weak to make pursuit, so the men dismounted, and crawling over ice and snow managed to wound, and later to kill, one of the three. From sagebrush they made enough fire to cook some meat, which they ate, and they then lay down, under a single buffalo robe, to sleep. But the wind rose, scattering their fire; a hard, frosty snow began falling, and the rough, frozen earth proved a bed of pain. Numbed and sleepless, they waited through the long night, their faithful horses near at hand.

Next morning, being unable to maintain a fire, they headed for some timber four miles away. After struggling to this goal, they found dry wood, made a fire, and broiled a steak. The food and warmth brought revival and the two, bringing precious meat, rejoined their companions.

The men then crossed a low divide and apparently descending Willow Creek or Rock Creek, reached the Sweetwater, east-flowing branch of the North Platte. In the night the wind blew with such fury that the men had to stay awake to hold on to their blankets and robes to keep them from blowing away. In the morning they were unable to maintain a fire and had to resort again to their robes, "the wind still blowing all day and night without abatement." The following day some men wrapped themselves as fully as possible to go hunting. They moved downstream where "it became confined in a narrow Kenyon" (Sweetwater Canyon). Mr. Branch managed to tumble a mountain sheep from a cliff and it rolled to their feet. They carried the meat to camp and attempted to cook it, but "soon gave it up the wind still keeping up such a continual blast as to prevent even a starving mountaineer from satisfying his hunger we all took to our blankets again it being the only way to keep from perishing" (p. 23). When a lull finally came they got up, and cooked and ate during the rest of the night. In the morning some of the men went to hunt game; others to find a better camping place.

"I went down the sweet water some four or five miles," writes Clyman, "to whare the Kenyon opened out into Quite a valley and found plenty of dry aspin wood in a small grove at the Lower end of the Kenyon and likewise plenty of Mountain Sheep on the cliffs which bounded the stream. . . . the next morning we packed up and moved down to the Aspin grove whare we remained some two or three weeks Subsisting on Mountain sheep. . . . we did not leave this camp untill the Mountain Sheep began to get scarce and wild and before leaving we here made a cash of Powder Lead and several other articles supposed to be not needed in our Spring hunt and it was here likewise understood that should circumstances at any time seperate us we would meet at this place and at all event we would all met here again or at some navigable point on the stream below at or by the first [of] June acording to our recording" (p. 24).[14]

Upon leaving camp the party traveled up the Sweet-

---

[14] The location of their camp and cache is thus rather accurately determined. This canyon is shown on Section IV of the Frémont "Topographical Map of the Road from Missouri to Oregon," etc., drawn by Charles Preuss; and especially on the excellent map by Paul Henderson accompanying his *Landmarks on the Oregon Trail* (New York, 1953). The location is a little above the mouth of Turkey Creek and the later St. Mary's stage station. Henderson, Peter Decker and six others re-explored this section of the Oregon Trail in July 1951, and Henderson says that Peter Decker a little later explored the region in a Jeep.

"According to Decker's findings," writes Henderson on page 49, "the camp was at the eastern end of the Sweetwater Canyon, some thirty miles above the Three Crossings. Below the mouth of Willow and Rock Creeks, the Sweetwater for some miles and then moved westward where that stream turned to the north. They were approaching, almost imperceptibly, the continental divide. It was a barren region of gradual rises and low hills, where the backbone of the continent had been flattened out to a desert-like contour. The weather was dry and cold, and the snow had been swept from much of the surface and piled in the gullies and on the leeward side of knolls and hills. No streams were to be seen, and melted snow was used to quench the thirst of men and horses. For several days they moved westward, not knowing they had left the watershed of the Atlantic until they found streams flowing westward, when they realized they had traversed the long-sought South Pass.[15]

---

water debouches for some five miles through a steep, narrow and majestic canyon. The presence of clumps of aspen near the eastern end of the canyon seems to substantiate the location of the trappers' camp [and cache] as stated by Clyman."

The location of the cache is also substantiated by measurements from the other direction. Clyman gave them in his diary of 1844, recording his emigrant trip westward of that year. His distances traveled August 16 to 20 totaled sixty miles from Independence Rock to the site of the camp and cache.

From Clyman's diary of Aug. 20, 1844, we quote: ". . . made 7 miles and encamped clos below another Kenyon through which the creek [Sweetwater] passes and near to whare we encamped in January 1824, at which time we were under J. Smith and T. Fitzpatrick first traversed the now well known South Pass" (p. 96).

The location of the camp and cache at the east end of Sweetwater Canyon is given also in *The Rocky Mountain Journals of William Marshall Anderson*, edited by Dale L. Morgan and Eleanor Towles Harris (San Marino, Calif., 1967), pages 122 and 180, where the place is called "Fitzpatrick's Cache." The accuracy of this identification is assured by the fact that Anderson was traveling eastward with Fitzpatrick on this trip over the Oregon Trail in 1834. Morgan, in his *West of Ashley*, p. 94, says the site was sixty miles above the Three Crossings; Henderson and the maps show the correct distance as thirty miles.

[15] In July 1939, my wife, son, and I tried to take Herbert E. Bolton over South Pass. Bolton, after giving the Commencement Address at the University of Denver had expressed the desire to go to historic South Pass, so we undertook the journey. We drove to the North Platte, to Fort Laramie and Independence Rock. But two days of steady rain had so glazed the ungraveled clay road that it was so slick we were compelled to turn back before reaching our goal.

If other white men had been there before them — such as Robert Stuart's eastbound Astorians in the fall of 1812 — nothing immediately came of the event. The effective discovery and utilization of the Pass dates with its crossing on a March day in 1824 by the party of Smith and Fitzpatrick. Little did these hardy pioneers dream that they were marking a trail destined to be, for nearly half a century, the most important route to the Pacific. It was to be trodden into a pathway by the trappers and the missionaries, and broadened into a great avenue by the Oregon emigrants, the Mormon colonizers of the Salt Lake Valley, and the swarms of California Argonauts of 1849.

There has been some question as to who was leader of the party when it crossed South Pass. John S. Robb, in an article which he wrote under the pseudonym "Solitaire," in the St. Louis *Weekly Reveille* of March 1, 1847, makes a strong statement that the leader was Thomas Fitzpatrick (see the entire article reproduced in Appendix B of this volume).

James Clyman, whose account we have been following, does not mention either Jedediah Smith or Thomas Fitz-

---

Years later, while retracing the route of the Mormon handcart migration to Utah, my wife and I followed the oiled highway over the Pass. I mention this to emphasize the nature of the country. I drove from the west side and watched for a supposed marker on the summit. The ground was so nearly level that not until I reached the Sweetwater did I realize that I had crossed the summit. Upon returning westward I found no historical marker, so again turned eastward. At the remnant of South Pass City, east of the continental divide I found an "oldtimer" who explained that the present highway crossed the divide about two miles north of the original emigrant road. He said that the Highway Department had placed a marker on the summit, but that history-minded people voiced such a vigorous protest against having the monument inscription call this the crossing of the Oregon Trail that the Highway people moved their marker southward to the true emigrant crossing. We induced our South Pass guide to get in our car and pilot us to the original site. We followed a winding dirt road through the sagebrush and finally came to the Oregon Trail and Whitman-Spaulding markers at the historic Trail crossing.

patrick in his narrative of the trip from the Wind River to the Sweetwater and over South Pass to Green River, being principally concerned with the experiences of himself and William Sublette. But in his diary of the wagon trip over the Oregon Trail in 1844 he mentions the place "whare we encamped in January 1824 at which time we under J. Smith and T. Fitzpatrick first traversed the now well known South Pass" (p. 96). This would infer co-leadership. But when the party gets to the Green River Clyman refers to Smith as "Capt." But as with the famous co-leaders, Lewis and Clark, the first named man was ranked first; so with Smith and Fitzpatrick, the first named is usually given the primacy.

From the summit of the pass, still enduring hunger and cold, the men moved on to the Little Sandy, the Big Sandy, and followed the latter to the eagerly awaited river they sought. They reached the Seeds-kee-dee (with numerous spellings) about which the Crows had told such luring tales. This was the *Rio Buenaventura* (Good Fortune) River of the Escalante Expedition of 1776 and the *Rio Verde* (Green River) of subsequent Spanish traders, who reached the river ahead of the Americans. The British fur hunters coming from the distant Columbia referred to it as the Spanish River. But American usage was to make it the Green River.

Now in the fabled land of the beaver, they prepared for an energetic campaign. The party divided — Smith with perhaps half of it moving downstream, and Fitzpatrick with Clyman and the remainder setting out to trap the branches to the north. The land lay snowbound, and the river was locked in ice. Before many days, however, flocks of wild geese began flying upstream, the sun came out, the ice and snow melted, and Fitzpatrick's little party settled down to its work. Beaver were plentiful, and day after day the men piled up a store of fur.

Everything looked promising, until on a certain night the party suffered a staggering loss. In the valley nearby was a small band of Shoshones — "Digger" Shoshones, Clyman termed them in distinction from the better sort of that nation — comprising some eighteen or twenty warriors, with a rather disproportionate quota of women and children. The trappers had befriended them with the gift of all the beaver meat they did not want for themselves and therefore feared no injury at their hands. Suddenly, one night, the village disappeared, and with it all the trappers' horses, leaving no trail. A search proved unavailing, and the trappers, though sobered by a loss which left them isolated in the mountains nearly a thousand miles from the Missouri, doggedly returned to their work. Perhaps they might meet some other Shoshones or some Crows from whom they could obtain horses, or perhaps Smith might return, or perhaps by some miracle of chance they might come upon this same thieving band and force the return of their property. Peril and loss were inevitable in the life of the trappers, and they must make the best of things as they found them.

April had gone, May was passing, and the time was at hand to set out for the rendezvous on the Sweetwater. The men *cached* their traps and furs, hung their saddles and other equipment high up in the trees and on a certain morning started on their journey. About noon, on turning the point of a ridge, they came face to face with five or six mounted Indians. Instantly the trappers recognized their stolen animals. Rifles were levelled, lariats were seized, and the Indians were compelled to lead the way, a mile or so up the steep mountain, to their village. Overawed by this little band of well-armed and determined men, the Indians gave up all the remaining horses but one, which evidently they had hidden. But Fitzpatrick and his men were in no mood for trifling. They seized one of the Indians, tied him up and threatened to shoot him unless the missing animal was returned, and it was soon in their hands. Then, giving the Indians some presents as a balm for their wounded feelings, the trappers joyfully rode back to their former camp, took down their saddles, dug up their furs and traps and packed up for the march.

With horses well laden, Fitzpatrick, at the head of the party, led his men back east through South Pass. A proud and happy young mountain man we may picture him. His days of apprenticeship were past; he had been successful in his first hunt for beaver, and a loss that had seemed irreparable disaster had been overcome by the recovery of his stolen horses. From now on he was to be a leader among men. He was to command trappers in Indian fights and on journeys through regions never before seen by white men; he was to guide missionaries and homeseekers, official explorers and United States troops; he was to take a foremost part in making treaties between his Government and the wild tribes of the plains, and not infrequently was to be called to Washington for conferences on the matters he knew so well. One may question if any distinction that came to him in after years yielded half the measure of gratification that he felt as he conducted this trapper band to the meeting place.

But when he arrived at the designated point on the Sweetwater neither Smith nor any of his men were there. The problem of getting his furs to market now prompted him to examine the course of the stream and ascertain if it could be navigated by light-draft boats. With Clyman as companion, he followed it some fifteen miles, only to decide that boats could not be used; and leaving Clyman to continue farther downstream, he returned to camp. They were not to see each other again for nearly three months. Clyman, intercepted by Indians rightly supposed to be hostile, wandered about, lost his way, and seeing no other course, determined to make his way eastward to the Missouri. Following the general course of the Platte, he arrived after almost incredible hardships at Fort Atkinson some time in September.

Fitzpatrick, returning to camp, opened the cache stored away in early spring. The goods were found in perfect order, but the powder was damp and had to be spread and dried. Smith and his party finally came in. Some search was made for Clyman, but given up in the belief that he had been killed by Indians. It was now near the end of June, and the two leaders made their plans for the future. It was agreed that Fitzpatrick would take the furs to the Missouri, report to Ashley and bring back supplies, and that Smith should remain in the mountains with most of the men and conduct the fall trapping.

Encouraged by a slight rise in the Sweetwater, due to the melting of snow in the mountains, Fitzpatrick decided to construct a bullboat for carrying the furs eastward. The bullboat, which may have been invented by the Mandans, and which looked in the water something like an upturned umbrella without its handle, was made of willow framework, tightly covered with sewn buffalo skins, the seams calked with tallow mixed with ashes. In this awkward, unwieldly craft, heavily laden with furs, Fitzpatrick, Stone, and Branch started their voyage. Troubles must have dogged them from the start — sandbars, a shifting current, snags, and shallows. Clyman says, ". . . the three men hauld the boat down stream untill it was nearly worn out and the water still falling so they cached the furs on Independence rock" (p. 29).[16]

Nearly five miles west of Independence Rock is Devil's Gate, which must have given the boatmen serious trouble. This deep narrow gorge cut through a mountain ridge by the docile-looking little Sweetwater during many millennia, was indeed a hazard. In walking through its half-mile length on August 22, 1933, I noted the big rocks and other hazards in the rugged canyon and concluded that Fitzpatrick's party here decided to give up the boat transportation of their furs and to cache them in the vicinity of Devil's Gate and Independence Rock.

The Rock, a large rounded granite mass that rests like a huge turtle on the plain, was to become a famous landmark on the Oregon Trail, and to be labeled by Father De Smet the "Register of the Desert." It is possible that Fitzpatrick and his two fellow voyageurs were at the Rock

---

[16] Clyman says the cache was "on" Independence Rock, but it is hardly conceivable that this would be correct. Although the Rock (upon which I have clambered several times) has depression and crevices, there is no place where furs could be safely hidden. The cache must have been at or near Independence Rock.

on July 4, 1824, and that the impressive landmark received its name at that time. But it is more likely that the name was given by William Sublette and his large party that celebrated the national holiday at the Rock in 1830.[17] Matthew C. Field, in 1843, saw Fitzpatrick's name inscribed on Independence Rock in three places; and James Clyman mentions seeing it on the Rock in 1849.[18]

With their boat lightened by the cached furs, the three men set out for a farther voyage. They were soon in another canyon, worse than Devil's Gate. In spite of conflicting stories of the wreck they suffered, it almost certainly occurred in the canyon and rapids of the North Platte immediately below the mouth of the Sweetwater. Here they lost two guns and all of their bullet-lead.[19] The disaster might well have crushed the spirit of weaker men, but with these it only inspired to greater resourcefulness. With a stone they broke from the remaining gun the brass mounting, hammered it into balls, and with these brass bullets killed a buffalo or two. Continuing down the Platte, like the lost Clyman before them, they made their way eastward. Ten

---

[17] See the discussion on the naming of Independence Rock in Morgan's note on page 118 of the Anderson *Journal, op. cit.;* and for the Devil's Gate name see *ibid,* 182.

[18] M. C. Field, *Prairie and Mountain Sketches,* Collected by Clyde and Mae R. Porter, Edited by Kate L. Gregg and J. F. McDermott (Norman, Okla., 1957), 174–75; and Camp, *Clyman, op. cit.,* 95.

[19] Frémont ran these rapids in a rubber boat in 1842 and on that occasion wrote: "Eighteen years previous to this time, as I have subsequently learned from himself, Mr. Fitzpatrick, somewhere above on this river, had embarked with a valuable cargo of beaver. Unacquainted with the stream, which he believed would conduct him safely to the Missouri, he came unexpectedly into this canon, where he was wrecked, with the total loss of his furs." — J. C. Frémont, *Report of the Exploring Expedition, etc.* (Washington, 1845), 73.

Inasmuch as Fitzpatrick had previously cached his furs (which he was subsequently to recover and pack to the Missouri River), Frémont misinterpreted the facts. Clyman is doubtless right in saying they lost two guns and their lead (p. 29).

days after Clyman reached Fort Atkinson, as he tells the story, the three arrived, "in a more pitible state if possible, than myself" (p. 29).

This was in September, probably about the middle of the month. Fitzpatrick wrote to Ashley at St. Louis, telling of the discovery of South Pass, the arrival at Green River, and the successful harvest of fur cached near Independence Rock.[20] Then he obtained horses from Lucien Fontenelle and started back at once. The party must have traveled the fourteen hundred miles there and back with unflagging speed, for the diary of James Kennerly, sutler at Fort Atkinson, under date of October 26, 1824, has this entry: "Fitzpatrick & party have come in & brot Beaver."[21] He sold the furs to Fontenelle, and was thus acting largely as a free trapper.[22]

---

[20] See Solitaire's statement, in Appendix B in this volume.

[21] Missouri Historical Society *Collections,* VI, no. 1 (Oct. 1928), 78.

[22] Dale L. Morgan, "The Diary of William H. Ashley," in *Bulletin of the Missouri Historical Society,* XI (Oct. 1954), 13.

Chapter 3

Ashley and the Rendezvous

TO WILLIAM HENRY ASHLEY, depressed by two years' reverses on the Missouri and no doubt anxious about the fate of his companies in the West, Fitzpatrick's letter must have been joyful news. It may not have been the first word the General received, for Major Henry had sent men from the upper Missouri country into Absaraka and over the continental divide into the Green River area. Some word of their success had probably reached the General. In any event, he decided to set about promptly to reach the new rich field. He would not wait for another spring, but move out in the fall of 1824. Getting together a small force of men and equipment, Ashley went up the river to Fort Atkinson, arriving on October 21. Here he picked up some recruits and further equipment, sending the party forward mounted, with fifty pack horses and a wagon (the latter doubtless soon abandoned), under the command of Fitzpatrick. Clyman was in the party, and there was also

42

James P. Beckwourth, a mulatto and a new man to the mountains, but later to become noted as a trapper and a chief among the Crows, and thirty-two years later to attain the distinction of a published biography.

On November 3 Ashley set out from Fort Atkinson westward, overtaking his party two days later.[1] Because of the expectation that food supplies could be obtained in the Pawnee villages, he carried but a meager stock of provisions. But the Grand Pawnees had started on their migration to the wintering grounds on the Arkansas, and their villages were found to be deserted. Through deep snow, facing stiff winds, amid cold so intense that some of the horses froze to death, the party pushed on. Though a horse was now and then killed for food, the men suffered greatly from hunger. "Our allowance," said Beckwourth, "was half a pint of flour a day per man, which we made into a kind of gruel; if we happened to kill a duck or a goose, it was shared as fairly as possible . . . a duller encampment I suppose never was witnessed. No jokes, no fire-side stories, no fun; each man rose in the morning with the gloom of the preceding night filling his mind; we built our fires and partook of our scanty repast without saying a word."[2]

On November 22 they passed near the Loup Pawnee villages and found these also deserted. A little farther on they found game and forage. Now they moved more rapidly, and on December 3, near present Kearney, Nebraska, they found the temporary encampment of the Grand Paw-

---

[1] Ashley's letter of Dec. 1, 1825, published in H. C. Dale, *The Ashley-Smith Explorations*, etc. (Glendale, Calif., 1941), 115–57.

[2] T. D. Bonner, *The Life and Adventures of James P. Beckwourth* (New York 1931), 21. Hereinafter cited as Beckwourth.

nees. Though some of the Indians committed thefts, the chiefs and principal men proved friendly and compelled a restitution of the property. They warned Ashley, however, against proceeding farther; the attempt, they said, would endanger the loss of all the men and horses. But the warning went unheeded, and in the extreme cold, with frequent snow flurries, the party proceeded. Eight miles farther the whites fell in with the Loup Pawnees, with whom they traveled to the forks of the Platte. Here for eleven days the white men remained to recruit and trade. Fortunately they were able to obtain from these Indians twenty-three horses, some buffalo robes, and dried meat.

The weather moderated, herds of buffalo appeared, and two days before Christmas they started to ascend the South Platte along a course approximating that of Major Stephen H. Long in the summer of 1820. The weather turned cold again; snow fell; and had it not been for the paths through the snow made by the buffalo, further progress would have been impossible. The buffalo also served to keep the horses alive, for they pawed the snow away from the grass. On January 1, 1825, the men came to a grove of sweet cottonwood, the inner bark of which is relished by horses and is highly nutritious. Here the party remained for ten days, recuperating from its fatigue and privations. Again it set forth, and January 20, near a small island clothed with cottonwood (later known as Fremont's Orchard), in the present Morgan County, Colorado, the men had their first view of the peaks of the Rockies, deemed to be some sixty miles distant.

What part Fitzpatrick had in the conduct and movements of this heroic company we do not know. The course, the marches, the weather encountered and the sufferings endured by men and horses are told in detail in the long report to General Henry Atkinson, written by Ashley at the end of 1825, and referred to above. Ashley, however, was no distributor of praise, he says much of himself, but little of anyone else. Yet we may be sure that in this expedition, nominally led by a man new to the wilderness, the business of management rested largely, if not wholly, upon the shoulders of the sturdy young man who had so quickly mastered the technique of the mountaineer and the plainsman and but recently had twice traveled a part of the route. Fitzpatrick was blessed with a strong frame, with good common sense, a ready adaptability to all circumstances, a keen eye for trails, an alert sense of watchfulness. We may fairly look upon him as the second in command, the executive of the commanding officer, busy with all the details of the march and the bivouac, the effective agent of the expedition and its safeguard from disaster.

Leaving the South Platte and ascending the Cache la Poudre the party reached the base of the Front Range of the Rockies, in the region west of present Fort Collins, Colorado. Here the party spent two or three weeks trapping and hunting. Then it turned northwestward towards the Laramie Plains, continuing the search for beaver. Rounding Medicine Bow Mountain and descending Pass Creek it reached on March 26 the North Platte, about six miles southwest of present Walcott.[3] The route taken from the

---

[3] "The Diary of William H. Ashley," edited by Dale L. Morgan, in *Bulletin of the Missouri Historical Society*, XI, 26. This important diary (first published in 1954), begins on Mar. 25, 1825. Since the preceding was written, the Diary has been republished in *The West of William H. Ashley . . . 1822–1838* (Denver, 1964), and in this more accessible form will be cited hereafter as Morgan, *Ashley*.

Fort Collins region northwestward to the Rawlins area was generally that followed by Frémont in 1843,[4] by the California-bound Cherokees (Cherokee Trail) in 1849 and 1850, and by the Overland stagecoach in 1862. The route from Fort Collins to Laramie City was generally along modern US 287, and thence to the Rawlins area was near US 30.

Traveling west and then northwest from the North Platte crossing, the party crossed the route of the present Union Pacific a little south of Rawlins and upon moving generally westward crossed the Great Divide Basin and the Red Desert. On this near-level plain the men could detect no drainage pattern — in fact there is no outlet to the sea in this inland basin atop the continental divide. Had it not been for falling snow they would have suffered from thirst in this generally dry, desert area. West of the Great Divide Basin on April 5 a band of Indians ran off seventeen of the party's best horses and mules. Of the nine men sent in pursuit, Fitzpatrick was probably the leader, for he and Clyman were the two men who knew this region from the previous year's experience. They followed northward as far as the Sweetwater but were unable to overtake the Indian thieves, whom they concluded were Crows.

The men now had to carry the packs of the missing horses. Staggering on, the party struck the Big Sandy, on April 19, 1825.

The Green, wrote Ashley, was a "beautiful river. Its margin and islands are wooded with large long leafed (or bitter) cottonwood, box-elder, willows, etc., and judging from the quantity of wood cut on its banks, and other appearances, it once must have contained a great number

---

4 Frémont, *op. cit.*, 123–25.

THE SUMMER RENDEZVOUS

(From Victor's *River of the West*)

of beaver, the major part of which (as I have been informed) were trapped by men in the service of the North West company some four or five years ago."[5] Those foreign trappers had been led by Donald McKenzie, who had penetrated so early and so far from the British outposts of the far Northwest.[6]

Here on the Green, for the main course of the expedition, was journey's end. It was the breakingup place — the point from which smaller parties were sent out to their work — and it remained a pivotal point of the operations of the trappers during most of the trapper period. The day after reaching Green River, Ashley sent out nine hunters to procure buffalo skins for making a bull-boat, with which he planned to descend the river on a tour of exploration. Skins were procured and a boat seven feet wide and sixteen feet long was constructed.

The Ashley men were now divided into four detachments to engage in trapping. Fitzpatrick led a party of six southwestward to the Uinta Mountains; Clyman with an equal number went up the river northward; Zacharias Ham took a party of seven westward; and the fourth party, led by Ashley, was to explore the lower Green by water. Before parting, the men were told that a general rendezvous of all trappers in the mountains would be held the first of July, at a downstream point that Ashley would suitably mark by peeling trees or raising a five-foot mound of earth.[7]

[5] Ashley's Narrative in H. C. Dale, *op. cit.*, 134.

[6] Alexander Ross, *The Fur Hunters of the Far West,* edited by Kenneth A. Spaulding (Norman, 1956), 135, 153.

[7] These arrangements are given in Ashley's Diary, April 20–22, in Morgan, *Ashley,* 106–07. The detailed information, if not otherwise identified, is from this source.

Near the Wyoming-Utah border of today Ashley found a suitable site, and at the mouth of a western affluent which he called Rendezvous Creek (now Henry's Fork) he selected and marked the place for the rendezvous. After caching merchandise and supplies here, he continued his voyage.

Of the experiences of the land parties we know but little. Fitzpatrick rode southward along Green River, keeping in touch for several days with the boatmen. A little below the mouth of Black's Fork he left the Green and headed for the Uinta Mountains, the only major range in the United States that runs east and west. He undoubtedly ascended and trapped Henry's Fork, which heads in the Uinta Mountains and flows northward and then eastward, paralleling the mountain range. Enroute eastward it receives the waters of Beaver Creek, Burnt Fork, and other affluents. These were all good beaver streams; and even today the ranchers there trap the beaver that dam their ditches and cause trouble (as told to the author in September, 1962).

Clyman, some time after the division of the parties, was attacked by Indians and lost one man. He thereupon beat a hasty retreat southward to join Fitzpatrick.[8] Ham, in going westward would reach Muddy and Bear rivers, and the branch of Black's Fork that now bears Ham's name.

In the meantime Ashley, in his two bullboats, floated down Green River, and soon was involved in the winding and treacherous course of the mighty stream. He threaded the deep canyons of Flaming Gorge, Lodore, Whirlpool,

---

[8] Camp, *Clyman*, 38.

and Split Mountain; braved Ashley Falls, Disaster Falls, and lesser cataracts that forced him to make sixteen portages around obstructions. Below present Dinosaur National Monument he emerged into more open country. Here he encountered Ute Indians and some of Etienne Provost's trappers out from Taos, New Mexico.[9] A little below Ashley's Fork, upon which modern Vernal, Utah, is located, he cached most of his remaining goods — including 150 pounds of tobacco, 200 pounds of coffee, 130 pounds of sugar, 150 pounds of gunpowder, 120 pounds of lead, and the fifty beaver skins garnered along the Green River.[10]

He passed the wintering place of Provost's trappers at the mouth of White River, near present Ouray, Utah,[11] and continued down some twenty-five miles farther, to the mouth of Minnie Maud Creek. Now faced with the forbidding geography of Desolation Canyon, he gave heed to the discouraging reports of the Indians and trappers about the lower country, and decided to turn back. Obtaining a few horses from the Indians and trappers he retraced his route to the mouth of the Indian-named "Euwinty"

---

[9] Beckwourth's report of this encounter with Provost and his men (Beckwourth, *op. cit.*, 44), was ridiculed by Bernard de Voto, in his edition of the mulatto's work, p. 377. Ashley's early Narrative (Dale, *op. cit.*) did not mention Provost, but his Diary (Morgan, *Ashley*, 113, 116) later discovered, does. So Beckwourth is vindicated.

[10] Morgan, *Ashley*, 112.

[11] Here the White River comes in from the east and the Duchesne (Uinta of Ashley) from the west. On the east side of the Green and especially north of the White, is an area of several hundred acres covered with round-leaf cottonwoods. These undoubtedly helped to determine Provost's winter site, as the bark and twigs of the sweet cottonwood were well known as good food for horses. When we visited the site in September 1962, we noted that many of the ancient trees were dead, but the area is still an impressive park, known now as Chipeta's Grove — Chipeta was the wife of Ouray, the famous Ute Chief who died in 1880.

(Uinta, and later Duchesne)[12] and proceeded up this stream on June 3.

Following the general route of the historic Escalante party of 1776, he ascended the Duchesne River and on June 7 met Etienne Provost and twelve men. Provost had been blazing trails and making history. From his native Canada he had come early to St. Louis and accompanied the ill-fated Chouteau-DeMun Expedition up the Arkansas and into New Mexico, 1815–17. Later he had returned to Santa Fe and in 1823 was conducting beaver-trapping expeditions north-westward to the Green River and the Great Basin, where he was treacherously attacked while in council with presumably friendly Indians. This occurred on Provo River, a stream named for him and this incident.[13] The attacking Shoshone Indians, under Chief Bad Lefthand, had been ill-treated previously by British traders and were taking revenge on white men.

The meeting with Provost was fortunate for Ashley, because Provost knew well the Indians and the country and in addition could supply horses and pack-animal transportation. From Provost Ashley learned that John H. Weber and other Americans had wintered on Bear River or the Snake.[14] Anxious to meet these trappers whom partner Andrew Henry had sent out from the upper Missouri River, Ashley induced Provost to go to the Green, near the mouth

---

[12] At the Ute Indian Agency of Fort Duchesne, Utah, we interviewed some Ute Indians on Sept. 27, 1962. Francis McKinley, Director of Education and an educated Ute, explained that Euwintey (as Ashley rendered the term) means lodgepole pine, and referred to a grove near White Rocks on the upper waters of the Uinta River.

[13] W. A. Ferris, *Life in the Rocky Mountains* . . . (Denver, 1940), 308–09. See also my sketch of Provost in my *Mountain Men Series* (Glendale, Calif., 1962–72), VI, 371–85.

[14] Morgan, *Ashley*, 116.

of Ashley's Fork, open the Ashley cache and return with the goods to the junction of the Duchesne and Strawberry, at the site of the town of Duchesne, Utah.

Upon Provost's return with the cached supplies, the party moved up the Strawberry and over the beautiful high country to the summit of the Wasatch Mountains and descended to the Provo River drainage in the vicinity of present Heber. Crossing a low divide they descended to the Weber River, another Great Basin stream. Here they met Johnson Gardner, a free trapper associated with Weber. About a month before, both he and Provost had met and defied Peter Skene Ogden and the British traders on the Weber River. Gardner had induced more than twenty of Ogden's men to desert the British leader, taking with them about 700 beaver skins.[15]

It is remarkable how competing trappers had concentrated here in the Weber River area in the summer of 1825. Provost had come from the southeast, from Taos, New Mexico, with his band; Ogden had traveled from the northwest, from the Columbia River with his Snake River brigade; and Ashley's men had flooded in from the east, from the upper Missouri and up the Platte to the Green River Valley and beyond. Both the Americans and British contended that they were within their legal domain. The Oregon treaties of 1818 and 1827 had provided joint occupancy of the Oregon Territory for the two nationals; hence fertile grounds for dispute. But what the partisans did not know was the fact that they were all interlopers, being well below the 42nd degree of latitude, which was the northern

---

[15] Ogden's Journal, as edited by David E. Miller in *Utah Historical Quarterly*, XX, 181.

boundary of Spanish territory, having been fixed by the Adams-Onis Treaty of 1819.

Eager to contact Gardner and the British deserters with their valuable packs of beaver fur, Ashley turned east to follow these parties (who had learned of Ashley and his cached goods, probably from Fitzpatrick or Ham) to the rendezvous site on Green River.

Here the various trapper bands were to assemble on July 1, 1825. Jedediah Smith and his small party were back. Since leaving Fitzpatrick in the summer of 1824, Jedediah had trapped westward to the Bear River and the Snake, where he had encountered some British Iroquois who had suffered at the hands of other Indians and were ready to give Smith pelts if he would give them needed supplies and escort them to the nearest British post. Smith acceded, doubtless eager to survey the country with guides who knew it and to learn from the experienced British the fur-gathering devices of these trappers. After spending some weeks at Flathead Post, on Clark's Fork, west of Flathead Lake, Jedediah accompanied Ogden's Snake River brigade back to the Bear River and Salt Lake region, and then he pushed on to the Green.

Fitzpatrick, Clyman, and Ham, who had left Ashley in late April, came in to the rendezvous. Of their experiences we have no detailed reports. The results of Fitzpatrick's trapping are briefly told in one line in the Ashley accounts: "140 Fitzpatrick." Whether this was the number of beaver trapped by Fitzpatrick alone or by his party is not made clear. Clyman is credited with 166 and Ham with 461.

This rendezvous, the first of the great mountain fairs

that for sixteen years were to be the annual "big event" in the trapper country, was in all respects a success. Before now there were no supplies in the mountains. For refitting themselves with even the barest necessities the trappers were compelled to journey all the way to some trading post on the Missouri. Ashley's innovation brought supplies to the country in which the trappers operated. It was thus an economizer of time and labor, and it was also a profitable thing for the man who sold the supplies. "Mountain prices" were high, and they were to continue so throughout the trapper period.

Records of this epoch-making assemblage are scant. Ashley's fine diary ends abruptly on June 27. None of the other American participants kept journals that have survived. Ogden and his clerk Kittson kept good diaries, but these men had been turned back from Weber River in May and did not attend the rendezvous. Ashley's summary narrative, previously referred to, provides some data, and his financial accounts copied in his diary give valuable information on goods and prices. From these sources we learn that 120 men assembled in this first fair of the wilderness. Twenty-nine were deserters from H.B.C., twenty or so were associated with Provost, and the rest were Ashley-Henry men, who as employees or free trappers were relying on Ashley for supplies.

Ashley had come well stocked. From his caches had been unearthed supplies of powder, lead, and knives; quantities of tobacco, coffee, and sugar; and miscellaneous trade goods such as colored beads, bright-colored cloth, finger rings, earrings, ribbons, sleigh bells, red paint, tomahawks, needles, awls, buttons, combs, scissors, thread, fish hooks, and gun flints. Goods were sold at mountain prices — coffee and sugar, $1.50 per pound; knives at $2.50; tobacco, $2.00 per pound; scissors at $2.00 apiece; cloth, $6.00 per yard, etc. Beaver skins were credited at an average of $5.00 apiece, or $3.00 per pound. Ashley's total trade amounted to nearly 9,000 pounds of beaver skins, which would be worth near $50,000 if safely brought to St. Louis.

The rendezvous was of short duration, and was tame as compared to those of subsequent years. Very little spirits or rum were available, but the calls must have been urgent, for ampler supplies were to be brought in the supply caravans of subsequent years.

The location of this first great rendezvous in the Rocky Mountains (1825) has been a matter of considerable speculation. Ashley, in boating down the Green, had cached goods and marked the rendezvous site at the mouth of Henry's Fork. But the actual rendezvous, he says (Dale, *op. cit.*, 152) was held "about 20 miles distant from the place appointed by me as a general rendezvous." The twenty miles would have to be up the Green or up Henry's Fork. Twenty miles up the Green would place the site near the mouth of Black's Fork. This is an unlikely location for this stream through practically all of its course below the Fort Bridger location is a treeless and grassless river flowing through barren land. Henry's Fork, on the other hand, which I have examined, is supplied with grass and trees through most of its course. Especially in the area about twenty miles up the stream, near the mouth of Burnt Fork, there was and is an extended area of good meadow land, such as would be necessary for a rendezvous location.[16]

The selection of the site probably came about in this fashion. Ham, who went westward to trap in the spring of 1825, undoubtedly encountered Weber and other Ashley-Henry men in the Bear or Weber River valleys. Fitzpatrick could well have met these trappers also. Ham and Fitzpatrick would have told Weber and the others about Ashley's cached supplies and the appointed rendezvous. As recounted in Ashley's diary, Weber and the Hudson's Bay Company deserters had headed for the rendezvous site before Ashley and Provost reached the Weber River. Learning of this, Ashley turned back to Chalk Creek and followed those trappers eastward to Henry's Fork. I have traversed this route, over country roads and difficult terrain.

Now we get help from James P. Beckwourth, whose remarkable biography was so embellished in the telling that historians do not rely upon it if there are other sources. But the boastful mulatto, despite his exaggerations and some confusion of events in his reminiscent account — dictated more than thirty years after the earlier events recounted — has much of value. Beckwourth was with Clyman's trapper detachment and encountered the Weber-Gardner men. Of the rendezvous event he writes:

We then proceeded to *uncache* our goods, which we had buried at the "Suck" [where the Green River enters Flaming Gorge Canyon, and very near the mouth of Henry's Fork], and prepared to move up the river to a point where the Canadians and Indians had engaged to meet him [Ashley] with their peltry. . . . On arriving at the rendezvous, we found the main body of the Salt Lake party

---

[16] Gen. Albert Sidney Johnston, when stalled with his Utah Expedition during the winter of 1857–58, sent his stock from the Fort Bridger area over to the better grass on Henry's Fork. See LeRoy R. and Ann W. Hafen, *The Utah Expedition, etc.* (Glendale, 1958), 83.

already there with the whole of their effects. The general [Ashley] . . . opened his goods, and there was a general jubilee among all at the rendezvous.[17]

The rendezvous over, Ashley loaded his bundles of skins on pack animals and headed his train eastward. He planned to carry the furs to navigable water of the Bighorn and thence boat down that stream, the Yellowstone, and the Missouri. Despite two clashes with hostile Indians enroute, he reached his place of embarkation, near present Thermopolis, Wyoming, on August 7. Now he sent back half of his fifty men and all of their horses to pursue trapping. At the mouth of the Yellowstone he was happy to see the newly-arrived Atkinson Expedition with United States troops.[18] On the Government boats the furs were freighted to St. Louis, where Ashley arrived October 4, 1825.[19]

At the rendezvous, apparently, Ashley had made a deal with Jedediah Smith, taking him in as a field partner. Smith accompanied Ashley to Missouri and the partners quickly assembled a big outfit with ample supplies to continue the profitable trade. Ashley was also busy with other arrangements; on October 26 he was married to Eliza, a daughter of Major William Christy. So Ashley was glad to remain in pleasant St. Louis and have Smith lead the supply caravan on the winter trip to the mountains.

At the end of October Jedediah was ready to set out from

---

[17] Beckwourth, 46–47.

[18] See Russel Reid and C. G. Gannon (Eds.), "Journal of the Atkinson-O'Fallon Expedition," in *North Dakota Historical Quarterly,* IV (Oct. 1929), 10–40. The Journal records on Aug. 19, 1825: "Three men from Gen. Ashley's party arrived this morning at 9 – at 11 Gen. Ashley with a party of 24 men arrived with 100 packs of Beaver. . . . Gen. Ashley's Beaver was put on board of the Buffalo [one of the keelboats] this morning."

[19] Reports of Ashley's arrival and fur trade success are given in the Missouri newspapers. See the reprints in Frost., *op. cit.,* 190–42.

St. Louis with seventy men, 160 horses and mules, and merchandise valued at $20,000.[20] He traveled as far as the Pawnee villages and spent the winter there. In the spring he was joined on the Platte by Ashley.[21]

While Ashley and Smith were boating their furs to St. Louis and Smith was starting back with fresh supplies, 1825–26, the fur men in the field were busy with their fall trapping. Divided into several small bands, they were pursuing beaver in the valleys of the Green, Bear, Snake, and other likely areas. Fitzpatrick presumably was again head of a party. The routes of none of the bands are known in detail. But as winter closed in, several parties, probably by prearrangement, assembled in what they called Willow Valley, now known as Cache Valley, Utah. This is a grassy, mountain-encircled area, one that had been trapped in 1824 by Ashley's men and in the spring of 1825 by Ogden. No where are the golds and reds of autumn more gorgeous than on the low hills bordering this beautiful valley.

Daniel T. Potts, one of the Ashley free trappers who wintered in Cache Valley, 1825–26, gives us excellent contemporary descriptions of the valley of Bear River, Bear Lake, Great Salt Lake, Utah Lake, and the region generally. In his letter headed "Rocky Mountains, July 16, 1826," he accurately describes the circuituous course of Bear River and says that Willow [Cache] Valley "has been our chief place of rendezvous and wintering ground."[22]

---

[20] *Missouri Advocate* and *St. Louis Enquirer,* Oct. 29, 1825, and *Missouri Republican* of Oct. 31, 1825, reprinted in Frost, 142–43.

[21] The hitherto confused situation as to Smith's and Ashley's return to the mountains has been cleared by discovery of the Robert Campbell dictation of 1870. See Morgan, *Ashley,* 143–45.

[22] Frost, *op. cit.,* 62–63.

Louis Vasquez, already becoming an important Mountain Man,[23] was in the assemblage and said that the winter was so severe and the snow so deep that the trappers moved down into Salt Lake Valley, which was free from snow and was supplied with buffalo.[24] Beckwourth also was there and agrees with Vasquez about the move to Salt Lake Valley. He tells of this and a subsequent encounter:

Our present rendezvous was in Cache Valley, but Sublet gave orders for all to remove to Salt Lake, which was but a few miles distant, and then go into winter quarters. We according moved to the mouth of "Weaver's Fork" [Weber's], and established ourselves there. When all were collected together for the winter, our community numbered from six to seven hundred souls (from two to three hundred consisting of women and children), all strong and healthy as bears, and all having experienced very good success.

Shortly after we had become well settled down, we had the misfortune to lose about eighty horses, stolen one dark, stormy night by the *Pun-naks* [Bannocks], a tribe inhabiting the head-waters of the Columbia River. On missing them the next day, we formed a party of about forty men, and followed their trail on foot — the ground was covered with snow at the time. I volunteered with the rest, although fortunately my horses were not among the missing. After a pursuit of five days we arrived at one of their villages, where we saw our own horses among a number of others. We then divided our forces, Fitzpatrick taking command of one party, and a James Bridger of the other.

The plan resolved upon was as follows: Fitzpatrick was to charge the Indians, and cover Bridger's party, while they stampeded all the horses they could get away with. I formed one of Captain Bridger's party, this being the first affair of the kind I had ever witnessed. Every thing being in readiness, we rushed in upon the horses, and stampeded from two to three hundred. Fitzpatrick at the same time engaging the Indians, who numbered from three to four hundred. The Indians recovered a great number of the horses from us, but we succeeded in getting off with the number of our own

23 See "My Mountain Men — Louis Vasques," in the *Colorado Magazine,* X (1933), 14–21.
24 *San Francisco Evening Bulletin,* Oct. 29, 1858.

missing, and forty head besides. In the engagement, six of the enemy were killed and scalped, while not one of our party received a scratch. The horses we had captured were very fine ones, and our return to camp was greeted with the liveliest demonstrations.[25]

So far as we know this was Fitzpatrick's first Indian fight in which he acted as a leader. Soon after the trappers' return, a large village of Snake Indians pitched their tepees in the locality. Here at the mouth of Weber River, near the site of Ogden of today, was a favorite wintering ground of the Snakes. These friendly Indians and the white fur men comprised one of the largest winter gatherings of the trapper period. The winter was passed peaceably and comfortably.

After the Indians and whites parted, the Snakes were encountered on March 24, 1826, by Peter Skene Ogden. He records: "These fellows have spent the winter with the Americans and from their own accounts have made peace with them and this I am inclin'd to believe is the case as they have received an American Flag and appear pleased and contented with the reception they have received from them."[26] They told Ogden the American camp comprised twenty-five tents.

With the opening of spring the fur men moved back into Willow Valley. Here they dug caches for their furs. The making of a safe cache was everywhere and always a work of art and skill. The choosing of the ground, the digging of the pit, the storing of the goods, demanded wisdom and care, for the least failure to observe the well-attested rules

---

[25] Beckwourth, 60–61. Some allowance should probably be made for Beckwourth's usual exaggerations as to numbers involved.

[26] *Peter Skene Ogden's Snake Country Journals, 1824–25 and 1825–26* (London, 1950), 146.

might result in disaster. Everything done must conduce to keeping the goods dry and to obliterating all traces of the work, so that the practiced eye of the most canny savage would be foiled in the search for the buried treasure. The surface opening was usually small — the better to be hidden — but as the pit deepened it was bellied out like a cistern to enlarge the capacity. The location was generally beside a stream, into which the dirt could be disposed.

While digging one of these pits a cave-in of the bank buried two of the diggers. Thereafter, and ever since, the locality has been called Cache Valley. There was, according to Beckwourth, another fatal casualty at the time — one that might have been followed by wholesale reprisals. One of the trappers, while out hunting, saw what appeared to be an antelope and shot it. Upon going up to it he found that he had killed a friendly Shoshone hunter who as a decoy had put on an antelope's head and skin. The resentment of the Indians was feared, and Fitzpatrick hurried to the Snakes with an explanation. The chief, realizing what had occurred, amicably replied:

> You and the Snakes are brothers; we are all friends; we cannot at all times guard against accidents. You lost two of your warriors in the bank, the Snakes have just lost one. Give me some red cloth to wrap up the body. We will bury the fallen brave.[27]

A scarlet blanket was given him to shroud the body, which, with appropriate funeral ceremonies, was hoisted into a high tree. Peace between the reds and the whites was not disturbed.

For the spring trapping, according to Beckwourth, Fitz-

---

[27] Beckwourth, 63. It is possible that this event and the cave-in of the cache may have occurred in the winter of 1826–27. Beckworth did not always keep his chronology straight.

patrick led his band (which included Beckwourth) north-ward across the low divide to the Portneuf, a small branch of the Snake River. Many beaver were found, and for three weeks the men trapped with success. But at the mouth of the Portneuf, near present Pocatello, they ran into a band of Blackfeet, who this time, as they often did, professed friendship. The whites, who were not deceived, set a heavy guard at night, but despite all their watchfulness three tether ropes were cut in an attempt to spirit away the horses. The ruse was instantly discovered, and the whole camp was aroused. Rifles cracked, and five of the Indians were killed, while a sixth, mortally wounded, crawled into the river, which swept him away. The five bodies were scalped, for many trappers were ready to retaliate in kind.

Signal fires sprang up on the nearby hills, and the whites realized that swarms of Blackfeet were advancing upon them. Accordingly they hastily packed up and retraced their way along the Portneuf and over to the Bear. Again they resumed trapping. At the mouth of the Sage River, on the Wyoming border, they met two couriers sent by General Ashley to find the trappers and apprise them of the goods being brought to the rendezvous. Fitzpatrick now moved his party toward the designated place and after some trapping on the way arrived without further note-worthy incident.

One party, of 28 trappers, had contacted Ogden and his party on the Snake River on April 9. With these Americans were a few British men who the year before had deserted to the Americans, but were now ready to return to Ogden. The two parties soon separated and Ogden gloated over the fact that he had already trapped the region into which the Americans were heading. He gives no names, so the identity of the Americans is undisclosed.[28]

The various trapping parties drifted in to the summer (1826) rendezvous site to meet the Ashley-Smith supply train that had wintered on the Platte River and was headed for the mountains. From this train Smith and Black Harris went as couriers to find the trappers and apprise them of the coming of the train of supplies.

There has been some disagreement among writers as to the site of this rendezvous of 1826 — whether it was in Cache Valley or adjacent to Great Salt Lake. Beckwourth says it was at the latter site, but his recollections and statements are not always dependable. The most specific contemporary record is that appearing in the *Missouri Herald and St. Louis Advertiser* of November 8, 1826, presumably written by Charles Keemle, former fur trader who became an important newspaperman. This report of "General Ashley's Expedition" was reprinted widely, including appearance in the *National Intelligencer, Niles Weekly Register*, and others. The statements therein that bear on the site of the rendezvous are: "He [Ashley] went to the station of the party he had left beyond the mountains, when he came in a year ago, and thence descended a river believed to be the Buenaventura [Bear], about one hundred fifty miles to the Great Lake. . . . *The lake which terminated the expedition westward* [my italics] is a most remarkable body of water . . ."[29]

---

[28] Ogden's Journal, *op. cit.*, 181. It is likely that this party was a band led by Johnson Gardner; for it was he who had had a brush with Ogden in the summer of 1825 and to whom the British trappers had deserted.

[29] The reprint in Frost, *op. cit.*, 147–48, is from the *Alexandria Gazette* (Virginia) and is identical with that appearing in *Nile's Weekly Register* of Dec. 9, 1826. This article is also reprinted in Morgan, *Ashley*, 153.

Robert Campbell's reminiscent account, dictated in 1870, says the rendezvous of 1826 was held in Cache Valley. "We remained in Cache Valley only a couple of weeks," he says, "long enough to complete the traffic with the trappers. After we left Cache Valley, Jackson and Sublette met us on Bear river. Ashley then sold out his interest in the fur trade to Smith, his partner, and to Jackson and Sublette, the new firm being known as Smith, Jackson and Sublette."[30] The arrival in Cache Valley and the trading with the trappers occurred in June,[31] but Ashley remained in the region for about a month, continued on to Great Salt Lake, sold out to Smith, Jackson and Sublette "near the Grand Lake West of the Rocky Mountains in the month of July."[32]

Ashley apparently quit the mountains without regret. He was never a Mountain Man at heart; his interests were with politics and business in Missouri. With a fortune in hand, he would give up the hazards of trapping and take over the surer business of supplying the trappers and marketing their furs.

Two of the purchasing partners — Smith and Sublette — have become well known to historians, but David E. Jackson has heretofore been almost unknown. This led to the question why Fitzpatrick did not become the third partner with Smith and Sublette in the partnership that succeeded Ashley. That question has been largely resolved by the publication of Carl D. W. Hays' biography of Jackson, in which he is shown as a competent experienced man, older

---

[30] In Morgan, *Ashley*, 145.
[31] Jedediah Smith's statement, reprinted in Morgan, *Ashley*, 145.
[32] Ashley's statement, in Morgan, *Ashley*, 171.

than the other partners, and one who gave balance and stability to the new company.[33]

Under the terms of the Agreement of July 18, 1826, between Ashley and Smith, Jackson, and Sublette the partners were to take over Ashley's stock of merchandise, amounting to about $16,000. They were to pay for it in beaver fur delivered at the rendezvous at $3 per pound or else have him sell it for them at St. Louis, they paying the cost of transportation at $1.12½ per pound. The partners were to deliver to Ashley all the beaver skins collected by them before July 1, 1827, these to be used to pay for the merchandise of 1826 and 1827. Regarding the merchandise wanted for 1827 — to cost $7,000 to $15,000 — the partners were to notify Ashley by March 1, 1827. Ashley agreed to furnish no other persons merchandise except those who might be in his immediate service, thus confining to the partners the control of supplies to the trappers.[34]

The negotiations finished, Ashley delivered, according to Beckwourth, a farewell address to his men, thanking them for their kindly labors in his behalf,[35] and then with an escort set out for St. Louis. He arrived in late September, having spent about 70 days enroute. He brought in about 125 packs of beaver, valued at some $60,000.[36] The mountains were never to see him again, for though in the following spring (1827) he decided to accompany the

[33] Carl D. W. Hays, "David E. Jackson," in LeRoy R. Hafen (ed.), *Mountain Men and the Fur Trade of the Far West* (Glendale, Calif., 1972), IX, 214–44.

[34] The terms are specified in Ashley's letter of Oct. 14, 1826, and the Agreement is found in the Sublette Papers, Mo. Hist. So. See also, Morgan, *Ashley*, 150–52, 158–59.

[35] Beckwourth, 70.

[36] *Missouri Intelligencer* of Fayette, Sept. 28, 1826. Other newspapers also carried reports of his arrival and praise for his success.

supply train and started with it, he became ill en route and returned home.

He was now, with all debts paid, the owner of a fortune, considering the time and place. Moreover, he was assured a good annual income by reason of his contract to furnish supplies. He aspired to a political career. In 1824 he had been an unsuccesful candidate for Governor, and five years later he had failed to be elected to the United States Senate. But in 1831, in a special election to fill a vacancy, he was elected to the national House of Representatives, and he held the seat until March 3, 1837. A little more than a year later he died.

Chapter 4

Smith, Jackson and Sublette

FOLLOWING THE RENDEZVOUS of 1826 and the departure of Ashley for St. Louis with the accumulated furs, the newly-formed partnership of Smith, Jackson, and Sublette launched its program. The new "bushways" were to undertake an intensive search for beaver and a wide range of exploration. Jedediah Smith, with a party of fifteen men, set out from the Salt Lake rendezvous on a trail-breaking journey of great importance. From it and his other searchings he was to emerge as perhaps our greatest single explorer of the Far West.

His little party rode south to Utah Lake and, continuing generally southward, ascended the Sevier and its Clear Creek branch, then descended the Virgin to its junction with the Colorado River and thence to the Mojave villages. Then crossing the Mojave Desert and the San Bernardino Range he pushed westward to San Gabriel Mission. Here he found himself an unwelcome intruder in Mexican territory. With difficulty he was able to explain his presence and extricate himself from official restrictions. He then journeyed northward, through the San Joaquin Valley. After leaving most of his men on the Stanislaus River, he effected the difficult crossing of the High Sierra and the even more hazardous transit of the Nevada desert, and reached the Great Salt Lake area. He was able to join his partners and the other fur gatherers at the rendezvous on Bear Lake in early July, 1827.[1] He was the first to open a route to the Pacific through present United States territory. The country traversed was generally barren, but in California he had found beaver. However, the furs accumulated were still on the Pacific Coast.

The other two partners had done better. They led brigades of trappers into rich beaver country and had made good catches. The route of one party — probably Sublette's — has been recorded for us by Daniel Potts, who gives us our most important contemporary record of events. This brigade left the rendezvous of 1826 and moved northward to the Snake River and up this stream to Henry's Fork. Here, writes Potts, they "were daily harassed by the Blackfeet."[2] After ascending Henry's Fork thirty miles they crossed the Teton Range to the main Snake River and ascended to its source. Crossing the low divide they reached a beautiful expanse of water which they called Sublette's Lake, now known as Yellowstone Lake. Potts gives us

---

[1] Maurice S. Sullivan, *The Travels of Jedediah Smith* (Santa Ana, Calif., 1934); and Dale L. Morgan, *Jedediah Smith and the Opening of the West* (Indianapolis, 1953), hereafter cited as Morgan, *Smith*.

[2] Potts' letter, written at Bear Lake on July 8, 1827, and reprinted in D. M. Frost, *Notes on General Ashley, the Overland Trail, and South Pass* (Worcester, Mass., 1945), 63–64.

our earliest printed account of the marvels of the region.

> On the South border of this Lake is a number of hot and boiling springs, some of water and others of most beautiful fine clay, resembling a mush pot, and throwing particles to the immense height of from twenty to thirty feet. The clay is of a white, and of a pink color, and the water appears fathomless, as it appears to be entirely hollow underneath. There is also a number of places where pure sulphur is sent forth in abundance. One of our men visited one of these whilst taking his recreation — there at an instant the earth began a tremendous trembling, and he with difficulty made his escape when an explosion took place resembling that of thunder. During our stay in that quarter I heard it every day.[3]

This appears to establish the Potts group as the first certain visitors to Yellowstone Park. "From this place," he continues, "by a circuitous route to the North West we returned." Where they went into winter quarters he does not report, but it was probably in Cache Valley or near Salt Lake, their locations of the previous winter.

Of the route and accomplishments of David Jackson and his party we have no record. It is likely that Fitzpatrick accompanied this party, for in 1828 he was Jackson's clerk (see below, page 78) and he may have been serving in this role as early as 1826–27. Robert Campbell says he accompanied Jackson and Sublette and reports that they "ascended the Snake river and tributaries near the Three Tetons and hunted along to the forks of the Missouri, following the Gallatin, and trapped along across the head waters of the Columbia," before coming back to winter in Cache Valley.[4] Upon counting their catch and surveying

---

[3] *Ibid.*, 64. See also Merrill Mattes, "Behind the Legend of Colter's Hell," in *Miss. Val. Hist. Rev.* (Sept. 1949), 271.

[4] Campbell's dictation of 1870 in the Missouri Historical Society Library, quoted in Dale L. Morgan, *The West of William H. Ashley* (Denver, 1964), 161; hereafter cited as Morgan, *Ashley*.

their prospects they decided to send an express to St. Louis to apprise Ashley of their trade and supply needs, in accordance with the Agreement made with him at the preceding summer rendezvous.

William Sublette agreed to carry the winter express, so taking "Black" Harris and a dog as companions, the hardy mountaineers set out from Salt Lake Valley on January 1, 1827. Their hazardous and exhausting journey has been detailed for us by Matt Field.[5] Over the mountains and down the Platte they edged their way. The winds were so fierce, the snowdrifts so deep, the food and fuel so scant, that the men at times despaired of getting through. Their lame and exhausted dog was finally sacrificed, the difficult killing and eating of it being one of the ordeals of the journey.

Upon finally reaching St. Louis, on March 4, Sublette found that Ashley had made an arrangement with B. Pratte & Company to join in the project of taking out supplies to the Mountains. Sublette obtained from Superintendent of Indian Affairs, William Clark, a two-year license to trade with the Indians in the mountain area.[6] The supply company left St. Louis late in March with a party of forty-four men, under the direction of James Bruffee and Hiram Scott.[7]

Of the spring trapping operations of Jackson, Fitzpatrick, and the majority of the mountain fur men we have no information. Our sole, but very interesting contemporary report is by Daniel Potts. With five companions he set out

---

[5] Matthew C. Field, *Prairie and Mountain Sketches,* edited by K. L. Gregg and J. F. McDermott (Norman, Okla., 1957), 165–66.

[6] Licenses to trade with the Indians, listed in *Sen. Doc. 96,* 20th Cong., 1 sess. (Serial 165).

[7] Morgan, *Ashley,* 164–66.

from the winter camp in mid-February "to explore the country lying southwest of the Great Salt Lake." They passed Utah Lake, which Potts reports accurately, and proceeded to Rabbit [Sevier] River. The "Utaw" Indians of the region he described graphically. The party ascended the Sevier some distance, crossed the Wasatch Mountains to Green River drainage and after losing some of their horses to the Indians returned northward.[8] Potts says that a few days before reaching the summer rendezvous site on Bear Lake, the white camp and friendly Indians were attacked by a band of 120 Blackfeet.

Snakes, Utaws and whites sallied forth for battle — the enemy fled to the mountain to a small concavity thickly grown with small timber surrounded by open ground. In this engagement the squaws were busily engaged in throwing up batteries and dragging off the dead. There were only six whites engaged in this battle, who immediately advanced within pistol shot and you may be assured that almost every shot counted one. The loss of the Snakes was three killed and the same number wounded; that of the whites, one wounded and two narrowly made their escape; that of the Utaws was none, though they gained great applause for their bravery. The loss of the enemy is not known — six were found dead on the ground; a great number besides were carried off on horses.[9]

The summer rendezvous of 1827, as agreed to the year before, was held at Bear Lake. This hill-encircled lake is one of the beautiful ones in the mountains. It is especially famous for its changing colors, with the blues and greens remarkably vivid. And in a storm, with the surface covered with sparkling whitecaps, as we witnessed in 1962, the ef-

[8] Potts' letter from Sweetwater Lake [Bear Lake] July 8, 1827; in Frost, *op. cit.*, 66.

[9] *Ibid.*, 64–65. Campbell also tells of the battle (Morgan, *Ashley*, 182). One of the numerous battles described by Beckwourth, always embellished, probably refers to this encounter; his account in T. D. Bonner, *The Life and Adventures of James P. Beckwourth* (New York, 1931), 73.

fect is exhilarating. The lake lies astride the 42nd parallel, which is the present boundary between Idaho and Utah, and was then the international boundary line between Mexico and the Oregon Territory (held jointly by the United States and Great Britain, 1818–46). Thus the trappers were intruders on the soil of Mexico, being at the southern end of the lake. But who knew or cared among the Mountain Men? They were more concerned with the rich meadow area about the site of present Laketown.

The assembled trappers welcomed the supply train as it came over the hill from the east. Goods were now ample and the trappers, having made a fine catch of beaver, were free spenders. Indians, especially the Utes and Snakes who had recently fought with the whites against the Blackfeet, were colorful parts of the rendezvous scene. The fair and fiesta were to last about two weeks. When Jedediah Smith, after his long year's absence in California, came in on July 3, there was special jollification.[10] The four-pounder brought up from St. Louis with the trade goods was fired in salute. Smith took time to write a long letter telling of his exploration and fortune on the California trip.[11] Potts wrote the informative letter we have referred to.

The furs brought in to the rendezvous made a sizable pile, even though Smith's catch was still in California. Sublette and Jackson's men turned over 7,400 pounds of beaver at $3.00 per pound, 95 pounds of castor at the same price, and 102 otter skins at $2.00 each — for a total credit of $22,690.[12] The partners had experienced a good year.

[10] Sullivan, op. cit., 26.

[11] Reproduced in H. C. Dale, The Ashley-Smith Explorations (Glendale, Calif., 1941), 182–90.

[12] Morgan, Smith, 233, citing the Ashley Papers, Mo. Hist. Soc., St. Louis.

The bundles of pelts were packed eastward and upon reaching western Missouri were turned over to the Ashley-Chouteau interests. Mountain supplies and trade goods, brought from St. Louis to this point by prearrangement, were taken over by the caravan, which about-faced and again headed westward. By this arrangement the horses needed by the trappers were being taken back to the mountains, carrying now the supplies required for the winter trading and spring trapping.[13] But the supplies did not reach their destination that fall.[14]

At the close of the 1827 summer rendezvous Jedediah Smith set out on the return trip to his men left in California. His long, disastrous journey, in which the Mojaves and the Umpquas killed most of his men has been told by others. Of the journeys of the other Mountain Men we have but meager records. The experiences of the American trappers who came in contact with the British fur men in the Snake River country have survived in the journals of Peter Skene Ogden. Few men are named, and we are not sure whether Fitzpatrick was in the parties.

Forty Americans encountered Ogden on the Weiser River of west-central Idaho in late September, and some Americans were with or near the British leader on the Payette, Boise, and other streams of southern Idaho through the autumn. By late October the American trappers were short of supplies and gladly traded beaver pelts to the British at low prices.

---

[13] *Niles Weekly Register,* Dec. 1, 1827; J. E. Sunder, *Bill Sublette, Mountain Man* (Norman, Okla., 1959), 75; Don Berry, *A Majority of Scoundrels; an Informal History of the Rocky Mountain Fur Company* (New York, 1961), 159.
[14] P. S. Ogden so reported in his journal (Feb. 17, 1828); see below; and in Morgan, *Ashley,* 180.

From the Portneuf fork of Snake River, the Americans left Ogden on November 30 and "started for Salt Lake," where there was probably a depot of supplies. The next day began "with a wild storm of wind and snow. . . . The trappers came in covered with ice and nearly froze."[15] On Christmas Eve Samuel Tullock, with men of Kenneth McKenzie's upper Missouri outfit, came into Ogden's camp. On New Year's Day they set out for Salt Lake, intending to return in fifteen days with trade goods. But they failed to get through, because of the deep snow, and returned to the British camp. They tried to buy snow shoes, but Ogden prevented sales.

On January 23 Ogden writes: "The American is now very low spirited. He cannot hire a man to go to his cache nor snow shoes nor does he suspect that I prevented. This day he offered 8 beaver and $50 for a pair and a prime horse to anyone who would carry a letter to the American camp. In this he also failed. I have supplied the Am with meat as they cannot procure it without snow shoes. The Americans are starving on Bear River according to report, no buffalo in that quarter, they are reduced to eat horses and dogs. We could not learn from Indians if the American traders had come up from St. Louis." The Americans finally made some snow shoes and tried to get through in late January, but again failed. On a third attempt, they succeeded. On the upper Portneuf they met Robert Camp-

---

[15] The Journal of P. S. Ogden, 1827–29, as copied by Agnes C. Laut in 1905 from the original in Hudson's Bay Company House in London, is edited by T. C. Elliott and published in the *Quarterly of the Ore. Hist. Soc.* of December 1910. Dale L. Morgan made a copy from the H.B.C. original manuscript and has reproduced sections of it in his Jedediah Smith biography. There are variations in the two versions. The quotes are from Miss Laut's copy, as hers covers a longer period.

bell coming north with supplies. He reported that the traders from St. Louis had not arrived due to the severe weather. Campbell now went north to open trade with the Flatheads.

Tullock and his companions who had been with Ogden since December, set out for Salt Lake on March 26. A few days later, on the upper Portneuf they were attacked by Blackfeet, who killed three of the party, including Pinckney Sublette, youngest of the five famous brothers.[16]

Campbell reached the Flatheads and conducted a profitable trade. Upon his return, and just before reaching the summer rendezvous site, he had a brush with Blackfeet. "They would no doubt," wrote Ashley, "have ultimately succeeded in cutting off the whites, had they not been so near the place of rendezvous, where, in addition to 60 or 70 white men, there were several hundred Indians friendly to them, and enemies to the Blackfoots. This fact was communicated to the assailants by a Flathead Indian, who happened to be with Mr. Campbell, who spoke the Blackfoot language. At the same time, the Indians saw two men mounted on fleet horses pass through their lines, unhurt, to carry the information of Mr. C.'s situation to his friends. This alarmed the Indians and produced an immediate retreat."[17]

Jim Beckwourth, who apparently was one of the two emissaries, gives a vivid and florid account of the ride

---

[16] Ashley's letter to T. H. Benton, Jan. 20, 1829, in 20 Cong. 2 sess., *Sen. Doc. 67* (Serial 181), 14, cited by Morgan. A monument to Pinckney Sublette has been placed on the hill overlooking the Green River rendezvous site, near Daniel, Wyoming. A memorial chapel to Father De Smet has been erected nearby. My wife and I visited them in the summer of 1963, with Dr. and Mrs. Jesse Weight of Provo, Utah.

[17] *Ibid.*, 14.

and the battle.[18] Verification of the incident has come from a recently found letter of Daniel Potts, written October 13, 1828, after his return to St. Louis: "A couple of our men mounted two of their swiftest horses dashed through the ranks of the horrid tribe where the balls flew like hail and arrived with the express at our camp in less than one hour a distance of more than sixteen miles." He also tells of the terrible preceding season: "Winter remained gentle untill the first of December, when the power vengence was poured out on us . . . and continued to snow untill the first of March when it somewhat abated the snow remained upwards of four feet deep on the level the sweet [Bear] lake was bridged over on the 8 of may for twenty days in succession."[19]

The supplies being brought out for Smith, Jackson, and Sublette, in the fall of 1827, did not reach the mountains until late November and apparently did not reach their destination until the following spring.[20] Details are lacking.

Some competition for S. J. & S. had developed for the 1828 rendezvous. Joshua Pilcher had launched a new organization with Lucien B. Fontenelle, W. H. Vanderburgh, Charles Bent, and Andrew Drips, and was again in the field. In late summer of 1827 they had set out from Council Bluffs with forty-five men and one hundred horses, bound for the mountains. East of South Pass, the Crows made off with most of their horses, so the partners cached their goods and pushed on to Green River to spend the winter. In the

---

[18] Bonner, *Beckwourth,* 68–70.

[19] Potts' letter in National Park Museum at Mammoth, Wyoming.

[20] Ogden's journal and Ashley's letter of March 1829. See Morgan, *Ashley,* 180, 194.

spring, having procured horses from the Snakes, one party returned for the cached goods, but found most of these spoiled. Pilcher reports:

> The remnant saved from this misfortune was carried across the mountains to the small lake called *Bear Lake*, a little to the west of the sources of the Colorado, then a rendezvous for hunters and traders. Here our traffic with these people was completed. My partners and myself, with nine men, commenced a tour to the northwest, with the view of exploring the region of the Columbia river, to ascertain the attractions and capabilities for trade. This was in July, 1828.[21]

At the close of the summer rendezvous of 1828, Pilcher's company broke up, and three of his companions returned to Missouri with the meager results of their venture — only about seventeen packs of beaver.[22] Smith, Jackson, and Sublette had done better. From the rendezvous of 1828, Sublette had carried their furs back to Missouri. These comprised over seven thousand pounds of beaver, twenty-seven pounds of castorum, forty-nine otter skins, and seventy-three muskrats, the whole valued at $35,810.75. This paid the S. J. & S. debts to Ashley and left a balance of $16,000.[23]

In the fall of 1828 Fitzpatrick again comes clearly into the records. He is serving as clerk for David Jackson's brigade. Probably encouraged by Robert Campbell's success the preceding spring in trading with the Flatheads, Jackson and Fitzpatrick pushed trapping operations north to Flathead Lake, some sixty miles north of present Mis-

---

[21] 21 Cong., 2 sess., *Sen. Doc. 39* (Serial 203), 7–8. See also H. H. Bancroft, *History of the Northwest Coast* (San Francisco, 1884), I, 516; II, 456.

[22] Letter written in French to P. Chouteau Jr. on Oct. 14, 1828. — Chouteau-Papin Collection, Mo. Hist. Soc.

[23] Sublette Papers, Mo. Hist. Soc.

soula, Montana. Here too was Pilcher. Neither of the competing American parties, Jackson's nor Pilcher's made much headway with the Flatheads. The entrenched H.B.C. took the principal business. Gov. George Simpson, head of the veteran British company, reported at Fort Vancouver on March 1, 1829:

> Jackson, accompanied by a clerk Fitzpatrick, and a Major Pilcher with a Clerk Gardner & 40 Trappers . . . visited the Flat head Post last Winter; they had very few Skins, and of those few, about half fell into our hands in exchange for some necessary supplies. . . . "The Major" and Smith Jackson & Siblit, are in hot opposition to each other, and both court our protection and countenance, while we contrive to profit by their strife. Pilcher, has made a formal tender of his Services to the Hon. Co. by letter addressed to me, but I have rejected his strange proposition.[24]

Pilcher had asked for H.B.C. backing and apparently offered to lead a trapping party to the headwaters of the Missouri, being the front for a British operation into American territory. After misfortunes at the hands of the Indians, Pilcher gave up trapping and most of his men joined Jackson and Fitzpatrick.

While with the Flatheads, or shortly thereafter in the spring of 1829, Jackson and Fitzpatrick were delighted to welcome Jed Smith to their camp. He had left Fort Vancouver on March 12, having emerged from his long and hazardous experiences in California and Oregon. Together they worked their way southward to reach Pierre's Hole country, west of the Tetons, and there to join partner William Sublette in early August.[25]

While Jackson and Fitzpatrick were in the Flathead

---

[24] Simpson's report as quoted in Sullivan, *op. cit.*, 144–45.
[25] Smith, Jackson, and Sublette letter to William Clark, Dec. 24, 1829, in Morgan, *Smith,* 341.

country, Robert Campbell led a trapping party into the Crow lands of present Wyoming. With him went Jim Beckwourth, who reports that the party comprised thirty-one men, including Jim Bridger. They trapped the Powder River and Bighorn country. Beckwourth says he was captured by the Crows, who claimed him as a long-lost member of their tribe. An old woman examined the mulatto and removed all doubt when she discovered a mole on his left eyelid.[26] In any event, Beckwourth now began his exciting life with the Crows. It was probably at this time that Campbell released him and gave him some supplies, as recorded in a promissory note which Beckwourth signed with a cross, acknowledging indebtness of $275.17½, which he promised to pay in beaver fur at $3.00 per pound.[27] Beckwourth became a warrior and then a chief of the Crows.

Sublette spent the winter, 1828–29, in St. Louis, gathering goods and men for the supply train he would lead westward in the spring. Among the raw recruits were three young men — Joe Meek, Robert Newell, and George Ebberts — who would supply historians with valuable information on subsequent events. According to Newell and Ebberts the company comprised fifty-four or fifty-five men, as it set out from St. Louis in early March.[28]

On horseback and with pack mules the caravan moved

26 Bonner, *Beckwourth*, 94.

27 This note is preserved in the Sublette Papers, Mo. Hist. Soc. It was dated at "Wind River [torn] 6, 1829."

28 Dorothy O. Johansen (ed.), *Robert Newell's Memoranda*, . . . (Portland, Ore, 1959), 31; G. W. Ebberts, "A Trapper's Life in the Rocky Mountains and Oregon, from 1829–1839," manuscript in the Bancroft Library, University of California. Joseph Meek, in Frances F. Victor, *River of the West* . . . (Hartford, Conn., 1870), 43, says "about sixty men." Harvey E. Tobie has given us a good re-study of Meek's life in *No Man Like Joe* (Portland, Ore, 1949).

up the Platte and Sweetwater. Of the routine Meek said (as reported by Mrs. Frances F. Victor):

When the large camp is on the march, it has a leader, generally one of the Booshways, who rides in advance, or at the head of the column. Near him is a led mule, chosen for its qualities of speed and trustworthiness, on which are packed two small trunks that balance each other like panniers, and which contain the company's books, papers, and articles of agreement with the men. Then follow the pack animals, each one bearing three packs — one on each side, and one on top — so nicely adjusted as not to slip in traveling. These are in charge of certain men called camp-keepers, who have each three of these to look after. The trappers and hunters have two horses, or mules, one to ride, and one to pack their traps. If there are women and children in the train, all are mounted. Where the country is safe, the caravan moves in single file, often stretching out for half or three-quarters of a mile. At the end of the column rides the second man, or "little Booshway," as the men call him, usually a hired officer, whose business it is to look after the order and condition of the whole camp.[29]

From the upper Sweetwater Sublette's party turned northward to the Popo Agie, a branch of Wind River. Here, in the vicinity of present Lander, Wyoming, they met Robert Campbell's party returning from the trapping tour in the Crow country, briefly reported above. Here, about July 1 occurred what might be called the first summer rendezvous of 1829.[30] Meek speaks of it as a hilarious affair, but he appears to be generalizing on the rendezvous as an institution, rather than about this particular meeting.[31]

Jackson did not show up at this July rendezvous; instead, he appears to have sent Fitzpatrick to find Sublette and direct him to a meeting with Jackson farther west. On

---

[29] Victor, *River of the West,* 52–53.

[30] See accounts of Ebbert and Meek and the discussion in Morgan, *Smith,* 303 and 429.

[31] Victor, *River of the West,* 48–52.

June 20, 1829, Fitzpatrick was at the point where the Wind River becomes the Bighorn. Here he witnessed an unusual atmospheric disturbance that in 1834 he described to William M. Anderson: ". . . . all of a sudden the air became of a dull smoky appearance so excessively heated that the skin seemed to be blistered at its touch. He states that he believed that his eyes would melt from his head."[32]

At the Popo Agie and before continuing his journey westward, William Sublette made arrangements for Robert Campbell to carry his forty-five packs of furs back to Missouri. (This he did successfully, reaching Lexington in late August.)[33] Then Sublette organized a large trapping party, which he placed under his brother Milton and two other men who were gaining prominence in the business. One of these was a German named Henry Fraeb (usually called Frapp), and the other a Frenchman, Jean B. Gervais (with a variety of spellings in the literature). We shall presently see these three as partners in the Rocky Mountain Fur Company. The triple-headed party, doubtless to be broken up later into smaller groups, was to move down the Bighorn River and trap that stream and other affluents of the Yellowstone.[34]

Fitzpatrick and William Sublette traveled up the Wind River, over Togwotee Pass and down into Jackson Hole country. Here, Meek says, they met Jackson.[35] Other sources indicate that Jackson and Smith, still together, were not encountered until later, after Fitzpatrick and Sublette

---

[32] Dale L. Morgan and Eleanor T. Harris (eds.), *The Rocky Mountain Journals of William Marshall Anderson* (San Marino, Calif., 1967), 176.

[33] Morgan, *Smith*, 306, 430.

[34] Victor, *op. cit.*, 57.

[35] *Ibid.*, 58.

had crossed the Teton Range and descended into Pierre's Hole.[36] In this beautiful valley of eastern Idaho, immediately west of the Grand Tetons, a general rendezvous (the second of 1829) was held in August. Newell says there were 175 present,[37] and if this number is correct, it must have included many free trappers.

For the fall hunt of 1829 Sublette led his men up Henry's Fork and over the divide northward to the head of the Madison Fork of the Missouri. Enroute they were harassed by Blackfeet. One morning early, just as the horses and mules were being turned out to graze, the Indians attempted to stampede and run off the animals. Fitzpatrick's courage and ability were soon in play. As Meek relates, the Indians were

too hasty by a few minutes . . . only a few of the animals had been turned out, and they had not yet got far off. The noise of the charge only turned them back to camp.

In an instant's time, Fitzpatrick was mounted, and commanding the men to follow, he galloped at headlong speed round and round the camp, to drive back such of the horses as were straying, or had been frightened from their pickets. In this race, two horses were shot under him; but he escaped and the camp-horses were saved. The battle now was to punish the thieves. They took their position, as usual with Indian fighters, in a narrow ravine; from whence the camp was forced to dislodge them, at a great disadvantage. This they did do, at last, after six hours of hard fighting, in which a few men were wounded but none killed.[38]

Despite Blackfeet threats, the trappers pushed deeper into the territory of those hostiles, crossing from the Madison to the head of the Gallatin and then over the range

---

[36] Smith, Jackson, and Sublette Letter to William Clark, Dec. 24, 1829; reprinted in Morgan, *Smith,* 341.

[37] Johansen, *Newell, op. cit.,* 31.

[38] Victor, *op. cit.,* 70.

to the Yellowstone. In the late fall the party moved south to the Stinking (now called Shoshone) Fork of the Bighorn. Here was a volcanic region of sulphur springs and pungent smells that gave the name to the river. It was, as Meek states, the original Colter's Hell. After descending this stream to the Bighorn they encountered Milton Sublette and his forty men.[39]

With winter closing in, the combined parties trekked up the Bighorn to the region where the stream becomes the Wind River. Here they settled into winter camp. The partners and their men had had a successful fall hunt, so it was decided to have new goods and supplies brought up from St. Louis for the summer rendezvous. The assignment went to experienced William Sublette. As three years before on a similar mission, he chose Moses Harris for companion, and the two set out on Christmas Day. However, instead of taking one dog, as before, they now took a train of pack dogs and snowshoes. They had learned something from the British Canadians. They were to make it through safely, and apparently without undue difficulties.

It was at this winter camp, on the day before Christmas, that Jed Smith wrote the letter, now famous, that reveals the character of this religious man. To his brother Ralph he gives a short report of his travels and tragedies, and continues:

As it respects my Spiritual welfare, I hardly durst Speak. I find myself one of the most ungrateful; unthankful, Creatures imaginable. . . . It is, that I may be able to help those who stand in need, that I face every danger — it is for this, that I traverse the Mountains covered with eternal Snow — it is for this that I pass over the Sandy

---

[39] *Ibid.*, 80.

Plains, in heat of Summer, thirsting for water, and am well pleased
if I can find a shade, instead of water. . . . I entangle myself altogether too much in the things of time — . . . pray for me My Brother
— & may he, before whoom not a Sparrow falls, without notice,
bring us, in his own good time, Together again.[40]

The Wind River Valley, usually hospitable to the trapper
bands, was not so this winter. The weather was cold, the
game scarce. So in early January, after caching their accumulated furs, the trappers moved northeastward to the
better buffalo country along Powder River. Here the groves
of sweet, round-leafed cottonwoods were the lure. On the
twigs and bark of the young limbs, horses thrived, and the
buffaloes came to the river valley for the same fare — for
shelter from storms, and for water. Here was a hunter's
paradise. Tents, rude cabins, and tepees sprang up, and
a bustling village appeared in the wilderness.

Through the day, hunting parties were coming and going [as
Mrs. Victor has Meek say], men were cooking, drying meat, making
moccasins, cleaning their arms, wrestling, playing games, and, in
short, everything that an isolated community of hardy men could
resort to for occupation, was resorted to by these mountaineers.
Nor was there wanting, in the appearance of the camp, the variety,
and that picturesque air imparted by a mingling of the native element; for what with their Indian allies, their native wives, and
numerous children, the mountaineers' camp was a motley assemblage; and the trappers themselves, with their affectation of Indian
coxcombry, not the least picturesque individuals. . . .
Instead of Nature's superb silence and majestic loneliness, there
was the sound of men's voices in boisterous laughter, or the busy
hum of conversation; the loud-resounding stroke of the axe; the
sharp report of the rifle; the neighing of horses, and braying of
mules; the Indian whoop and yell; and all that not unpleasing
confusion of sound which accompanies the movements of the creature man. . . .
If the day was busy and gleesome, the night had its charms as

---

[40] Printed in Morgan, *Smith,* 352–54.

well. Gathered about the shining fires, groups of men in fantastic costumes told tales of marvelous adventures, or sung some old-remembered song, or were absorbed in games of chance. Some of the better educated men, who had once known and loved books, but whom some mishap in life had banished to the wilderness, recalled their favorite authors, and recited passages once treasured, now growing unfamiliar; or whispered to some chosen confrere the saddened history of his earlier years, and charged him thus and thus, should ever-ready death surprise himself in the next spring's hunt.[41]

A Bible and Shakespeare somehow turned up in camp — books we may believe well known to men like Fitzpatrick, Smith, and Campbell. Groups formed about the campfires as men read aloud from the volumes, and some of the listeners here obtained a knowledge — perhaps the first knowledge — of the marvels of the printed page. Classes were organized and Meek avers that he was one of the pupils. Fitzpatrick may well have been one of the helpful teachers, for though he had left school at an early age he had already acquired, as his later writings show, a training in the use of the English language probably unmatched by that of any other man at the encampment.

Came the first of April, time for the trappers to be up and about their spring hunt. Jackson, with about half of the men went westward to the Snake River country. Smith and the other half, including Bridger and Meek, moved over to the Tongue, then to the Bighorn, and — crossing the Yellowstone — tarried for a time about the site of present Livingston, Montana. The lure of the Blackfeet country drew him on northward to the Mussellshell and the Judith Basin, but the savages kept up a close investment, stealing traps and horses and making trapping difficult. Smith

---

[41] Victor, *op. cit.*, 83–84.

finally retreated, and by way of the Bighorn reached the point on the Wind River agreed upon as the place of the summer rendezvous. This was doubtless near the point where the Popo Agie enters Wind River, and thus not far from present Riverton, Wyoming.

Of the adventures of Jackson's trapping band, doubtless including Fitzpatrick, we have no record, but they showed up at the summer rendezvous, as Meek says, "with plenty of beaver."[42]

To this rendezvous of 1830 came William Sublette with the supply train — this time a caravan of ten wagons and two Dearborn carriages, the first wheeled vehicles (except the small cannon of 1827) ever to travel a large part of the course which later was to become the Oregon Trail. (It was the centennial of this epochal event — the beginning of wheeled traffic on the Oregon Trail — that, through the efforts of the Oregon Trail Memorial Association, was widely recognized in 1930, and with a special celebration at Independence Rock on the Sweetwater.) Sublette, with eighty-one men, made a very successful trip, one widely reported in the press.[43]

There was a large gathering at the rendezvous; the year had been in the main, prosperous; and the trappers, with ample funds of beaver, bought extravagantly for themselves and their Indian wives. They drank, gambled, and gave themselves up to a season of pleasure and dissipation.

The partners had made a good profit, but they were ready to retire. They could see ahead a diminution of the furs and keener competition in the trade. Important de-

---

[42] *Ibid.*, 89.

[43] Some of the news stories are reprinted in Frost, *op. cit.*, 152–54.

velopments had occurred. Astor's powerful American Fur Company had come into the Missouri River trade. As early as December 1826, Astor had begun the transformation of the Pratte and Chouteau company into the Western Department of his American Fur Company. The next year the Columbia Fur Company, with skillful leader Kenneth McKenzie, joined Astor to form the Upper Missouri Outfit. In 1828 their traders began to push into the Crow country of Wyoming, with knowledgeable Etienne Provost as pilot. That year the Western Department bought out Joseph Robidoux, and later W. H. Vanderburgh. Then, in May 1830, it sent from Council Bluffs a trapping and trading party, headed by Fontenelle and Drips, to the Green River country of the central Rockies.[44] These developments looked ominous and the outlook not bright. Also, Smith wanted to go home, his mother having died. He had a modest fortune and he probably saw this as an appropriate time to retire from the mountains. Jackson had also had deaths in his family. William Sublette, like Ashley before him, saw a safer and surer business career in supplying the trappers, rather than in risking trapping ventures.

In any event, on August 4, 1830, Smith, Jackson, and Sublette sold their mountain fur interests to five of their most competent brigade leaders — Thomas Fitzpatrick, James Bridger, Milton G. Sublette, Henry Fraeb, and Jean Baptiste Gervais. These were to operate under the firm name of the "Rocky Mountain Fur Company."

Smith, Jackson, and Sublette loaded their furs into their wagons and turned back towards Missouri. Their route

---

[44] A discussion of these developments is found in Chittenden, *op. cit.*, 328–31; and in Phillips, *op. cit.*, 417–20.

down the Platte and across Missouri brought them to St. Louis on October 10, 1830. In an exultant report to the Secretary of War they praised the route and declared it entirely feasible for wagon transportation.[45] They had traveled from fifteen to twenty-five miles per day, their ten wagons loaded with about 1800 pounds apiece. They stated that the route on to the Pacific Coast was also practicable. Smith warned of the powerful British establishment on the Columbia River and of the vigor with which the British were trapping the beaver in the southern part of the Oregon Territory.

The three partners were to take a try in the Santa Fe caravan traffic, and Smith was to be killed by Comanches on the first trip out. Jackson was to go to California, engage in mule buying, and disappear from the fur trade story. Sublette would come back to the trade as a supplier and controller of the new Rocky Mountain Fur Company.[46]

---

[45] This report is reprinted in Morgan, *Smith*, 343–48.
[46] See Sunder, *op. cit.*

Chapter 5

Head of Rocky Mountain Fur Company

THE FIVE MEN WHO FORMED the Rocky Mountain Fur Company[1] at the rendezvous of 1830 were capable trapping brigade leaders, rather than experienced businessmen. "The brains of the firm was Thomas Fitzpatrick," writes Dale L. Morgan, "and to a lesser extent Milton Sublette."[2] The other three — Fraeb, Gervais, and Bridger — were competent as trappers and as fighters or traders with the Indians; but with little or no formal education. Whether or not the partners went through the formality of electing a president there is no word; but Fitzpatrick was the acknowledged leader and the executive. Together the five were not equal in business management to Smith, Jackson, and Sublett, nor to Astor and his giant organization.

---

[1] This term has been loosely applied to William Ashley's venture and to the Smith, Jackson, and Sublette firm. But this is incorrect; the name was used first and correctly only by the partnership of Fitzpatrick, Bridger, Fraeb, Gervais, and Milton Sublette.

[2] Morgan, *Smith*, 320.

The exact terms of transfer of the goods and assets of Smith, Jackson, and Sublette to the Rocky Mountain Fur Company have not been found. The agreement was made at the Wind River rendezvous (probably at the mouth of the Popo Agie) in early August 1830, and apparently was similar to that by which the three partners had succeeded Ashley in 1826. That is, the R.M.F. company was to take over the goods remaining at close of rendezvous and pay for them with beaver skins at the rendezvous next year. The obligation thus assumed was about $16,000.[3]

Before we follow the Rocky Mountain Fur Company men on their fall hunt of 1830, let us note the introduction of threatening competition they were to face of American Fur Company men. This opposition in the field was led by Lucien Fontenelle, Andrew Drips, and Joseph Robidoux. We have an excellent detailed account of this party's activities in the narrative of one of its men, Warren A. Ferris.[4] The company left St. Louis in February 1830, and reached Green River on June 21. In this valley they hoped to meet and trade with the free trappers of the region. Four sep-

---

[3] The amount of the note is revealed in subsequent business papers. In one document, signed on Aug. 23, 1831, Jackson and Sublette give David Waldo power of attorney to collect for them. This paper states that on or about Aug. 4, 1830, at the Wind River in the Rocky Mountains the five partners executed to Smith, Jackson, and Sublette a note or obligation for $16,000 and upwards to be due and payable on or about June 15, 1831. The other document, an Agreement made July 25, 1832, between William Sublette and the partners of the Rocky Mountain Fur Company, list the various obligations of the partners to Sublette. One of these is "a note to the late firm of Smith, Jackson, and Sublette amounting to Fifteen Thousand Five Hundred and Thirty-two Dollars 22/100." The two doubtless refer to the same obligation. Both of these papers are in the Sublette Collection, Missouri Historical Society, St. Louis.

[4] W. A. Ferris, *Life in the Rocky Mountains,* . . . edited by Paul C. Phillips (Denver, 1940).

arate parties they sent out at different times and in different directions, failed to locate any of the unattached fur men. Finally, giving up their trading venture for the time being, the new company cached their goods on Ham's Fork and separated into three trapping parties, led respectively by the three leaders. Fontenelle went southward toward the Uinta Mountains, Drips to the upper waters of the Green, and Robidoux northwestward to the Snake River. All finally wound up with Fraeb and Gervais' party and some free trappers at a winter camp in Cache Valley.

After the summer rendezvous of 1830 the Rocky Mountain Fur Company partners had divided into two major brigades for the fall trapping. Fraeb and Gervais, with thirty-four men plus Indian women and children, set out for the Snake River region.[5] Near the mouth of Salt River, which flows northward through Star Valley, Wyoming, to enter the Snake, they were met by the Robidoux party of the American Fur Company men. Although competitors, the two bands moved westward together, along the valley of the Snake and its tributaries. They ran into John Work and a band of Hudson's Bay Company men. The Americans finally made their way back in December to Bear River and to Cache Valley where the snow was three feet deep.[6] Of the spring activity of Fraeb and Gervais we have no positive record.

The other brigade of R. M. F. men under Fitzpatrick, Milton Sublette, and Bridger left the rendezvous of 1830 with a band of some eighty men. With this large force they

[5] *Robert Newell's Memoranda,* edited by Dorothy O. Johansen (Portland, 1959), 31; also Ferris, 59.
[6] Ferris, 58, 60, 64, 69.

dared to penetrate the fur-rich country of the Blackfeet, in present Montana. Robert Newell and Joseph Meek, who were of this band, give some information of movements and adventures. Newell, very sparing with words, says: "[We] went to the Blackfoot Country with 81 men myself one of the number went to the three forks of Missourie Returned took up winter quarters on the yellow Stone."[7]

Meek's report is full of interesting detail, much of which we cannot accept. Especially is his account of the brush with Ogden and the Britishers incorrect. His story of Ogden's Indian wife coming into the American camp and recovering the horse carrying her baby and also taking a pack horse laden with furs, cannot be true, or at least the dating is incorrect. Ogden at the time was on his long expedition through Nevada down to the Colorado River and back through California.[8] Joe's bear stories of this season need also to be taken with a grain of salt.

Fitzpatrick later reported that from the summer rendezvous (1830) he "proceeded to the Three Forks of the Missouri River, a section of country deemed the most dangerous by the trappers." His party reached their place of destination, succeeded in their hunting operations, and returned in safety to the Yellow Stone.[9]

From the Yellowstone camp Fitzpatrick set out in early March with one companion to go to St. Louis to procure supplies. Apparently they boated down the Yellowstone

---

[7] Newell, 31.

[8] See Ted Warner, "Peter Skene Ogden and the Fur Trade of the Great Northwest," M.A. Thesis, Brigham Young University, 1958. Nor does H. E. Tobie, Meek's latest biographer, in his *No Man Like Joe* (Portland, 1949), 21, accept the story.

[9] *St. Louis Beacon*, May 12, 1831, as cited in Morgan, *Smith*, 435.

to Fort Union and thence down the Missouri. He obtained some provisions en route at "Otter Post" on April 15, 1831,[10] and arrived at Lexington, Missouri, in early May.[11]

In the meantime the large R.M.F. company moved south from the Yellowstone to Tongue River. Here in the land of Absaraka those great admirers of horseflesh, the Crows, could not pass up an opportunity. They stole fifty-seven head of trapper horses. Newell records, ". . . this is the first time I went to war on foot." Meek enlarges the losses to 300 and other matters in proportion. Simplified — the trappers followed the Crows and in a surprise attack, recovered their mounts.

After the Crow encounter, Milton Sublette and Bridger led their men southward, up the Powder River and then separated. According to Newell: "Sublette went to the Park [North Park] on the Platte I being one of Bridgers number went with him to the head of Laramas fork met Sublette in the Park from thare to the Snake Country on Bear River near the Big [Salt] lake took up Summer quarters to wait the arrival of Mr. Fitzpatrick with Supplies but in vain."[12]

When Fitzpatrick reached Lexington in early May 1831, he was returning to the settlements for the first time since he set out for the mountains with Ashley in 1823. During

---

[10] Upper Missouri Outfit Ledger, 1831–35, p. 50, Missouri Historical Society. The charge for provisions was $17.45. J. B. Cabanne writing from Council Bluffs to Pierre Chouteau, Jr., on Apr. 19, 1831, says that Fitzpatrick had arrived at Yellow Stone and is going to St. Louis. — A two-page letter in French, in Missouri Historical Society papers. Heretofore it has been assumed that Fitzpatrick went back to Missouri by land, but this later evidence indicates that he boated down.

[11] His arrival at Lexington from the "Mountain region a few days since" is noted in the *St. Louis Beacon* of May 12, 1831.

[12] Newell, 32.

the eight years many changes had occurred. A new army post, Fort Leavenworth, had been established in 1827, thirty miles above the Bend of the Missouri, and in the same year historic Fort Atkinson had been abandoned. The fur trade of the West and the merchandise trade with Santa Fe had developed to great proportions, farming and stock-raising had rapidly increased, and the line of settlements had advanced along the Missouri up to the Bend. Lexington, founded in the year before he started out with Ashley, had grown into a rich and populous town as the frontier starting point of all the western expeditions; though now, in this year 1831, gradually losing its place to its four-year-old rival, Independence, founded near the Bend of the Missouri in 1827.

Fitzpatrick's arrival in Missouri was very late in the season for procuring supplies for mountain trappers. Whether the R.M.F. company had arranged at the summer rendezvous of 1830 for William Sublette alone or in association with his partners Jackson and Smith to bring out supplies to the mountains is not definitely known. Circumstantial evidence would indicate that such an arrangement had been made, in the pattern used preceding years. Otherwise it is likely that Fitzpatrick would not have waited until March to leave the mountains.

The potential suppliers having received no positive word in March or April, were left in doubt as to expectations. They had decided to enter the trade to Santa Fe and apparently figured that they could correlate this with the trade to the central Rockies.[13]

---

[13] See the discussion of the problem in John E. Sunder, *Bill Sublette, Mountain Man* (Norman, Okla., 1959), 93–95; and Morgan, *Smith*, 325–28.

By the time Fitzpatrick reached Lexington, forty miles east of Independence, the three new traders were well on their way towards Santa Fe. The only thing that Fitzpatrick could do upon meeting them was to make arrangements for supplies on their terms. Thus it was agreed that Fitzpatrick would accompany the wagon caravan to Santa Fe and that there the traders would provide him with the desired goods. This would make a long, roundabout route, but what alternative was there?

The twenty-three mule-drawn wagons, carrying an eighty-five-man party, rolled along the well-known Santa Fe Trail. It was an odd company, for by some strange circumstance none of the leaders was well acquainted with the Trail or traffic upon it. The Santa Fe caravans were in most respects different from the trapper trains. The leaders here were merchants, not trappers; they moved by wagon, and not by pack-train, for thus far wagons had been used but once on the Platte trail.

The appearance of the typical caravan and its men is preserved for us by Josiah Gregg, early historian of the Santa Fe Trail:

The most "fashionable" prairie dress is the fustian frock of the city-bred merchant furnished with a multitude of pockets capable of accommodating a variety of "extra tackling." Then there is the backwoodsman with his linsey or leather hunting-shirt — the farmer with his blue jean coat — the wagoner with his flannel-sleeve vest — besides an assortment of other costumes which go to fill up the picture.

In the article of fire-arms there is also an equally interesting medley. The frontier hunter sticks to his rifle, as nothing could induce him to carry what he terms in derision "the scatter-gun." The sportsman from the interior flourishes his double-barrelled fowling-piece with equal confidence in its superiority. . . . A great many were furnished beside with a bountiful supply of pistols and knives of every description, so that the party made altogether a very brigand-like appearance.

Cooking and dining utensils, says the Trail historian, consist "of a skillet, a frying-pan, a sheet-iron campkettle, a coffee-pot, and each man with his tin cup and a butcher's knife." And when the meal is prepared "the pan and kettle are set upon the grass turf, around which all take a 'lowly seat,' and crack their gleesome jokes, while from their greasy hands they swallow their savory viands — all with a relish rarely experienced at the well-spread tables of the most fashionable and wealthy."[14]

The caravan moved at the pace of about twenty miles a day. Before reaching the Arkansas it lost a man, killed by the Pawnees. After crossing the Arkansas, already low in a dry season, the party headed over the waterless Cimarron Desert. Fitzpatrick and Smith went ahead of the wagons to look for water. While Fitzpatrick was scooping a shallow well in a dry stream bed, Smith pushed on toward the Cimarron. He found it dry. While digging into the wet sand he was pounced upon by a band of Comanches and killed.[15] Thus was the heroic trailblazer, the survivor of the bloody Indian massacres by the Mojaves and the Umpquas, and of the Nevada desert terrors, finally cut down at the age of 32 by the mounted raiders of the high plains. His body was never found by white men; but his pistol and other personal equipment was said to have later shown up in the hands of Mexican traders at Santa Fe. The wagon train continued on and eventually reached the waters

---

[14] Josiah Gregg, *Commerce of the Prairies,* edited by Max L. Moorhead (Norman, Okla., 1954), 33, 39.

[15] The information is pieced together from fragmentary facts and plausible conclusions.

of the Cimarron and then in due time arrived at the New Mexico capital.

Somewhere in the region south of the Arkansas River Fitzpatrick had a strange experience. While riding apart from the wagons he noticed in some brush a movement as of an animal or Indian. Advancing cautiously and examining carefully, he discovered a small Indian boy, emaciated with hunger and too helpless to run. The kind traveler picked up the waif, soothed his fears, and carried him to the wagons, where with sympathetic ministrations the little fellow rapidly recovered strength and spirit. Fitzpatrick took a liking to the boy, whom he cared for and adopted. For the day on which the rescue was made, he named the boy "Friday." Later the boy, who was found to be an Arapaho, was taken to St. Louis and placed in school. He subsequently was returned to his parents and will appear from time to time in this narrative. The story of his life, unique in frontier annals, will be told in full later in this volume (see Appendix A).

The wagon train did not arrive at Santa Fe until July 4; at a time when the supplies should have reached the trappers' summer rendezvous. All that could now be done was to make the best of a bad situation. Fitzpatrick bought from Sublette and Jackson and from a representative of Jedediah Smith's estate, equipment and supplies totaling nearly $6,000.[16] Of these Fitzpatrick afterwards wrote: "I took such articles as you could not dispose of in Mexico and articles which you were glad to get rid of." He promised to bring in to the Taos vicinity by December 31 in

---

[16] Documents in the Sublette Collection, Mo. Hist. Soc.

payment "good clean, well handled mountain fur at the rate of $4.25 per pound."[17]

In New Mexico Sublette and Jackson dissolved their partnership. Jackson went on to California to procure mules for the Missouri trade and Sublette remained to dispose of his goods. By September 1 he had succeeded in this, having traded for 55 packs of beaver and 800 buffalo robes.[18] On his return home he wrote from Walnut Creek near the Arkansas on the Santa Fe Trail, a letter to his friend Robert Campbell. In this he said, "we Equipt Mr. Thomas Fitzpatrick out from Taos with about 40 men and supplies and Expected if he had time he would have returned before we left there but the time was two short We heard from Mr. Milton Sublette he had taken about 50 packs of Beaver in the Spring hunt which was nearly one pack to the man."[19]

At Taos, frontier New Mexico town and favorite gathering place of mountain trappers, Fitzpatrick completed his outfit and took on his last recruits. Among them was one destined for fame, Kit Carson. Kit, having run away from the saddlemaker to whom he had been apprenticed in Franklin, Missouri, had joined a Santa Fe caravan and had launched his career in the Southwest. With Ewing Young, experienced trapper, and others he had learned something of the craft by trips into Arizona and California.

---

[17] The paper by which Jackson and Sublette appointed David Waldo their attorney, Aug. 23, 1831; correspondence of Fitzpatrick and Ira G. Smith (Jedediah's brother) and statement of Samuel Parkman (agent for Jedediah), relating to goods sold in New Mexico to Fitzpatrick; and Jackson's receipt to W. L. Sublette, Mar. 29, 1833 — all documents in the Sublette Collection, Mo. Hist. Soc. — examined by me in 1953.

[18] Sunder, *Sublette,* 99.

[19] Campbell Papers, 1825–31 (photostats, Mo. Hist. Soc.).

Now he was going for the first time into the central Rockies; and he was under the capable guidance of Thomas Fitzpatrick.[20] Kit was to continue in the fur trade for more than a decade, and would emerge as one of the notable Mountain Men.

On July 23 at Taos Fitzpatrick signed notes for his equipment and supplies.[21] Then with his party of about forty men he pushed the pack-horse train northward along the front range of the Rockies. They crossed the Arkansas, doubtless near present Pueblo, Colorado, and moved on to the South Platte and then to the North Platte.

In the meantime Fitzpatrick's partners had completed their spring hunt, as reported above, and were ready for summer rendezvous. One infers from Newell's statement that Sublette and Bridger came in to Cache Valley or the nearby Bear River near Great Salt Lake. Meek says his party went to Green River for rendezvous; and Fraeb was there in early July.[22] The assembled trappers waited anxiously but in vain for Fitzpatrick and the supplies. Meek reports: "The large number of men now employed, had exhausted the stock of goods on hand. The camp was without blankets and without ammunition; knives were not to be had; traps were scarce; but worse than all, the tobacco had given out, and alcohol was not! In such a case as this, what could a mountain man do?"[23]

---

[20] De Witt C. Peters, *The Life and Adventures of Kit Carson, etc.* (New York, 1858), 50.

[21] Statement in Jackson's receipt to W. L. Sublette, Mar. 29, 1833, in Sublette Papers, Mo. Hist. Soc.

[22] On July 9, 1831, at Green River, Fraeb signed, for the Rocky Mountain Fur Company a promissory note to William Gordon for $30.00. Original in the Sublette Papers, Mo. Hist. Soc.

[23] Victor, *River of the West,* 99. Hereafter cited as **Meek.**

As the men grew more restive, Fraeb, who like many trappers, had picked up some of the superstitions of the red man, decided to learn the whereabouts of Fitzpatrick by consulting an oracle. A medicine man of the Crows should be able to tell what had become of the absent "booshway." The prophet was not unwilling to help, but required a generous fee, of the value of a horse or two, to propitiate the unseen powers and to engage their assistance. This given, he began his ceremonial inquiry. Singing, dancing, screeching, violent contortions of the body and the beating of drums were continued for several days and nights until the exhausted prophet fell asleep. When he awoke he announced that Fitzpatrick was neither dead nor lost, but was on his way, though coming on the wrong road.[24]

Thus encouraged, Fraeb determined to find him, and taking a few companions, set out immediately. He went first in the direction of Wind River, then came down to the Sweetwater and the Platte. Here, to the great joy of the party, Fitzpatrick and his supply train were met. Fitzpatrick turned over to Fraeb the train of goods, and set his face for Missouri.[25] He must be certain that the next year's supplies arrive at rendezvous on time.

At the mouth of the Laramie, near where Fort Laramie was to rise three years later, Fitzpatrick was unhappy to come upon a newly-arrived party of competing trappers. This band had been organized by John Gantt and Jefferson Blackwell, who had obtained a license from Superintendent

[24] *Ibid.*, 99–100.
[25] Ferris, 124.

TRAPPER COMPANIONS OF FITZPATRICK

Upper left: James Clyman (courtesy Charles L. Camp)
Upper right: James P. Beckwourth (courtesy of the State Historical Society
 of Colorado)
Lower left: Joseph L. Meek (from Victor's *River of the West*)
Lower right: Kit Carson (courtesy of the State Historical Society of Colorado)

William Clark at St. Louis on May 5, 1831.[26] Inexperienced and with poor management they had proceeded slowly and with difficulty up the Republican River and then the Platte. Before separating into three parties for the fall hunt they dug a hole for storage of supplies. It was while caching their goods that they welcomed Fitzpatrick and his companions.

Writes Zenas Leonard, one of the Gantt and Blackwell men: "He was an old hand at the business and we expected to obtain some useful information from him, but we were disappointed. . . . He refused to give us any information whatever, and appeared to treat us as intruders."[27] It is easy to understand Fitzpatrick's attitude. He was one of the original band that had opened the fur resources of the Green River and central Rockies area. The Hudson's Bay Company had early challenged their primacy; then came the men from Santa Fe, and during the past two seasons the American Fur Company now had crowded in. He could hardly be expected to exult over added competition.

But he did accept Blackwell and his two men as traveling companions back to the states, even though Blackwell was going in for supplies to bring out the following summer. On their journey eastward, after setting out on September 3, we have no record. Fitzpatrick arrived in due course at St. Louis, where he spent the winter, making arrangements for supplies for 1832.

Now back to the trappers in the mountains. After a long

---

[26] A Spanish translation of the license is found in Henry E. Huntington Library, San Marino, Calif. It names 61 men of the proposed company, and for the first time in literature, gives us the full name of Captain Blackwell.

[27] J. C. Ewers, editor, *Adventures of Zenas Leonard, Fur Trader* (Norman, 1959), 8–9.

wait in the Cache Valley area for Fitzpatrick and supplies, Milton Sublette and Bridger concluded that their partner was not coming, and that the intended summer rendezvous for 1831 would not take place. So they finally set out for their fall trapping. Robert Newell of their party gives their general route. They moved northeastward from Bear River to Grey's Fork (which runs parallel to Salt River) and descended it to the Snake. They pushed across the Snake River Plains and on to Salmon River of western Idaho; then north to the Deer Lodge and Flathead areas of Montana; and finally back to Salmon River. Here they "met Mr. Fraeb with Supplies from Mr. Fitzpatrick and took up winter quarters with the flatheads and napercies [Nez Perces]."[28]

Ferris gives a colorful additional report: "Fraeb arrived . . . and camp presented a confused scene of rioting, and bebauchery for several days, after which however, the kegs of alcohol were again bunged, and all became tranquil. . . . The men provided themselves with lodges, and made preparation for passing the winter as comfortable as possible."[29]

A party of fifty men from Fort Union, at the mouth of the Yellowstone, had come out in the fall of 1831 and passed the winter in Cache Valley. It was led by W. H. Vanderburgh.[30] Here was evidence of the vigorous competition that the powerful American Fur Company people were putting into the central Rockies region.

Another party, of forty-eight A.F.C. men under Andrew

---

[28] Newell, 32. Ferris also gives information as to the movements of the R.M.F. company men. See pages 96, 121, 124, 128.

[29] Ferris, 126.

[30] *Ibid.*, 138.

Drips, had come out during the fall with supplies. They had left Council Bluffs about the first of October and were able to reach only to the Laramie River area before being forced to hole up for the winter.

The R.M.F. company men, for their spring trapping of 1832, went from Salmon River to Henry's Fork and then up Snake River. They trapped Salt and Grey's forks of the Snake and crossed to Bear River.[31] Here Drips and the opposition trappers caught up with them. Ferris gives us a good contemporary description of Bridger's band:

> Their encampment was decked with hundreds of beaver skins, now drying in the sun. These valuable skins are always stretched in willow hoops, varying from eighteen inches, to three feet in diameter, according to the size of the skins, and have a reddish appearance on the flesh side, which is exposed to the sun. Our camps are always dotted with these red circles, in the trapping season, when the weather is fair. There were several hundred skins folded and tied up in packs, laying about their encampment, which bore good evidence to the industry of the trappers.[32]

The rivalry between the R.M.F. and the A.F.C. was now keen and bitter. The former had the more experienced field men, but the latter had ample financial backing and were determined to profit from the know-how of the Fitzpatrick men. Meek describes the situation:

> The American Company's resident partners were ignorant of the country, and were greatly at loss where to look for the good trapping grounds. These gentlemen, Vanderburg and Dripps, were therefore inclined to keep an eye on the movements of the Rocky Mountain Company, whose leaders were acquainted with the whole region lying along the mountains, . . . the rival company had a habit of turning up in the most unexpected places, and taking advantage of the hard-earned experience of the Rocky Mountain Company's

---

[31] Newell, 32; Meek, 103.
[32] Ferris, 144.

leaders. They tampered with the trappers, and ferreted out the secret of their next rendezvous; they followed on their trail, making them pilots to the trapping grounds; they sold goods to the Indians, and what was worse, to the hired trappers. In this way grew up that fierce conflict of interests, which made it "as much as his life was worth" for a trapper to suffer himself to be inveigled into the service of a rival company, which about this time or a little later, was at its highest, and which finally ruined the fur-trade for the American companies in the Rocky Mountains.[33]

The R. M. F. company men had set Pierre's Hole as the place of summer rendezvous, 1832. To this picturesque valley, in the shade of the high, sharp Three Tetons, the trappers began to gather in June. The A. F. C. men, not to be outdone, gathered in to the same place also. They expected Fontenelle to bring in supplies, and Vanderburgh awaited trade goods to be brought from Fort Union by Etienne Provost. But neither arrived at Pierre's Hole.[34]

The weather was cold as the trappers waited for the supply trains to arrive. Ferris writes: "Throughout the month of June, scarcely a day passed without either rain, hail, or snow, and during the last three days of the month, a snow storm continued without intermission, the whole time, night and day; but disappeared from the earth a few hours after the sun reappeared."[35]

Then in early July a man sent in quest of the supply trains, returned and reported that Sublette with a big caravan was on the way.

---

[33] Meek, 103–104.
[34] Ferris, 150, 156.
[35] *Ibid.*, 151.

Chapter 6

Fitzpatrick's Perilous Ride

DURING THE WINTER OF 1831–32 in St. Louis Fitzpatrick had plenty of time to procure supplies, but no money with which to buy the goods or equip a train for the coming spring. Although the fur catch of his Rocky Mountain Fur Company had been fair in 1831, the partners had been unable to make a return of furs to the Missouri market. Under the circumstances, the best Fitzpatrick could do was to make a deal with William Sublette, largely on the latter's terms. Sublette, as merchant and supplier, was in a good position. Money from his own ventures and credit with William H. Ashley, recently elected to Congress, enabled him to drive a hard bargain.

Sublette offered to buy the necessary trade goods and supplies and to transport them to the summer rendezvous at Pierre's Hole. This was the beginning of Sublette's control over the Rocky Mountain Fur Company. His advantageous position was to be formalized and perpetuated in an Agreement to be signed at the rendezvous in July, 1832 — more of this later. Sublette advanced Fitzpatrick money to see him through the winter, to purchase some supplies, and to employ four men.[1]

On April 25, 1832, William Sublette obtained from William Clark, Superintendent of Indian Affairs at St. Louis, a license to trade with the far western Indians. The license, which was to run for two years, names 39 employes and says the capital employed was $1,300.[2] He also received a special permit to carry 450 gallons of whisky "for the special use of his boatmen." Inasmuch as his party was to travel by land and had no boatmen, this permit was merely an excuse to take liquor for trade at the rendezvous.[3]

Apparently, Fitzpatrick and the R.M.F. company did not procure a trading license. Presumably they would operate under Sublette's license, or else consider themselves as trappers, and not traders.

With a train of about fifty men, including his brother Andrew, and 65 horses and mules, Sublette set out from St. Louis in late April, 1832. With him went Fitzpatrick with four men, and Robert Campbell with five.[4] The rains were heavy and the mud deep as they sloshed across Missouri. Near Independence the final recruiting and outfitting camp was made. Here on the frontier the Sublette-Fitzpatrick party was joined by Nathaniel Wyeth and his company of Far Easteners now venturing into the Far West.

---

[1] Letter of Sublette to W. H. Ashley, from Independence, Missouri, May 12, 1832. — Campbell Papers, Mo. Hist. Soc. Sublette says he has advanced Fitzpatrick $1373.70, besides a draft for $500.

[2] The original license is in the Sublette Papers, Mo. Hist. Soc. Papers.

[3] John E. Sunder, *Bill Sublette, Mountain Man* (Norman, 1959), 102–03.

[4] Sublette's letter to Ashley of May 12, 1832, *op. cit.*

These newcomers were happy for the opportunity to go along with well-seasoned packers and Mountain Men.

The combined parties, leaving Independence on May 13, numbered about 85 men, with some 300 head of stock, as they pushed up the route soon to be known as the Oregon Trail. They traveled in two columns and under strict discipline. Beef and sheep on the hoof provided larder until the buffalo range was reached.

At the mouth of Laramie's fork of the North Platte the caravan came upon a detachment of Gantt and Blackwell's trappers, waiting in vain for the return of their chiefs. Fitzpatrick, with whom Blackwell had traveled to the States the preceding fall, informed the disappointed fur men that their leaders' company was bankrupt. So Stephens, head of the local party, sold their 120 beaver skins to Fitzpatrick and agreed to go along with the R.M.F. supply train to the rendezvous in Pierre's Hole.[5] Fitzpatrick cached the purchased furs on the spot and then raced ahead of the train to carry to the rendezvous news of the approach of the company's supply caravan.

After crossing South Pass and before reaching Green River, the pack train met some of Drips and Fontenelle's men and also had a brush with the Indians, in which they lost a number of horses killed or stolen. But the supply train arrived safely at Pierre's Hole on July 8. What was their surprise to learn that Fitzpatrick had not arrived.

---

[5] J. C. Ewers (Ed.), *Adventures of Zenas Leonard, Fur Trader* (Norman, 1959), 28–29. The Leonard narrative, after being run in the newspaper of Clearfield, Pa., was issued as a small book at the same place in 1839. Leonard is the principal historian of the Gantt and Blackwell venture. Captain Wyeth also mentions the new group in his "The Correspondence and Journals of Captain Nathaniel Wyeth, 1831–6," edited by F. G. Young, in *Sources of the History of Oregon*, I, 156. Hereafter sited as Wyeth.

Later that day he was found, but so emaciated as to be hardly recognizable. After food and rest he reported his experiences. The fullest contemporary account is given by Zenas Leonard, who purports to render it in Fitzpatrick's own words.[6]

With two fleet horses, which he rode alternately, Fitzpatrick felt himself secure from pursuit by Indians. Unmolested he crossed South Pass and descended the western slope. Suddenly he was confronted by a band of Grosventres (often spoken of as Blackfeet), and he realized that he must race for his life. Shifting his course and losing one of his horses, he made for the nearby mountains. Up a mountain path, steep and rough, he started on a gallop, but soon found his flagging mount weakening under the strain. The Indians dismounted and followed on foot. In vain he applied the whip; and seeing that his horse would soon be overtaken he abandoned it and ran on. He found a hole in the rocks, crept in, and hastily closed the mouth of it with sticks and leaves. In a few minutes he heard the yells of triumph of his pursuers as they captured his horse, and soon after their scurrying footsteps as they passed his hiding place. In despairing silence he waited for hours. Darkness came, and he knew that the pursuit had for the time been abandoned.

He crawled out, surveyed the country as well as the darkness would permit, and started off in what he deemed the safest direction. But he soon found himself on the

[6] The story that follows is based primarily on Leonard's account. Other briefer reports are found in Irving's *Bonneville*, 54–55; Ferris, *Life in the Rocky Mountains*, 152–53; and W. H. Ellison, ed., *The Life and Adventures of George Nidever* (Berkeley, Calif., 1937), 24–25. These all agree substantially with Leonard's account.

border of the Indian camp. Fortunately it was quiet, with no watchers awake, and so he was able unpursued to get back to his hiding place.

Early the next morning the search for him was renewed, but after a time abandoned for good. When the sound of the Indians' voices no longer reached him, he again crept to the mouth of the hole and at a distance saw them running races with his horse. The second night came, and he made another effort to escape. He descended the mountain to the creek that flowed some distance below the Indian camp, and followed it till daylight. Secreting himself in some brush, he then waited for the third night.

Again he passed a night in traveling onward, and at daylight, feeling that he was now outside the range of pursuit, he kept on. He found berries and roots to sustain him, but did not dare to fire his rifle at game. He came to a stream which he must cross, so he improvised a crude raft. But the raft broke in two against a rock, and though he swam to the other shore, his rifle and shot pouch disappeared in the water. He had now no weapon but a butcher knife.

He pushed on, weak and staggering, toward the haven of Pierre's Hole. One night, while digging for an edible root in a swamp, a pack of wolves came down upon him, and he escaped only by climbing a tree, where he remained till daylight. Then they moved off, intent upon some other quest, and he descended and went on. He came upon the carcass of a buffalo that had been killed and partly eaten by wolves. Scraping from the bones what meat remained, he cooked it in a hollow of the earth by a fire made by rubbing two sticks together. His hunger for the time appeased and his strength regained, he went on. But as the days passed he found food scarcer; there were no berries and no roots, and he became so weak that he was no longer able to walk. He now gave up hope and expected death. At the last extremity of weakness and despair, he was discovered by two men sent from the camp at Pierre's Hole to look for him. He was hardly recognizable; his body was a mere skeleton; his eyes were sunken, his face was drawn and emaciated, and his hair seemed to have turned white. Food was given him, and he soon recovered.

The Sublette supply train was not only the first to come in to renezvous; it was the only one that arrived. The American Fur Company goods were back on Green River. But at the rendezvous were Vanderburgh and Drips with a large contingent of A.F.C. men impatiently waiting for supplies.[7] With the Sublette train had come Wyeth's party and the Stevens group of Gantt and Blackwell's company men. Just before their arrival, a remnant of the Bean-Sinclair company from Arkansas had reached the rendezvous. There were also other small independent groups.

And as though there was not enough competition for the gradually diminishing beaver colonies in the mountains, another company had come out this year. Though it was not to figure in the stirring midsummer events at

---

[7] Ferris gives the fullest and most accurate account of American Fur Company activities. Vanderburgh and Drips were at the Pierre's Hole rendezvous and waited in vain for Provost and Fontenelle with supplies. Since they did not come, the Vanderburgh and Drips party, including Ferris, finally set out on August 2 and went southeast in search of their supply train. A week later they found Fontenelle and Provost on Green River. Fontenelle had brought up goods by boat from St. Louis to the mouth of the Yellowstone and thence packed them to Green River. He and Provost had a party of 50 men and about 150 horses.

On August 12 Fontenelle, with 30 men and the accumulated furs began his return trip to the mouth of the Yellowstone. Vanderburgh and Drips (and Ferris) set out to find and follow the R.M.F. trappers. See Ferris, 150–59.

Pierre's Hole, it was for three years to prove a source of constant irritation to Fitzpatrick's men. This was the party of Captain B. L. E. Bonneville, who with 110 well-equipped men and 28 heavily laden wagons, had set out from Fort Osage, on the Missouri, on May 1, 1832. In due time it arrived in the valley of the Green, and near the mouth of Horse Creek (at present Daniel, Wyoming) Bonneville erected a stockade and began to scatter his trapping parties throughout the region.

The rendezvous of 1832 at Pierre's Hole was one of the largest and most picturesque gatherings ever held in the mountains; and it was further distinguished as the occasion of one of the most famous battles of the fur trade period. Perhaps a thousand trappers and Indians were present.[8] The trappers of the various companies had separate camps, and friendly Indians had set up their skin lodges along the banks of the streams.

Supplies were abundant; beaver pelts were plentiful, and the mountaineers and Indians bought freely. Cups and camp kettles of whisky went the rounds and hilarity was unbounded. Writes Joe Meek's biographer:

When Captain Sublette's goods were opened and distributed among the trappers and Indians, then began the usual gay carousal; and the "fast young men" of the mountains outvied each other in all manner of mad pranks. In the beginning of their spree many feats of horsemanship and personal strength were exhibited, which were regarded with admiring wonder by the sober and inexperienced New Englanders under Mr. Wyeth's command. And as

---

[8] Meek, p. 110, says not less than 1000, with 2000 to 3000 horses. Wyeth, 159, says there were about 120 lodges of Nez Percés and 80 of Flatheads, 90 A.F.C. trappers under Drips, and 100 R.M.F. men. Then there were the small parties of Wyeth, Stevens, Sinclair, Perkins, and other independent groups. Nidever, 25, says there were about 500 hunters and trappers; Leonard says 400 whites (p. 41); Newell says 600 men, white and Indian.

nothing stimulated the vanity of the mountain-men like an audience of this sort, the feats they performed were apt to astonish themselves. In exhibitions of the kind, the free trappers took the lead, and usually carried off the palm, like the privileged class that they were.

But the horse-racing, fine riding, wrestling, and all the manlier sports, soon degenerated into the baser exhibitions of a "crazy drunk" condition.[9]

By mid July the goods were all sold, the fur packs gathered in, and plans were made for the fall hunt. Milton Sublette and Henry Fraeb, with Wyeth's reduced party, and a few independent trappers were the first to set out. They headed southeastward for Teton Pass and the Snake River on July 17. Eight miles out and still within the basin they camped for the night. Next morning a long line of horsemen was seen emerging from a canyon into the valley. Thought at first to be the long-expected supply train of the A.F.C., it soon took on a more colorful appearance. Wyeth, studying the men through a field glass, soon recognized them as an Indian party, plumed and painted for war. They proved to be Grosventres.

With blankets waving and feathers streaming they came whooping into the plain, as though they meant war. However, their chief rode forward unarmed, holding up a peace pipe. This gesture would normally be respected by red and white alike; but the Blackfeet and the Grosventres were notorious for treachery and a ruse was suspected. To meet the chief out rode Antoine Godin, an Iroquois half-breed, whose father had been killed by the Blackfeet some time before, and a Flathead — one of a tribe whose enmity against the Blackfeet and Grosventres was

---

[9] Victor, *Meek,* 110–11.

ingrained. As the three met, and the chief put forth his right hand in token of friendship, Godin told the Flathead to fire. The command was obeyed, and the chief fell dead; while Godin seizing his scarlet blanket as a trophy, galloped back with the Flathead amid a hail of bullets, to the trappers' camp.

The Battle of Pierre's Hole was on. The hostiles took a position in a jungle of willows, where their women threw up a breastwork of logs while the warriors kept up a fusilade of arrows and bullets. After sending a courier to the main camp for reinforcements, Milton Sublette entrenched his men in a ravine, while Wyeth posted his men behind their baggage.

At first the fighting was at long range and rather ineffective. But soon the trappers and friendly Indians from the main camp came to the rescue and began to move in closer. The hostiles, amazed to see so many enemies, withdrew behind their breastworks, while their women and children hurried into the mountains.

Fitzpatrick, according to Leonard, acted as commander-in-chief of the attacking force. But the excited and undisciplined trappers seem to have shown little concert of action. William Sublette favored an immediate charge, and started for the jungle. Robert Campbell went with him; each making his oral will to the other as they crept forward through the underbrush. Alexander Sinclair and some others followed. Sublette was stunned by a bullet in the shoulder, and Campbell dragged him back to safety. Sinclair was shot dead. George Nidever reports:

One of the trappers of Frapp's [Fraeb's] company got very near the rear of the fort, almost up to it in fact, by crawling flat on the ground and pushing and rolling a large log so as to protect his head. Several shots struck the log but the trapper got into the position and abandoned his log for a tree without being harmed.

Another one of Frapp's men, a Canadian half-breed, tried to distinguish himself by rashly crawling up to the very wall of the fort and then peeping over the top. He paid for his temerity with his life. He had barely raised his head above the breastworks of logs when he received two bullets in his forehead. He was half drunk at the time, liquor having been distributed among the men during the early part of the fight.[10]

As the trappers pressed forward in a crescent, the lines almost surrounded the Indian fort, and a dangerous cross-fire resulted. Gradually the trappers' rifles silenced the firing from the fort, and it seemed evident that the red warriors would be exterminated. Some one proposed to set fire to the jungle and burn the defenders out, but the friendly Indians objected; they wanted the blankets, guns, and trinkets of the Grosventres for trophies.

So the battle continued until late afternoon. The beseiged must have about lost hope. Then a voice arose in a high-pitched harangue, extolling the virtues of the Grosventres and shouting defiance to their enemies. Some of the friendlies translated this defiant utterance into the exulting statement that their enemies in overwhelming numbers were already attacking the unguarded main camp, with its hundreds of women and children and its stores of goods. The attack at once weakened, as the men withdrew from the lines, rushed for horses and sped back toward the camp. Finding everything there quiet and safe, they returned, but it was now too dark to resume the fight. In the morning they found that the surviving hostiles had fled. They had left ten dead bodies, taking with them many that were

---

[10] Nidever, 28.

wounded. Thirty or more horses were killed, and others were abandoned. Among the latter, Fitzpatrick was delighted to find one of the two that had been taken from him at the time of his recent gruelling experience with the hostile Indians. The losses of the whites has been variously stated. Sinclair was killed, and perhaps four or five others; while the wounded may have numbered five or ten. The losses of the Indian allies were seven killed, and perhaps as many more wounded.[11] The trappers returned to their rendezvous encampment, where the wounded were cared for and business was resumed.

Fitzpatrick and William Sublette drew up and signed a formal agreement that is so important as to justify its reproduction here:

Articles of Agreement made and entered into on the Teton Fork of the Colombia River and under the Three Teton mountains this Twenty fifth day of July in the Year One Thousand Eight Hundred and Thirty Two, by and between William L. Sublette of the first part and Thomas Fitzpatrick Milton G. Sublette John Baptiste Jarvie James Bridger and Henry Fraeb trading under the name and Style of the Rockey Mountain Furr Co. of the Second part witnesseth

That whereas the said William L Sublette has delivered as per contract a certain Invoice of Merchandise to said Rockey Mountain Furr Co and is now about to return to St. Louis missouri The said Rockey Mountain Furr Co have bargained with said William L. Sublette to transport on their account to St. Louis all their Beaver Furr, Beaver Castors, Otter, Musk rat & to St. Louis Missouri at their risk and to pay said William L. Sublette for so doing Fifty cents per pound with the following understanding viz.

---

[11] Early eyewitness accounts of the battle are to be found in the letters of W. L. Sublette (published in the *Missouri Republican* of Oct. 16, 1832, and the *Missouri Intelligencer* of Oct. 20, 1832), in the journals of N. J. Wyeth and of J. B. Wyeth, 43–46; Nidever's account, 26–29; and John Ball's *Autobiography*, 77–79. One of the best accounts is by Irving in his *Bonneville*, 58–63.

The said Rockey Mountain Furr Co owe said William L. Sublette for the merchandize above alluded to the sum of Fifteen Thousand Six Hundred and Twenty dollars. Also one note due June first for One Thousand Four Hundred and Thirty Eight Dollars and one Note for Five Hundred Dollars due July 29th besides a settled account of Two Hundred and Six Dollars 44/100 and also a note to the late firm of Smith Jackson & Sublette amounting to Fifteen Thousand Five Hundred and Thirty Two Dollars 22/100 and to the late firm of Jackson & Sublette a Note of Three Thousand and Thirty-two Dollars 75/100 and also another Note of One Hundred and Three Dollars and also an amount of their orders and notes to men now going to St. Louis which orders are accepted by said William L. Sublette and to be paid by him on the arrival of this Beaver Furr in St. Louis Missouri. They amount to Ten Thousand Three Hundred and Eighteen Dollars 47/100. And the said Rockey Mountain Furr Co. have delivered to said William L Sublette Eleven Thousand two Hundred and Forty six pounds Beaver Furr (including Two Hundred Musk rat skins and Fifty seven otter skins. And they have also delivered Two Hundred and Forty seven pounds Beaver Castors all of which together with Three Thousand pounds or thereabouts in caches on the river Platte, which the said William L. Sublette is to weigh and transport (with the Furrs etc received at this place) to St. Louis Missouri on their account and risk they paying him at the rate of Fifty cents per pound for same And on his arrival in St. Louis Missouri should he deem it advisable and to the advantage of said Rockey Mountain Furr Co he is authorized to dispose of it there on their account or should he deem it more to their advantage to ship it to another market he is there authorized to do so and when sold the nett proceeds are to be appropriated as follows viz

The said William L Sublette in the first place is to pay himself the before mentioned sum of Fifteen Thousand Six Hundred and Twenty Dollars and also for the transportation of the Beaver & to St. Louis at the rate of fifty cents per pound with interest at the rate of Eight per cent per annum from first november next until paid.

Secondly . . . [other obligations numbered and listed in sequence to] Sixthly.

And there is a perfect understanding that all expenses attending the Furrs & after their arrival in S. Louis are to be paid by the said Rockey Mountain Furr Co.

And as there is an uncertainty as to the price Beaver Furr etc.

may sell for an understanding exists between the parties before mentioned that should the nett proceeds of the Beaver amount to more than will pay off the foregoing obligations the said William L Sublette is to pay off any of their just notes now in St. Louis or that may be taken there as far as money remains in his hands and should a surplus still remain it is to be subject to the order of the said Rockey Mountain Furr Co. But should the nett proceeds of the Beaver not more than discharge the foregoing obligation — then should the said William L Sublette pay out money in taking up their notes now in St. Louis then the said Rockey Mountain Furr Co are to pay the said William L. Sublette at the rate of eight per cent per annum until paid.

In witness whereof the parties have hereunto set their hands and seals the day and year before written

Witness	Wm L Sublette Seal
R. Campbell	Thos Fitzpatrick for
A. W. Sublette	Rockey Montn fur Co Seal

Attached also is a statement by Robert Campbell and Louis Vasquez that they weighed and marked beaver fur, etc., raised out of caches on Sweetwater and Platte River, weighing: Beaver, 2,473 pounds; 10 otter skins weighing 15 pounds, and forty-five pounds of beaver castors.[12]

Many of the drafts and notes made out to trappers at the rendezvous and signed by Fitzpatrick are preserved in the Sublette Collection, Missouri Historical Society.[13] The accounts of the R.M.F. company with William Sublette, September, 1832, to January, 1833, contain the names of persons to whom orders were made, with amounts.[14]

---

[12] The original document is in the Sublette Collection, Mo. Hist. Soc.

[13] The following one is typical: "Mr. W. L. Sublette please pay Louis Vasques or order on the arrival of the beaver fur now on hand at St. Louis the sum of thirteen hundred thirty three dollars. Charge the same to account. Rocky Mtm Fur Co. Thos Fitzpatrick. Teton fork Columbia, July 24, 1832 [Written across the note] St. Louis, October 3, 1833 Recd of Wm L. Sublette the full amount of this order. Louis Vasquez. Test R. Campbell."

[14] The names and amounts are as follows: Poliet Dejurdy, $375.00; Miller Francis, $202.50; George Ennis, $781.85; Strother Coleman, $80.75 and $30.00;

At the rendezvous Fitzpatrick took over the employment of certain men who had come out with Sublette and wished to remain and trap.[15]

Since the A.F.C. supplies had failed to reach the rendezvous at Pierre's Hole in July, 1832, Vanderburgh paid some of his debts to trappers and others by orders on P. Chouteau, Jr., at St. Louis.[16]

William Sublette set out from rendezvous with 169 fur packs on July 30. He reached Lexington, Missouri, on September 21 and St. Louis on October 3. There he prepared the furs for market and soon began sales. His extensive accounts, nicely preserved in the Missouri Historical Society archives, tell an interesting story. He sold muskrat skins at 20 cents apiece, beaver skins at $4.25 per pound. Six sacks of beaver castors brought $1,204.06. On three hogsheads of beaver shipped by steamer to Louisville, Kentucky, and valued at $7,000 he paid insurance at the rate of one-half of one per cent. Sixteen hogsheads, each containing from 375 to 449 skins, he shipped to F. A. Tracy

---

Louis Vasquez, $1333.00; Rut D. Lewis, $392.75; Francis Lajones, $311.29; Joseph Wash, $82.08; Isaac Lyonsa, $620.67; L. Underwood, $274.42; Julian Lacont, $208.70; David Carson, $439.12; Louis Clermo, $123.37½; Baptist Lapage, $324.00; William C. Hutton, $333.25; Charles Dufon, $746.00; Jefferson Smith, $400; Joseph Pilkey, $460.75; Tessant Demet, $197.70; Robert Campbell, $50.00; a Spaniard (on Bent and Savory), $77.62; Charles Adams, $608.00; James White, $371.12½; John Robinson, $100.00; Thomas Eddie, $40.00; and for other notes and expenses. Also there is a list of expenses in attending to furs of Rocky Mountain Fur Co. after their arrival in St. Louis, Oct. 5, 1832, totaling $315.87. — Sublette Papers, Mo. Hist. Soc.

15 These men were Christian Shotts, Alfred R. Shute, William M. Price, John A. Mytinger, and John C. Hawains. They were to receive $14 to $16 per month and remain until September or November 1833.

16 Some of these drafts, preserved in the Chouteau-Maffitt Collection of the Mo. Hist. Soc. are: Antoine Janice, $12.00; Fuller P. Sinclair, $86.50; Jacob Foreman, $46.00; "Thomas Fitchpaterick," $71. Also an order to S. H. Everitt for $400, signed by Joshua Palen.

at New York, at a total price of $40,929.63. Rum he bought at 60 cents per gallon.

The figures in the accounts cannot be given here. But a reading of them and the Agreement given above, shows the stranglehold Sublette had over Fitzpatrick's R.M.F. company. The debts of the company enumerated in the Agreement totaled $46,751.13. Sublette carried eastward, as the R.M.F. company fur catch for two years, 13,719 pounds of beaver; 247 pounds of beaver castors, and a few muskrat and otter skins. The beaver skins alone would amount to $58,305.75, at St. Louis prices. But the difference of nearly $12,000 was eaten up fast. In the first place the transportation cost to St. Louis at 50 cents per pound was over $7,000. Then there were charges for cleaning and packaging, for fire and shipping insurance, dealers' commissions, and interest charges running from 6 to 10 per cent. By the time the accounts were carried to completion they would show Fitzpatrick's company in debt to Sublette.

Chapter 7

Passing of Rocky Mountain Fur Company

THE ROCKY MOUNTAIN FUR COMPANY and William Sublette had enjoyed a monoply of trade at the rendezvous of 1832. The company's accumulated furs, 169 packs for the two years of trapping, were on the way to market. But all was not well. Numerous competitors had entered the field — Gantt and Blackwell, Wyeth, Bonneville, and others. These independents, however, did not constitute a real danger; the powerful American Fur Company did.

The R.M.F. partners had offered to divide the trapping territory, but the A.F.C. men declined the offer.[1] So the veteran fur men of the central Rockies had no choice but to "take on" the tenderfeet. The great advantage A.F.C. had on market facilities and financial backing must be balanced by the superior skill of Fitzpatrick's men in the trapping game.

With the breakup of the rendezvous camp, the parties

---

[1] Irving, *Bonneville*, 75.

made ready for fall trapping. The brigade of Milton Sub-lette, Fraeb, and Gervais, with the remnant of Wyeth's men in tow, were the first to set out. After laying in a supply of buffalo meat on Portneuf River and caching six horse loads of goods, the party moved down the Snake River to the westward. They probably trapped on the Humboldt and Owyhee rivers also. Near the mouth of Boise River they divided into three parties to trap various streams, while Wyeth headed for Oregon.[2] Later the other R. M. F. men moved north to the Salmon River, where they were to meet their partners.

Upon moving out from Pierre's Hole, Fitzpatrick and Bridger steered generally westward to the upper waters of the Salmon. Here Fitzpatrick cached his goods and began his fall hunt. His men trapped the Bitter Root and other southern branches of Clark's Fork, and then moved eastward into Blackfoot country.[3]

In the meantime Vanderburgh and Drips hurried over to Fontenelle's camp on Green River, turned over their furs, and received fresh supplies. Returning to Pierre's Hole they picked up the trail of Fitzpatrick and Bridger and with hunting-dog noses followed the scent as best they could. Ferris, who was in the party of trailers, tells of find-ing the competitors' camp sites at Big Hole on August 27 and again on September 4. Two days later, he writes, "We again intersected the trail of the Rocky Mountain Fur Co., and judging from the fresh appearance of their traces, that they were but a short distance before us, we immediately followed, determined to overtake them, and by this means

---

[2] See *Wyeth*, 160–71.
[3] *Newell*, 32.

share a part of the game, which is usually found in advance of a company, but *never* behind."[4] On the upper waters of the Missouri they caught up with the R. M. F. men and continued to dog their steps. Both parties reached the Three Forks of the Missouri and here, according to Irving's Bonneville:

They accordingly took up their line of march down the course of the Missouri [northward], keeping the main Blackfoot trail, and tramping doggedly forward without stopping to set a single trap. The others beat the hoof after them for some time, but by degrees began to perceive that they were on a wild-goose chase, and getting into a country perfectly barren to the trapper. They now came to a halt, and bethought themselves how to make up for lost time and improve the remainder of the season. It was thought best to divide their forces and try different trapping grounds. While Dripps went in one direction, Vanderburgh, with about fifty men, proceeded in another. The latter, in his headlong march had got into the very heart of the Blackfoot country, yet seems to have been unconscious of his danger.[5]

Presently he was ambushed, and at the first fire of the savages his horse fell, pinning him to the ground. He managed to kill one of his foes with his rifle, but was immediately afterward tomahawked and slain. Another of his company, a Frenchman named Pilou, was killed, and the remainder, most of whom were wounded, saved themselves by flight.[6]

Of the fall hunt and the Vanderburgh affair Fitzpatrick gives his own account in a letter of June 4, 1833, to his friend Robert Campbell:

Immediately after our separation last summer I repaired to

---

[4] Ferris, 164, 166, 167.

[5] Bonneville, 91.

[6] Ferris was one of the survivors of this party, but was shot in the shoulder. — Ferris, 178. See also the accounts by Joe Meek and by Bonneville.

Salmon river and there made a deposit of all our goods &c from thence to the Blackfoot country and further north in it than a company of whites ever has been before in search of beaver but found them much scarcer than I had any Idea of our party in that section consisted of about 60 men we made a very extensive tour and caught only about 20 packs of beaver Mr. Vanderburgh overtook us with a party of 112 men on Dearborn river which was a great disadvantage to us altho in all they caught about 5 packs of fur while we got 20 they remained and camped with us until we arrived at the three forks of the Missouri where we separated — we up the Galletin and they the Madison and soon after we both had a fight with the blackfeet Mr Van der burgh was killed in a few days after we parted in our fight Bridger was shot in 2 places with arrows we lost one horse one squaw & the gun which you sold Bridger Besides one man who was killed out a trapping.[7]

Regarding the Fitzpatrick and Bridger brush with the Blackfeet more information is given by Joe Meek, especially about the Blackfoot woman and Bridger's gun. Upon meeting the party of Blackfeet, as Mrs. Victor writes Meek's story:

one of the chiefs came out into the open space, bearing the peace-pipe, and Bridger also advanced to meet him, but carrying his gun across the pommel of his saddle. He was accompanied by a young Blackfoot woman, wife of a Mexican in his service, as interpreter. The chief extended his hand in token of amity; but at that moment Bridger saw a movement of the chiefs, which he took to mean treachery, and cocked his rifle. But the lock had no sooner clicked than the chief, a large and powerful man, seized the gun and turned the muzzle downward, when the contents were discharged into the earth. With another dexterous movement he wrested it from Bridger's hand, and struck him with it, felling him to the ground. In an instant all was confusion. The noise of whoops, yells, of fire-arms, and of running hither and thither, gathered like a tempest. At first burst of this demoniac blast, the horse of the interpreter became frightened, and, by a sudden movement, unhorsed her,

---

[7] Letter of Fitzpatrick to Robert Campbell written from "River platte June 4th 1833." This is in the Campbell Papers, Mo. Hist. Soc. A copy was generously supplied to me by Dale L. Morgan.

wheeling and running back to camp. In the melee which now ensued, the woman was carried off by the Blackfeet, and Bridger was
wounded twice in the back with arrows. A chance medley fight now
ensued, continuing until night put a period to the contest. . . .

As for the young Blackfoot woman, whose people retained her
a prisoner, her lamentations and struggles to escape and return to
her husband and child so wrought upon the young Mexican, who
was the pained witness of her grief, that he took the babe in his
arms, and galloped with it into the heart of the Blackfoot camp,
to place it in the arms of the distracted mother. This daring act,
which all who witnessed believed would cause his death, so excited
the admiration the Blackfoot chief, that he gave him permission
to return, unharmed, to his own camp. Encouraged by this clem-
ency, Loretta begged to have his wife restored to him, relating how
he had rescued her, a prisoner, from the Crows, who would certainly have tortured her to death. The wife added her entreaties
to his, but the chief sternly bade him depart, and as sternly reminded the Blackfoot girl that she belonged to his tribe, and could
not go with his enemies. Loretta was therefore compelled to abandon
his wife and child and return to camp.

It is, however, gratifying to know that so true an instance of
affection in savage life was finally rewarded; and that when the
two rival fur companies united, as they did in the following year,
Loretta was permitted to go to the American Company's fort on
the Missouri, in the Blackfoot country, where he was employed
as interpreter, assisted by his Blackfoot wife.[8]

The arrowhead was to remain in Bridger's back until the
summer rendezvous of 1835, when Dr. Marcus Whitman
would exhibit his surgical skill by removing it.

Meek says the R. M. F. men continued their trapping on
the headwaters of the Missouri River, especially in Beaver
Head Valley, and took many skins. Then they crossed over
the continental divide and closed their fall trapping tour
by going into winter quarters on Salmon River, where they
met their partners.[9] There too was Bonneville, building

---

[8] Meek, 133–35. This account is so similar to that given by Bonneville that
it appears that Mrs. Victor merged Meek's and Bonneville's stories.
[9] Newell, 32.

a new fort; also a party of A.F.C. men and large groups of friendly Flatheads and Nez Percé.

Ferris says that Fitzpatrick went with him in December to find Drips "with whom he had some business to transact."[10] They went southeast to the Snake River, near the site of present Pocatello, and thence 70 miles up the river to Drips' camp. Of the business transacted we have no knowledge; it may have been regarding an arrangement that could be possible now that Vanderburgh was dead. Fitzpatrick soon returned to the camp of his men on Salmon River.

With too many horses for the available feed, the R.M.F. men moved over onto Snake River at the mouth of Portneuf. Of Fitzpatrick's subsequent spring trapping we have no adequate account, but by early June he was on the North Platte. Here, on June 4 he wrote a letter to Campbell in which he says, "We have now in our service in all about ninety men and is in 2 parties one of 60 and another of 30 the one of 60 I have under my command in this quarter and finds beaver much more plenty than I have in any part last fall we have done very well so far this hunt I put in cache a few days ago 40 packs of good fur I left [Milton] Sublette and Jervey in february last on the Columbia with the 30 men how they have done I dont know I hope well."[11]

This letter Fitzpatrick sent with his partner Fraeb, who was to go to St. Louis if necessary to get supplies. But happily, he met Campbell, now Sublette's partner, west-

[10] Ferris, 188.
[11] Letter to Campbell cited above, in footnote 7. In this letter he asks Campbell to send him a book or two, "such as you know may suit me."

126

bound on the North Platte five or six miles above the mouth of the Laramie. Campbell had set out from Lexington, Missouri, in early May, with forty men and a pack train of trade goods and supplies. With him went Louis Vasquez and Antoine Janise as assistants, and as guests William Drummond Stewart, noted Scot sportsman who was to figure prominently in the West during the next decade, General William Henry Harrison's son Benjamin (to break him of drinking), Edmund Christy, St. Louis businessman,[12] and Fitzpatrick's Indian boy Friday, now coming to visit his adopted father and his own people.

Campbell had sent out Louis Vasquez to find Fitzpatrick and arrange for a meeting. Instead, Campbell met Fraeb. This R.M.F. partner arranged to take over "the outfit with the exception of ten mules and ten Barrills of liquor and two bales of goods."[13] The supply caravan moved up the Sweetwater, over South Pass, and reached the rendezvous site on Green River on July 5.[14] Here, in the vicinity of Bonneville's "Fort Nonsense," built the year before, the trapper bands assembled. Fontenelle and Drips arrived on July 8, Bonneville on July 13, and other independent parties came in. Wyeth, returning from Oregon and bound for the States, gives the count thus:

Drips and Fontenelle arrd July 8th   160 men and a good supply of animals. Obtained 51 packs of 100 ea. Beaver.
Rocky Mtn. Fur Co. 55 packs   55 men well supplied   one party not in   Beaver sent home by Mr. Campbell.

---

12 Elliott Coues (Ed.), *Forty Years a Fur Trader on the Upper Missouri; the Personal Narrative of Charles Larpenteur, 1833–1872* (New York, 1899), I, 15–16. Hereafter cited as Larpenteur.

13 Larpenteur, 25.

14 *Ibid.,* 30.

Mess. Bonneville & Co. 22½ packs. Few goods few horses and poor Capt. Cerry goes home. B. remains.

Harris party now in hand 7 packs Beaver and are on foot.[15]

Warren Ferris, an A.F.C. man at the rendezvous, writes:

Some fifty or sixty lodges of Snakes lay encamped about the fort, and were daily exchanging their skins and robes, for munitions, knives, ornaments, etc., with the whites, who kept a quantity of goods opened for the purpose of trading in one of the block houses, constituting a part of the fort. This establishment was doubtless intended for a permanent trading post, by its projector, who has, however, since changed his mind, and quite abandoned it. — From the circumstance of a great deal of labor having been expended in its construction, and the works shortly after their completion deserted, it is frequently called "Fort Nonsense." It is situated in a fine open plain, on a rising spot of ground, about three hundred yards from Green river on the west side, commanding a view of the plains for several miles up and down that stream. On the opposite side of the fort about two miles distant, there is a fine willowed creek, called "Horse Creek," flowing parallel with Green river, and emptying into it about five miles below the fortification. . . . The fort presents a square enclosure, surrounded by posts or pickets firmly set in the ground, of a foot or more in diameter, planted close to each other, and about fifteen feet in length. At two corners, diagonally opposite to each other, block houses of unhewn logs are so constructed and situated, as to defend the square outside of the pickets, and hinder the approach of an enemy from any quarter.[16]

The rendezvous of 1833 was typical of that famous in-

---

[15] Wyeth's letter of July 18, 1833, to F. Ermatinger of the H.B.C., who did not come to this rendezvous. — in Wyeth, 69–70. In this letter Wyeth wrote that before the rendezvous Bridger and Fraeb's band had lost their horses to the Arikaras, as had Moses Harris' party; these Indians having moved from the Missouri River to the upper North Platte. Wyeth characterized the men at rendezvous as "a great majority of Scoundrels."

In his diary Wyeth wrote on July 15: "Made E.S.E. 12 miles to Green river and to Mr. Bonnevilles fort day clear and fine. Found here collected Capt. Walker, Bonneville, Cerry, and one Co. Dripps and Fontenelle of the Am. Fur Co. Mr. Campbell just from St. Louis Mess. Fitzpatric, Gervais, Milton Sublette of the Rocky Mountain Fur Co. and in all the Cos about 300 whites and a small village of Snakes" (p. 205).

[16] Ferris, 206–07.

stitution in its heyday. The picture of it drawn by the pen of Washington Irving has not been excelled:

> The three rival companies, which, for a year past had been endeavoring to out-trade, out-trap and out-wit each other, were here encamped in close proximity, . . . Never did rival lawyers, after a wrangle at the bar, meet with more social good humor at a circuit dinner. The hunting season over, all past tricks and manoeuvres were forgotten, all feuds and bickerings burried in oblivion. . . . This, then, is the trappers' holiday, when he is all for fun and frolic, and ready for a saturnalia among the mountains. . . . Here the free trappers were in all their glory; they considered themselves the "cocks of the walk," and always carried the highest crests. Now and then familiarity was pushed too far, and would effervesce into a brawl, and a "rough and tumble" fight; but it all ended in a cordial reconciliation and maudlin endearment. . . . Happy was the trapper who could muster up a red blanket, a string of gay beads, or a paper of precious vermilion, with which to win the smiles of a Shoshonie fair one. . . . The free trappers, especially, were extravagant in their purchases. For a free mountaineer to pause at a paltry consideration of dollars and cents, in the attainment of an object that might strike his fancy, would stamp him with the mark of the beast in the estimation of his comrades. For a trader to refuse one of these free and flourishing blades a credit, whatever unpaid scores might stare him in the face, would be a flagrant affront scarcely to be forgiven. In a little while most of the trappers, having squandered away all their wages, and perhaps run knee-deep in debt, were ready for another hard campaign in the wilderness.[17]

A special excitement at the rendezvous this year was the attack of one or more mad wolves upon the camp. Several men and horses were bitten and some of these died horrible deaths from hydrophobia.

At the rendezvous of 1833 the R.M.F. partners learned that William Sublette and Robert Campbell had entered into a partnership in December, 1832,[18] and had planned to challenge the supremacy of the A.F.C. on the upper

---

[17] Bonneville, 154–56.
[18] The Agreement, of Dec. 20, 1832, is in the Sublette Papers, Mo. Hist. Soc.

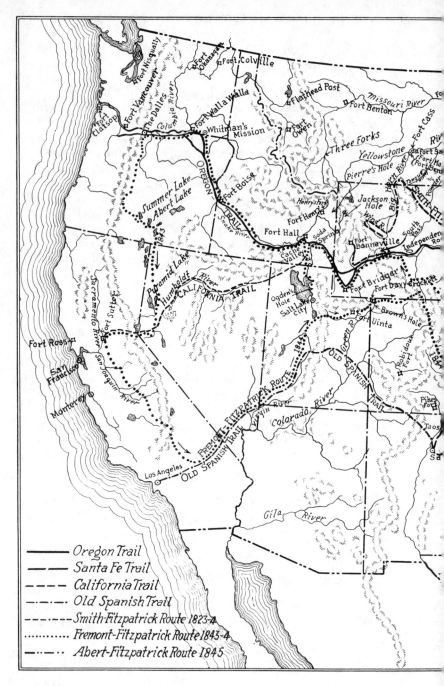

Fort Ross

San Francisco

Monterey

Los Angeles

Fort Clatsop

Fort Nisqually

Fort Vancouver

The Dalles

Fort Okanagan   Fort Colville

Fort Walla Walla

Whitman's Mission

Flathead Post   Fort Benton

Fort Owen

Missouri River

Three Forks   Fort Cass

Yellowstone

Fort Boisé

Summer Lake   OREGON TRAIL

Abert Lake

1843

Pyramid Lake

Humboldt   River

CALIFORNIA TRAIL

Sacramento River

Fort Sutter

San Joaquin River

Snake River

Fort Hall

Fort Henry

Henry's Fork

Pierre's Hole

Jackson Hole

Bear R.

Soda Spring

Cache Valley

Fort Bonneville

Ogden's Hole

Salt Lake City

FREMONT-FITZPATRICK ROUTE

OLD SPANISH TRAIL

Virgin River

OLD SPANISH TRAIL

Colorado   River

Gila   River

Independence Ro.

Fort Bridger

Fort Davy Crockett

Green R.

Fort Uinta

Brown's Hole

Robidoux Fort

OLD SPANISH TRAIL   1844

Pike's Fork

Taos

Sa.

1847

	Oregon Trail
	Santa Fe Trail
	California Trail
	Old Spanish Trail
	Smith-Fitzpatrick Route 1823-4
	Fremont-Fitzpatrick Route 1843-4
	Abert-Fitzpatrick Route 1845

130

FORTS AND TRAILS

(Prepared by LeRoy R. Hafen)

Missouri. Sublette had gone up the river to establish trading posts and Campbell was to go from the Green River rendezvous northeastward to the Bighorn and down that stream to the Yellowstone to join Sublette. Fitzpatrick and Milton Sublette agreed to go with Campbell as far as the Bighorn, whence Milton and Campbell would take the company's fur to St. Louis.

At the rendezvous also, the R.M.F. company had entered into an Agreement with Edmund T. Christy, who had come out with Campbell. The firm of "The Rocky Mountain Fur Company & Christy," was formed to operate for one year, to July 20, 1834.[19] Upon the breakup of the rendezvous, Christy led 25 men on a trapping expedition to the Snake River country; while Fraeb, with Bill Williams as guide, took 20 trappers down Green River.[20]

Fitzpatrick and Milton Sublette, accompanying Campbell to the Bighorn, took along 61 packs of furs, according to Wyeth, who also went along. Campbell had 30 packs, reports his clerk Larpenteur.[21]

On the Bighorn, August 14, 1833, Fitzpatrick and Milton Sublette made a contract with Wyeth to bring out supplies for them to the rendezvous by July 1, 1834. These were to cost not more than $3,000 in the States and weigh not over 8,000 pounds. Wyeth was to be paid the first cost of the goods plus $3,521 at rendezvous, with beaver skins at $4 per pound. The goods were to be selected by Milton Sublette, who was to accompany Wyeth and the goods

[19] This Agreement is in the Sublette Papers, Mo. Hist. Soc. See also mention of it in Larpenteur, 34.
[20] Fitzpatrick's letters of Nov. 13, 1833, to Milton Sublette, and to Robert Campbell, in Sublette Papers, Mo. Hist. Soc.
[21] Larpenteur, 35.

to rendezvous. The agreement was to be null in case Fitz-patrick and Sublette should sell out their fur business before November, 1833, and notify Wyeth of such action. Also, Wyeth, who was not certain he could get financial backing to buy the goods and procure equipment and men for another westward trip, would notify the R.M.F. company if matters turned out well for him, and Milton would then go East to select the goods for his company. Each party bound itself to fulfill the agreement or forfeit $500 in case of default.[22]

Upon reaching the point where the Wind River becomes the Bighorn, near present Thermopolis, Wyoming, the com-bined party stopped. The men constructed bullboats, of buffalo skins stretched over willow frameworks, and em-barked the furs. Louis Vasquez conducted a party with the horses by land. Milton Sublette and Wyeth rode a boat together. After passing Tullock's Fort Cass, built in 1832 near the mouth of the Bighorn, they floated on down the Yellowstone to the Missouri. Near here Milton found his brother William with goods to trade in opposition to the A.F.C. and its Fort Union. So he left Wyeth and joined his brother, to descend the Missouri later.

William induced Milton to sign a rather strange docu-ment:

Mouth of Yellowstone river Mo. T. September 8th 1833   We hereby acknowledge that William L. Sublette has accounted to us satisfactorily for the sales and proceeds of all the Beaver Fur Otter Skins Musk Rat Skins Catoram etc which he has transported for us from the Rocky mountains to St. Louis Mo. on our account last season as per Article of Agreement bearing date July the Twenty

---

[22] Agreement in Sublette Papers, Mo. Hist. Soc.

fifth One Thousand Eight hundred and Thirty two. And we hereby release him from all responsibility thereby incurred.

Given under our hands the day and year above written

M. J. Sublette, for himself and
Thos Fitzpatrick
H. Fraeb
Jas Bridger
J B Jervy   [23]

Wm L. Sublette

When the furs were safely embarked on the upper Bighorn, Fitzpatrick with his band of 20 or 30 trappers and over 100 horses moved eastward to trap the Little Bighorn, Powder, and Tongue rivers. With him went W. D. Stewart eager to see Absaraka, the land of the Crows. They came upon a large encampment of supposedly friendly Crows. The chief visited Fitzpatrick, suggesting that the parties camp together. But the white captain was wary, and declined, pitching his camp some three miles away. To maintain friendly relations, however, he then made a visit to the chief in his lodge. While absent from his camp, which he left in charge of Sir William, it was invaded by a band of young Crows, who overawed the captain and seized and carried off the stock and other property, which inclued 43 beaver skins. On their way back to the village the Crows met Fitzpatrick and took from him his clothing and personal effects, leaving him bare above the waist and altogether destitute.[24]

Returning to the village, Fitzpatrick protested against this treatment. Irving, in his *Bonneville*, writes:

---

[23] Found in the Sublette Papers. On the back of the paper is this notation: "Settled November 2nd 1836. Wm L. Sublette."

[24] Bonneville, 178, 207.

what eloquence and management Fitzpatrick made use of, we do not know, but he succeeded in prevailing upon the Crow chieftain to return him his horses and many of his traps; together with his rifles and a few rounds of ammunition for each man. He then set out with all speed to abandon the Crow country, before he should meet with any fresh disasters.[25]

Jim Beckwourth, who was living with the Crows at the time, according to his own account took a heroic stand in Fitzpatrick's behalf and an important part in recovering his property.[26]

Fitzpatrick was certain the robbery had been inspired by the A.F.C. The Indians confessed it and the company agents admitted it. The furs promptly found their way to Samuel Tullock's Fort Cass, near the mouth of the Bighorn. Later Kenneth McKenzie, head man for A.F.C. on the upper Missouri, wrote to Tullock on January 8, 1934:

> The 43 Beaver skins traded, marked, "R.M.F.Co.," I would in the present instance give up if Mr. Fitzpatrick wishes to have them, on his paying the price the articles traded for them were worth on their arrival in the Crow village, and the expense of bringing the beaver in and securing it. My goods are brought in to the country to trade and I would as willing dispose of them to Mr. Fitzpatrick as to any one else for beaver or beaver's worth if I get my price. I make this proposal as a favor, not as a matter of right, for I consider the Indians entitled to trade any beaver in their possession to me or to any other trader.[27]

To such depths had the rivalry gone; had degenerated into open robbery and warfare. Fitzpatrick appealed to his old friend and companion W. H. Ashley, now Congressman from Missouri. He told of the Crow robbery, charged it to the A.F.C. agents, and continued:

---

25 *Ibid.*, 208.
26 Beckwourth, 181–88.
27 Quoted in Chittenden, 303.

in short Genl if there is not some alteration made in the system of business in this country verry soon it will become a nuisance and disgrace to the U.S. So many different companies agoing about frome one tribe of Indians to another Each are telling a different tale besides slandering each other to Such a degree as really to disgust the Indians and will evidently all become hostile towards the Americans I now appeal to you for redress as the only person whom I know would be likely to have Justice done us I ask no more than the laws of the U.S. dictates in such cases it is because they [A.F.C.] are more powerful than we are that they are allowed to be instrumental to such acts of violence on people who are licensed and authorized according to law. . . . if I was disposed to become an out law I could verry soon have satisfaction for the injury done me but no I shall await Justice from the honorable members in Session I would have much more to say on this subject but the bearer of this Dr. Harrison is impatient to be off.[28]

Retreating from the Crow country, the Fitzpatrick men had crossed the South Pass into the Green River valley, where they found a friendly band of Shoshones, and the combined parties proceeded to a point on Ham's Fork of the Green. Here, at the end of October they met Bonneville, who had suffered a similar robbery somewhere to the east of South Pass. From this camp, on November 31, 1833, Fitzpatrick wrote to Milton Sublette, in St. Louis, telling of the robbery at the hands of the Crows, and then continued:

However it is not quite so bad as you may suppose Bridger and myself have on hand about twenty three packs of Beaver Furs Fraeb with about 20 men is Gone down the Seeckeedee [Green River] with Bil Williams for pilot and intends not to return before March 1st I think they may do well Jervey I have not heard from neither the understanding between you and My Self will have to remain in the Same State you left it until our meeting next Summer as the parties are absent I have been uneasy ever Since we parted about our arrangements with Wyeth however it may terminate well but still I dread it. I have an Idea we will stand in need

<hr>

[28] This letter, written from Ham's Fork on November 13, is in the Sublette Collection, Mo. Hist. Soc.

of a large supply of Madze at rendezvous as the Spanish companis will meet us there and there is now a party with Fraeb I wish you to work Wyeth as advantageous and Secure as possible Studdy well the articles of profit. Liquor will be much wanted I well know and indeed all groceris. Come as soon as possible to the rendezvous and look out for the Crows on your way up I believe they will be hostile to all partis here after. they have good encouragement from the A.F.Co.

perhaps they may not Kill but they will certainly rob all they are able and perhaps Murder also I intend to winter here and here about and will hunt nearly in the same Section where I did last spring dont gou so high up on Seekkiddee as horse Creek. strike some where about the Mouth of Sandy and remain until we come Harison is going after a small equipment you will if you alow him to take up make terms with him about it he will be among us considerable

Now I have given you a short sketch of the whole situation of our affairs and I expect you to act hereafter although according to your own dictations Mr. Guthery was killed last fall by lightning and Biggs since supplied his place Yours &c Thos F [29]

Following the summer rendezvous of 1833 Joseph R. Walker, with a party of Bonneville's men, had made his famous tour of California. On the return trip, according to Joe Meek, some of the men took a southern route and met Fitzpatrick's partners, Fraeb and Gervais, on the Bill Williams Fork of the Colorado, in present Arizona.[30] The beaver supply was gradually diminishing, and though Arizona and New Mexico had been repeatedly trapped in

---

[29] This is in the Sublette Collection, Mo. Hist. Soc. A copy of it was supplied to me more than 30 years ago by Mrs. Nettie Beauregard of the Society. In examining the original in October 1962, I altered the rendering of several words. In the archives of the Society the letter is recorded as written to William Sublette, but it is apparent from internal evidence and from Wyeth's correspondence (pp. 124, 128, 132, 421) that it was written to Milton Sublette. Don Berry also so concludes in his *A Majority of Scoundrels* (New York, 1961), 351.

This letter was carried east by Benjamin Harrison and Moses Harris. Dr. Harrison also carried an order on Sublette and Campbell for "$50. or thereabouts" signed by Fitzpatrick. — Sublette Papers.

[30] Meek, 152.

the years following 1824, it was now again sought, and this time by men from the supposedly richer fields of the North.

At Wyeth's urgent request, Milton Sublette went east in December, 1833, to select the supplies and trade goods which under the contract Wyeth was to take out to the rendezvous of 1834. The New Englander, having got financial backing from Henry Hall and Messrs. Tucker and Williams of Boston, was buying goods to send around the Horn. He hoped that he might supply the R.M.F. from a Columbia River base in 1835, for he figured that transportation by boat to the Columbia and thence to the Rocky Mountain rendezvous could be provided at a cheaper rate than from St. Louis to the mountains. In fact he offered to carry Bonneville's furs from the mountain rendezvous to the Columbia and thence by boat to Boston for 37½ cents per pound,[31] whereas the R.M.F. people had paid William Sublette 50 cents per pound for carrying furs from the rendezvous to St. Louis in 1831.

In Boston, New York, and Philadelphia the goods for 1834 were selected and were then shipped to St. Louis. Milton tried to prevent his brother William from learning of the R.M.F. deal with Wyeth for transportation of goods to rendezvous, but the word leaked out. Thereupon William and partner Campbell refused to honor some drafts unless Milton would remain in Missouri. Whereupon Wyeth lent Milton $500, and the two associates set out together with the R.M.F. supplies.[32]

Final preparations were made at Independence for the land journey. In addition to Wyeth's regular party he had

---

[31] Wyeth, 95–100.
[32] *Ibid.*, 130.

taken in tow the two naturalists, Thomas Nuttall and John K. Townsend, and the Oregon-bound party of five missionaries under Jason Lee. Milton had about 20 men of his immediate party. Mr. Townsend is a good historian of the journey. He begins:

On the 28th of April, at 10 o'clock in the morning, our caravan, consisting of seventy men, and two hundred and fifty horses, began its march; Captain Wyeth and Milton Sublette took the lead, Mr. N. [Nuttall] and myself rode beside them; then the men in double file, each leading, with a line, two horses heavily laden, and Captain Thing (Captain W.'s assistant) brought up the rear. The band of missionaries, with their horned cattle, rode along the flanks.[33]

On May 8 Townsend recorded:

This morning Milton Sublette left us to return to the settlements. He has been suffering for a considerable time with a fungus in one of his legs, and it has become so much worse since we started, in consequence of irritation caused by riding, that he finds it impossible to proceed. His departure has thrown a gloom over the whole camp. We all admired him for his amiable qualities, and his kind and obliging disposition.[34]

Not to be outdone in a trading venture, William Sublette had hurriedly assembled a packhorse company and set out for the mountains with a supply of goods for the trade. By unusual exertions he caught up with the Wyeth party, and then passed it during the night of May 12.[35] Thereafter he retained the lead.

Upon reaching the mouth of the Laramie he left William Patton and 14 men to build a fort at this good location. This trading post, which he named Fort William, was later

---

[33] Townsend's *Narrative*, in R. G. Thwaites (Ed.), *Early Western Travels* XXI, 141. Hereafter cited as Townsend.

[34] Townsend, 149.

[35] *Ibid.*, 151.

to become famous as Fort Laramie.[36] Sublette hurried on and reached the rendezvous a few days ahead of Wyeth.[37]

The rendezvous of 1834 shifted location a time or two on account of forage. The sites were in the Green River area, and the principal one was on Ham's Fork. For the fur trade in general, and especially for Fitzpatrick, this was an important occasion. Here on June 20 the R.M.F. company was dissolved. Just what caused this and how it was brought about have been the subject of considerable speculation and discussion. Fitzpatrick has heretofore been blamed for breaking the agreement with Wyeth and refusing to take the goods contracted for. It has been suggested that William Sublette bribed him.[38] An analysis by Don Berry, with very strong argument makes William Sublette the villian of the piece, setting out to break the R.M.F. company.[39] The known facts are still too incomplete for a definitive answer.

We know that William Sublette arrived at rendezvous several days ahead of Wyeth, and doubtless he used the pressure he could exert as principal creditor. The R.M.F. was dissolved by several steps, all on the same day (June 20, 1834), as shown by the papers preserved in the Sublette Collection, Missouri Historical Society. Henry Fraeb breaks first. "For and in consideration of forty head of horses, forty beaver traps, eight guns and $1,000 worth of mer-

---

36 *The Rocky Mountain Journals of William Marshall Anderson,* edited by Dale L. Morgan and Eleanor T. Harris (San Marino, Calif., 1967), 34, 108–10, 188. Hereafter cited as Anderson's *Journals.* Mr. Anderson accompanied William Sublette to the mountains in 1834 and gives us a contemporary record of the founding and naming of the post. For a history of this fort see LeRoy R. Hafen and Frank M. Young, *Fort Laramie,* etc. (Glendale, 1938).

37 Wyeth, 225.

38 Wyeth's letter of July 1, 1834, to Milton Sublette, in Wyeth, 140.

39 Don Berry, *op. cit.,* 352–53.

chandise," he sold and released to his remaining four partners all his "rights, title and interest" in the R.M.F. company, and was released "from debts due to and from the co." On the same date another note records the purchase of Fraeb's interest in the company by William Sublette, who assumes one-fifth of the debts of the company.

Then Jean B. Gervais sells his interest in the company for 20 horses, 30 beaver traps, and $500 worth of merchandise to Fitzpatrick, Milton E. Sublette, and James Bridger. Notice of dissolution of the partnership was formally given and this was added to the document: "The Public are hereby notified that the business will in future be conducted by Thos Fitzpatrick, Milton G. Sublette & James Bridger under the style and firm of Fitzpatrick, Sublette & Bridger."[40]

For himself and partners, Fitzpatrick on July 9 at Ham's Fork paid William Sublette the R.M.F. note for $1,258.66 which the company had given him and was dated September 10, 1833, together with interest on same. Also at Ham's Fork Fitzpatrick and partners received from Edmund T. Christy, who had entered the firm at the rendezvous of 1833, a note for $2,355. This was turned over to William Sublette and was not to be fully redeemed until 1836.

To summarize developments: In the previous year the R.M.F. partners had tried to get free of the William Sublette stranglehold on them. The furs they turned over to him had not been sufficient to pay their debts and buy needed supplies. So they necessarily gave him a further

---

[40] This and the above papers are in the Sublette Collection. Who signed for Milton Sublette in his absence is not clear — either his brother William or else Fitzpatrick.

note for $1,258.66. They then had made an agreement with Wyeth to bring out their goods for the rendezvous of 1834. Upon learning of the deal with the New Englander, William had hurriedly assembled a party and dashed out to the rendezvous ahead of Wyeth to present his claims and collect fur for the debts owed him.[41] The R. M. F. catch had not been large and the partners had little choice but to turn their furs over to William and fold up their organization.

So when Wyeth arrived they were not able to accept the goods, as they honestly told him, but they did pay the forfeit stipulated in their contract ($500) and paid also the $500 Wyeth had advanced to their partner Milton Sublette.[42] Wyeth, gravely disappointed at the refusal of his goods, wrote to Milton on July 1, 1834, from Ham's Fork:

> I arrived at Rendesvous at the mouth of Sandy on the 17th June. Fitzpatric refused to receive the goods he paid however, the forfeit and the cash advance I made to you   this however is no satisfaction to me. I do not accuse you or him of any intention of injuring me in this manner when you made the contract but I think he has been bribed to sacrifice my interests by better offers from your brother. Now Milton, business is closed between us, but you will find that you have only bound yourself over to receive your supplies at such price as may be inflicted and that all that you will ever

---

[41] This purpose is clearly expressed by Hugh Campbell to his brother Robert (partner of William Sublette) in a letter of April 5, 1834, in which he says that Sublette's expedition was "got up promptly with the view of collecting the debt and perhaps laying the foundation for future operations." — Quoted in Berry, *op. cit.*, 352.

[42] Wyeth wrote from Ham's Fork on July 1, 1834, to his Boston backers: "On arrival the Rocky Mountain Fur Co. refused to receive the goods allegging that they were unable to continue business longer, and that they had disolved, but offered to pay the advances made to M. G. Sublette and the Forfeit. These terms I have been obliged to accept." — Wyeth, 138.

It should be pointed out that the contract was conditional. Wyeth was to bring out the supplies if he could, and to pay a forfeit if he could not. Fitzpatrick's company was to accept the goods if they came, or pay the forfeit. Wyeth was himself uncertain, as he wrote in a letter at the time, of his ability to fulfill the contract. — Wyeth, 77.

make in the country will go to pay for your goods, and you will be kept as you have been a mere slave to catch Beaver for others.[43]

Wyeth moved on to Snake River and above the mouth of the Portneuf established in August, 1834, Fort Hall as a trading post for disposal of his goods. William Sublette left the rendezvous on July 10 or shortly thereafter, and stopped at Fort William on the Laramie to see the progress in construction at the post. He followed the regular route down the Platte and thence to St. Louis, which he reached at the end of August.[44]

After the 1834 rendezvous on Ham's Fork, Fitzpatrick and Bridger remained in the locality for a time. William M. Anderson, who had come out to the rendezvous with William Sublette, decided not to return with Sublette but to join Fitzpatrick and stay longer in the mountains. In his diary and journal Anderson gives a valuable contemporary report on Fitzpatrick's doings from July 10 to September 29, 1834. On July 19 Anderson journalizes: "Mr. Fitzpatrick and B[ridger] visited the A.F.C.'s [otherwise, Fontenelle and Drips'] camp, which has moved up within 8 or 10 miles, to transact some business which is as yet sub rosa."[45]

By August 3 he could write: "The arrangement some time contemplated between the two neighboring camps, has been this day effected. They are now una anima, uno corpore."[46] This marks the end of shortlived "Fitzpatrick, Sublette and Bridger" and the formation of "Fontenelle,

43 Wyeth, 140.
44 Sunder, 142–43.
45 Anderson's *Journals, op. cit.,* 160.
46 *Ibid.,* 172.

Fitzpatrick and Company," which was to continue a tenuous existence for two years.

Bridger and Drips remained in the mountains, leading trapping brigades,[47] while Fitzpatrick and Lucien Fontenelle took the furs down to the Missouri. Arrived at Bellevue (near present Omaha), Fontenelle reported by letter to his backer, Pierre Chouteau, Jr., on September 17, 1834: "The heretofore arrangement between him [William Sublette] and Messrs. Fitzpatrick, Milton Sublette and others having expired last spring, they concluded not to have anything more to do with William Sublette and it will surprise me very much if he takes more than ten packs down next year. I have entered into a partnership with the others and the whole of the beaver caught by them is to be turned over to us by agreement made with them in concluding the arrangement."[48]

The next day Fontenelle wrote a number of orders on Pratte, Chouteau & Company (successors of the Western Department of the A.F.C.) to pay balances owed to men of Fontenelle and Drips' Rocky Mountain Outfit. He also wrote on that day an order on the same firm to Fitzpatrick for $400. No explanation regarding the order is given.[49]

After the rendezvous of 1834 the trapper parties had moved up Ham's Fork to and past the present site of Kemmerer, Wyoming, and then took a northward and then an eastward course which brought them to Green River near the mouth of Cottonwood Creek. Thence they moved mainly eastward to South Pass.

---

[47] Newell, *Memoranda*, 33.
[48] Letter written at Bellevue and quoted in Chittenden, I, 309.
[49] Chouteau-Maffitt Collection, Mo. Hist. Soc., St. Louis.

Some fifty miles above Fort William [later Fort Laramie] Fitzpatrick and Anderson rode ahead as an express to the new trading post. On the farther journey eastward, Anderson mentions Fitzpatrick on several occasions (pp. 186–89, 198, 200, 201, 222, 223), and gives an interesting description of Fitzpatrick's boy Friday, who was returning east with his guardian. Anderson writes (p. 222): "Mr. Fitzpatrick's little foundling, Friday is becoming, every day, an object of greater and greater interest to me, his astonishing memory, his minute observation & amusing inquiries, interest me exceedingly. He has been from his band & kindred, 3 or 4 years, yet some scenes & incidents he describes with wonderful accuracy. He still remembers that he was called Warshinun which he tells me means 'black spot'."

Chapter 8

Last Years as Mountain Man

FITZPATRICK ARRIVED at St. Louis with Anderson and Friday on September 29, 1834.[1] During the winter, in St. Louis, Fitzpatrick and Fontenelle applied to Superintendent William Clark for a trading license for the new firm.[2] They also purchased Fort William on the Laramie River from Sublette and Campbell, and in the spring Fitzpatrick and Campbell, with Friday along, went out to effect the transfer of the fort. By this sale or otherwise Sublette and Campbell obtained a share in the Fitzpatrick, Fontenelle and Company venture of 1835.[3]

Fitzpatrick assumed control of the fort, for Fontenelle and Milton Sublette were back in the States, and Bridger

---

[1] Anderson *Journals, op. cit.*, 226.

[2] Letter of Clark listing licenses he issued; found in the Indian Archives, Washington, D.C. The license was dated April 21, 1835.

[3] They set out from St. Louis on April 9, 1835; Sunder, 145, 146.

was out leading a trapping band and had wintered on Snake River.[4]

Campbell remained at the fort for fifteen days and then with Andrew Sublette and others boated furs down the Platte.[5] Presumably Fitzpatrick stayed at the fort, for he was there on July 26 to greet Fontenelle and the company caravan coming up from the States.

Fontenelle had set out with the trade supplies from Bellevue on June 22. With him traveled the Oregon-bound missionaries, Dr. Marcus Whitman and Samuel Parker. The company included 50 or 60 men, 6 wagons, and nearly 200 horses.[6]

Upon reaching the fort on the Laramie, the customary "day of indulgence," as Parker calls it, witnessed much drinking and some shooting; but after the celebration, matters quieted down. A shift in transportation and a change in leadership was effected; the wagons were unloaded, and goods intended for the rendezvous were transferred to pack mules. Fitzpatrick now took charge of the party and conducted it onward. He set out from the fort on August 1, passed Independence Rock on August 7, and reached the rendezvous on Green River August 12. He brought along a letter from Fontenelle to his partner Drips, which reads in part:

---

[4] Newell, 33. At St. Louis on July 16, 1835, Milton Sublette wrote to Pratte, Chouteau & Co. asking them to honor a draft for $1900 drawn by Fontenelle on the part of their firm. Milton signs "for Fontenelle, Fitzpatrick & Co." — Document in the Chouteau-Papin Collection, Mo. Hist. Soc.

[5] *Missouri Republican,* July 18, 1835. *Niles Register,* August 8, 1835. Also Chittenden, 305, 941; and Sunder, 145, 146.

[6] "Journal and Report of Dr. Marcus Whitman," etc., in *Oregon Historical Quarterly,* XXVIII, 239–57. A good account of the journey is also given by Parker in his book, *Journal of Exploring Tour Beyond the Rocky Mountains* (Ithaca, N.Y., 1844).

I have concluded that it was better for our mutual interest for me to remain at this place [Fort William] until the return from the mountains should be in and then go down with them according to our agreement with Messrs. Fitzpatrick, Sublette & Bridger. . . . I wish that you would have the goodness to settle all accounts (separately) which regards our old and new concern and send me if you should not come down yourself a copy of the same. Inclosed is a copy of an acc Messrs Fitzpatrick Sublette & Bridger which you will please include in the arrangement. . . . You will also receive a bridle from Capt. Walker which I send up to you. Bridger has a fine coat, cap, pantaloons, etc. baled up for him among the goods, present him if you please my respects."[7]

Drips and Bridger, having brought in their trapper bands, were there to receive Fontenelle's letter and the presents.[8] Bridger availed himself of Dr. Whitman's services to have carved from his back the three-inch arrowhead which the Blackfeet had planted there three years before. The Doctor also operated on another trapper who had received a similar missile from the Blackfeet.[9]

Another notable incident at rendezvous introduced Kit Carson to Western history. The small, bandy-legged trapper accepted the boastful challenge of the French bully Shunar, and in the ensuing duel came out victorious.[10] Otherwise the rendezvous was not exceptional. Perhaps there were more Indians present than usual. Parker mentions the large bands of "Utaws, Shoshones, Nez Perces, and Flatheads, who were waiting for the caravan, to exchange furs, horses,

[7] The original in the Drips Collection, Mo. Hist. Soc. A copy was made available to me years ago by Miss Stella M. Drumm of the Society and was published in Hafen and Young, *Fort Laramie* (Glendale, 1938), 35–36.

[8] Drips on August 19 wrote an order on Pratte, Choteau & Co. for $300 in favor of Baptiste Godin and signed it for "Fontenelle, Fitzpatrick & Co." Drips, Bridger, and Milton Sublette were the "& Co." in the firm. This draft is in the Chouteau-Maffitt Coll., Mo. Hist. Soc.

[9] A. B. and D. P. Hulbert, *Marcus Whitman, Crusader* (Denver, 1936), 22.

[10] Rev. Parker writes the story and starts Kit on his road to fame (p. 84).

and dressed skins, for various articles of merchandise." He adds, "I was disappointed to see nothing peculiar in the Flathead Indians to give them their peculiar name."[11]

After the rendezvous broke up, Bridger led his band to Jackson Hole to begin his fall activities. He escorted Parker on the first part of his journey toward Oregon; then left him with the Flatheads and Nez Percé for the remaining distance to their country. Drips also led a band of trappers away for the fall hunt.

Fitzpatrick loaded up the packs of beaver skins and headed back to Fort William, taking with him Dr. Whitman, who was returning East for missionary reenforcements. On the Laramie Fitzpatrick and Fontenelle again exchanged positions, the former remaining at the fort, the latter hauling the furs eastward. With this home-bound caravan went former partners Fraeb and Gervais, and some eighty-five men from the mountains. Many men were quitting the business. William Sublette wrote that Fontenelle and Co. had about $40,000 to pay out to hands that came in to the States. Fontenelle took in 120 packs of beaver and 80 bundles of buffalo robes.[12] The furs were taken by land to Bellevue on the Missouri River and thence boated to St. Louis.

Fitzpatrick remained at the fort and traded with the Sioux; some fifty lodges were at the post and others coming in. D. D. Mitchell of the A.F.C. came over from the upper Missouri to make some deal for purchase of Fort

---

[11] Parker, *op. cit.*, 80.

[12] This information is from Sublette's letter to Robert Campbell, written from Fulton, Mo., Nov. 2, 1835. — Campbell Papers, Mo. Hist. Soc. Doc Newell went in with Fontenelle, but came out again next year. — Newell, 33.

William, and Fitzpatrick offered to sell on certain conditions; but apparently they were not agreed upon. Such was the word brought to Missouri by the "two Prevoes" who arrived there in late January 1836.[13]

Furthermore, William Sublette wrote in his letter of February 9, 1836: "Prevoe says Fitzpatrick talk of coming by the little Missouri as he spoke of selling out the fort on Laramie Fork in case they would furnish them goods there for the mountains on reasonable terms." This trip Fitzpatrick made, leaving the fort on the Laramie on January 3, 1836, with an unnamed companion, and arriving at St. Louis February 27.[14]

We now have bits of information gathered from William Sublette's letters of January 30, February 9, 27, and 29, 1836 (photostats of these letters obtained at the Missouri Historical Society by me in 1962), that fit into and give credence to the account of the adventurous trip on which Fitzpatrick suffered the accident that caused the crippling of his hand — the accident that induced the Indians later to give him the name "Broken Hand" (sometimes rendered "Bad Hand" or "Three Fingers").

This account, which appeared in the *Jefferson* (Mo.) *Inquirer* of December 25, 1847, is the only one found that gives details of the adventure and the accident. We present it here, despite its possible exaggeration (as to the height of the river bluff) and some possible variations as to facts.[15]

---

[13] Letters of William Sublette to Robert Campbell written Jan. 31 and Feb. 9, 1836. — In Campbell Papers, Mo. Hist. Soc. The two couriers were doubtless Etienne Provost and his brother or his nephew.

[14] Sublette's letter to Campbell, Feb. 29, 1836, Mo. Hist. Soc. This letter was written after Fitzpatrick's arrival at St. Louis and after Sublette's conversation with him.

[15] This important article was found by Dale L. Morgan when, some years

A ROCKY MOUNTAIN ADVENTURE

The following incident of mountain life has never appeared in print, but was communicated to the writer, by the party least conspicuous in the adventure.

In the year 1835, Mr. [Peter A.] Sarpy, the agent of the American Fur Company, and now stationed at Council Bluffs, and Capt. Fitzpatrick, the guide to the late United States exploring expedition in the Rocky Mountains, were out together on an excursion thro' these desert regions, and had occasion to separate, with an understanding of where they were again to meet. During the absence of Mr. Sarpy, his fellow-adventurer was discovered by a party of Black-Feet Indians, the inveterate enemies of the white man. The dreadful whoop of the savage was immediately raised, and pursued and pursuers started off in the direction of the Yellowstone River. Captain Fitzpatrick, mounted on a fleet horse, gained for a time on the Indians, without knowing his precise position or ultimate course. When within a short distance of the river, and without a single gleam of hope for escape by any other outlet, a steep bluff, about forty feet in height, suddenly presented itself to his view. Delay was dangerous in the case, and a dangerous experiment was to be tried. His trusty rifle encased, and arm elevated, with a firm hold of the bridle, he struck his heels to the horse's flanks, and horse and rider essayed a fearful plunge! That noble effort of the animal was succeeded by another, and his last! He yet breasted the current of the river, and only reeled from exhaustion, when he had safely landed his rider on a sand bar on the opposite shore. But the respite was momentary; and scarcely had the noble animal sunk beneath the waters, when the ruthless Indians, frantic with rage at the escape of their victim, took to the river — every moment lessening the distance between them and the Captain. The latter, conceiving that the present was his only available opportunity, had recourse to his

---

ago, he spent months gathering from newspapers and other sources a large collection of primary materials on Western history. So far as I know, this story has never before been republished. Mr. Morgan never fully accepted the authenticity or date of this account. In fact, in his biographical sketch of Fitzpatrick, accompanying his and Miss Harris' edition of the William M. Anderson *Journals, op. cit.,* 302, he says the "accident that crippled his left hand . . . may have occurred while he was trying to cross the Snake in Jackson Hole." This was on Fitzpatrick's disastrous ride to rendezvous of 1832, recounted at length above, in chapter 6.

Not one of the contemporaneous accounts of that ride, with all the details they give, mentions an accident that crippled his hand. Nor does any historical source tell of the accident before 1835.

rifle; but in his haste to pull off the cover, by some mismanagement received the contents of his piece in the left wrist, which was frightfully shattered with the discharge. Nothing daunted by the accident, he reloaded and fired, killing two of his pursuers before he left the spot. He then made for the woods, and dodged his enemies for some days, who with a rare sagacity peculiar to the children of the forest, kept on his trail, until wearied with the fruitless result of their efforts to make a prisoner of the fugitive. Thirty days after this adventure, he got up with Mr. Sarpy, and gave him the details of this most extraordinary escape.

The journey which Fitzpatrick took to the forts on the upper Missouri was in January 1836, rather than in 1835, an error that could have easily occurred in a recollection published eleven years after the event.

The only item found in Fitzpatrick's own writings that may refer to the accident to his hand and the loss of his horse is in his letter of March 18, 1836, to Pierre Chouteau:

"I need not undertake to give you a written account of our misfortunes, as you will too soon have a verbal one. . . . Our misfortunes in this expedition will be the cause of my making some extra expenses for horses or which I intend Drawing on you for and I hope you will honour."[16]

When Fitzpatrick reached St. Louis in February 1836, he found that William Sublette was trying to collect debts owed to him, and was especially having trouble in collecting on the "Fontenelle, Fitzpatrick, and Co." note. Fontenelle, upon arriving in Missouri in the fall of 1835 had continued drinking heavily. He would not put his accounts in order, preferred "sleigh riding," and wouldn't "leave off Frolicking." Sublette writes further: "The American Fur Co. apears determined to doe nothing more for Fontinill

---

[16] Fitzpatrick's letter in the Chouteau-Papin Papers, Mo. Hist. Soc.

and I cant blame them much . . . [they want to] get him out of the road."[17]

During this winter Milton Sublette was in Missouri, still suffering with his leg. But by means of a cork leg, sent to him by Hugh Campbell from Philadelphia, he managed to get about. Despite his handicap, he was eager to continue actively in the fur trade. Just what arrangements he and Fitzpatrick made with Fontenelle is not clear, but they got backing from Pierre Chouteau, Jr., and obtained goods for another venture to the mountains.[18] These supplies were shipped by steamboat to the Council Bluffs region, where they were packed into wagons and onto the backs of mules.

Fitzpatrick, with Milton Sublette along, headed his big trade caravan and set out from Bellevue on May 14, 1836. A famous missionary party, Dr. and Mrs. Marcus Whitman and Rev. and Mrs. H. H. Spalding and W. H. Gray, with Whitman's two Indian boys and sixteen-year-old Miles Goodyear, planned to join the trader company, but were late starting. Whitman rode ahead and asked Fitzpatrick to wait. The fur trade leader had no objections he said to having the missionaries along, but could not delay; they would have to catch up by added speed. This they accomplished, and on May 24 caught up at the crossing of Loup Fork of the Platte. The party was moving along the north bank of the Platte, on a route to be followed eleven years later by Brigham Young's pioneer band and to become known as the Mormon Trail.

---

[17] *Ibid.;* and Sublette's letter to Campbell of February 27. Sunder, 152, says Fitzpatrick dissolved his agreement with Fontenelle at this time, but of this there is some doubt, for the documents still carry the firm name.

[18] See Fitzpartick's letter of March 18, 1836, to Pierre Chouteau, Jr., in the Chouteau-Papin Collection, Mo. Hist. Soc.

The missionaries were good diarists, so we have excellent accounts of the 1836 journey to rendezvous.[19] Gracious, lively Narcissa Whitman pictures the caravan in motion:

The Fur Com. is large this year. We are really a moving village — nearly four hundred animals with ours, mostly mules and seventy men. The Fur Com. has seven wagons and one cart, drawn by six mules each, heavily loaded; the cart drawn by two mules carries a lame man [Milton Sublette], one of the proprietors of the Com. We have two waggons in our com. Mr. and Mrs. S. and Husband and myself ride in one, Mr. Gray and the baggage in the other. Our Indian boys drive the cows and Dulin the horses. Young Miles leads our forward horses, four in each team. Now E. if you wish to see the camp in motion, look away ahead and see first the pilot and the Captain Fitzpatrick, just before him — next the pack animals, all mules loaded with great packs — soon after you will see the waggons and in the rear our company. We all cover quite a space. The pack mules always string along one after the other just like Indians. There are several gentlemen in the Com. who are going over the Mountains for pleasure. Capt. Stewart, Mr. Lee speaks of him in his journal — he went over when he [Mr. Lee] did and returned. He is an Englishman, — Mr. Chelam. We had a few of them to tea with us last Monday eve — Capts. Fitzpatrick, Stuart, Mr. Harris and Chelam.[20]

Upon arriving opposite the mouth of the Laramie, the train was greeted by the fort's occupants — men, Indian wives, and halfbreed children. A ferryboat was constructed of two hollowed-out logs lashed together by means of poles and ropes and in this improvised craft the vehicles and goods were crossed over the Platte, and from thence were taken to the fort.[21] Here the company rested for a

---

[19] C. M. Drury (Ed.), *First White Women over the Rockies, Diaries, Letters, and Biographical Sketches of the Six Women of the Oregon Mission*, etc. 2 vols. (Glendale, 1963). Hereafter cited as *First White Women*.

[20] *Ibid.*, 51–52.

[21] *Ibid.*, 192 (Mrs. Spalding's diary); also W. H. Gray, *A History of Oregon* (1870), 116; and C .M. Drury, *Henry Harmon Spalding*, 139.

week, the white women being given the hospitality of the fort. Mrs. Whitman especially enjoyed the chairs; they were so comfortable, with their buffalo skin bottoms.[22]

According to plans, the wagons were to be left at the fort. But Whitman insisted on continuing farther with one of those belonging to the missionaries; so the company leaders consented for their cart to go along.

On June 20 a special party came to the fort. At its head was an important man in the fur business, a special representative of the A.F.C. — Joshua Pilcher. He had probably received some encouragement from Fitzpatrick when the latter was on the upper Missouri the preceding winter. Pilcher had hurried over from Fort Pierre on the Missouri, on a special mission — to try to buy out Fontenelle, Fitzpatrick & Co. and their fort on the Laramie. D. D. Mitchell, who had come to the post on a similar mission the preceding year, as noted above, had failed in his objective. This post had not only received a fair supply of goods in 1835 and had lured many Indians in to barter, but now, in June 1836, the big wagon loads of trade items were stored there. The competition with Forts Union, Pierre, and other posts on the upper Missouri would be more than the A.F.C. would relish. So they wanted this new fort.

This post on the Laramie, which was usually called Fort William at this time, Pilcher calls "Fort Lucien," in compliment to the first-named man in the owning partnership.[23]

---

22 Myron Eells, *Marcus Whitman,* 60–61.

23 See Pilcher's two letters of June 21, 1836, that follow, and which are in the Chouteau-Papin Collection, Mo. Hist. Soc. This explanation solves the puzzle that troubled Mr. Chittenden when he wrote his masterful history of the American fur trade. On page 939 he refers to Fort Lucien, but is unable to identify it.

To his chief, Pierre Chouteau, Jr., Pilcher wrote:

Fort Lucien 21st June 1836

P. Chouteau Jun. Esq.

Dear Sir In the afternoon of yesterday I reached this post and found Mr. Fitzpatrick and all hands still here, though they arrived some ten days ago — for *reasons* I enquire not — everything I see and hear admonishes me to move with caution and prudence. To enter into details might give unnecessary anxiety, but I cannot avoid stating that all my anticipations seem to be approaching a consumation. . . . The party for the mountains is about to move, not however without leaving a large outfit for this post for the Indian trade. . . . The miserable annimals with which I left the Missouri have nearly given out; and as far as I find an apparent reluctance to furnish others here, I am obliged to continue my rout with them; but now that I am with the party, I feel no uneasiness; for it is very certain that I never lose sight of them horses or no horses *until I put a period to this business.* . . . Adios   JOSHUA PILCHER

On the same day Pilcher wrote another letter:

To the Gentlemen of Fort Pierre

I reached this post yesterday and found all hands resting on their oars after a stay of ten days. If you can have some person here — say about the first of August or a little before — I may be able to give you some advise and information that will be of great importance to you; but it depends on the arrangements I make west of the mountains, Should I not compromise with those *fools* you will have opposition *heavy.*

A week after the caravan had headed for the rendezvous, Mr. L. Crawford, who was left in charge of the post (which he still calls Fort William), wrote a letter in which he said:

Major Fitzpatrick and Sublette left this seven days ago (& with them Mr. Pilcher) for the mountains. I am left in charge of this post, and my particular department is to trade with the Indians, Mr. Woods to keep the accounts and trade with the whites, under my directions. . . . I expect about 300 lodges in tomorrow of Sioux that I went after towards the South Fork. They have some robes to trade which will be sent down in waggons.[24]

---

[24] Crawford's letter to P. Chouteau, Jr., dated June 29, 1836. — Chouteau-Papin Collection, Mo. Hist. Soc.

156

Fitzpatrick led the caravan westward from the fort. Upon reaching the place for final crossing of the Platte (near present Casper, Wyoming) the company halted, constructed a bullboat of buffalo skins stretched over a willow framework, and boated the goods across the stream. Upon reaching and crossing South Pass on July 4, Mrs. Spalding prosaically recorded in her diary: "Crossed the ridge of land today, called the divide, which separates the waters that flow into the Atlantic from those that flow into the Pacific, and camped for the night on the head waters of the Colorado."[25] No other contemporary account makes anything special of the day's events. But this first crossing of the continental divide by white women and their entry into the Oregon country was too significant and potentially too dramatic to be retold later without embellishment. In 1870 it was rendered thus:

"And there — it was Independence Day, six years before Fremont, following in the footsteps of these women, gained the name of the Path-finder, — they [the women], alighting from their horses and kneeling on the other half of the continent, with the Bible in one hand and the American flag in the other, took possession of it as the home of American mothers, and of the Church of Christ."

A picture, representing this scene, appeared in O. W. Nixon, *Whitman's Ride through Savage Lands,* 1905, p. 56. The flag flies from a flagpole before the covered wagon as the mission party kneels in prayer. A different representation of the same incident is pictured in Eells, *Whitman,* p. 35. Here the artist pictures Spalding standing holding the United States flag on a shorter staff, with the two women, Whitman, and Gray kneeling.[26]

Today a rustic marker at South Pass fittingly commemorates the event.[27]

---

[25] *First White Women,* 193.
[26] *Ibid.,* Drury's footnote.
[27] The marker is on the old Oregon Trail crossing of emigrant days, about two miles south of where the present oil-top highway runs.

An express having been dispatched to Green River to announce the coming of the train, a motley band of trappers and Indians came out to greet it. Upon coming in sight of the caravan the leader of the greeting delegation tied a white cloth to the end of his gun and led the charge. On came the mountaineers, yelling and whooping, their horses jumping the sagebrush as they dashed past the train. Over the heads of the excited missionaries they sent a volley of bullets; then whirling back they circled the caravan and quieted down to handshake greetings.[28]

Arrived on July 6 at the rendezvous near the mouth of Horse Creek on the Green, the pack animals were unloaded and the goods placed in the log storeroom, a remnant of Bonneville's "Fort Nonsense." The clerks brought out their books and the trading began. Free trappers and Indians crowded around to barter their furs for powder and knives, sugar and coffee, bright colored cloth and spangles, and the numerous articles that appealed to primitive tastes.

The tents of the women missionaries became reception chambers. Braves admired the genial and gracious Mrs. Whitman, while the squaws were drawn to the enfeebled Mrs. Spalding. Trappers were reminded of mothers and sisters and homes long forsaken.

On the sixth day of the rendezvous, the Indians entertained with a gorgeous procession and a brilliant display of military maneuvers. The braves were painted and dressed (or undressed) for war, and with their weapons and battle paraphernelia needed only the presence of scalps to

---

[28] Victor's *River of the West*, 202; also, Gray, *op. cit.*, 118. The similarity of wording in these two accounts indicates that one was copied from the other.

make the war scenes complete.[29] The demonstration was enjoyed by the spectators almost as much as by participants.

The most significant business transacted at the rendezvous of 1836 was the sale by Fontenelle, Fitzpatrick & Co. of their business and of their fort on the Laramie to Joshua Pilcher, as agent for the A.F.C. or its successor. Dr. Whitman thus reports it:

Major Pilcher joined us at Fort Williams and came on to Rendezvoux, as agent of Pratt, Choteau & Co., in whose behalf he bought out the "mountain partners," so that the whole [fur] business now belongs to them.[30]

The terms of the sale have not been found. It appears that the principal provisions were for transfer of debts.[31] The partners, all good experienced brigade leaders, were now employed by the purchasing company. An indication of terms is revealed in a document in which Jim Bridger in July 1838 states that Pratte, Chouteau & Co. owe him $3317.13 (probably including interest) for services for the preceding two years.[32] Fitzpatrick would undoubtedly have been promised as much or more in salary.

In settling up with individual trappers Fitzpatrick gave drafts on Pratte, Chouteau & Co., chargeable to the Fon-

---

[29] Gray, 122.

[30] A. B. and D. P. Hulbert, *Marcus Whitman, Crusader* (Denver, 1936), 230–31.

[31] Pratte, Chouteau & Co. had been backing Fitzpatrick and his partners after their break with William Sublette in 1834, and had done the same for Drips and Fontenelle previously. So much was the supplying company involved that in the trading license obtained from William Clark on April 22, 1836, it listed among men authorized to trade for it the following: Thomas Fitzpatrick, M. G. Sublette, James Bridger, and Andrew Drips. — Copy of the license in the Newberry Library, Chicago.

[32] A document of July 13, 1838, in which Bridger appoints W. L. Sublette as his lawful attorney to receive the sum mentioned. Andrew Drips signs it as Agent for Pierre Chouteau & Co., at Wind River, Rocky Mountains.

tenelle, Fitzpatrick & Co. account.[33] The missionary party set out toward Oregon on July 18. It was being escorted by the H.B.C. leaders John L. McLeod and Thomas McKay, who had come in to the rendezvous six days before.[34]

Fitzpatrick, Milton Sublette and party returned with the furs from the rendezvous to Fort Lucien on the Laramie. Here on August 15 Fitzpatrick signed drafts to pay off some of the employes. Milton remained at the fort, apparently as major domo. Many Indians came in to trade, and the goods left there were insufficient to meet the demand. By mid-December Milton is disgusted, he cannot take up the buffalo robes and beaver skins offered, and numbers of the Indians are leaving to barter with traders on the South Platte.

To Pratte, Chouteau & Co. he writes December 13, 1836:

I have at this time near one hundred packs of robes, and nearly out of goods I am lacking tobacco whiskey and Blankets. . . . Fitzpatrick was to send me goods at all risk but after getting to the bluffs he concludes to have nothin more to do with me but I dont sencure the American Fur Company for this thow I have heard a great deal that your object was to brake up the post, but Fitzpatrick gives me his word he would return this winter though we were partners I shall neave have any thin more to do with him he left me with a few remnants from the summer trad.[35]

The cause of the friction is not revealed; and whether it was Fitzpatrick or the Company that neglected or de-

[33] Such drafts were made out at the rendezvous in July and at Fort Williams on August 15. Included are those to Toussaint Racine, for $320 (less previous advances) and "for his trip to Fort Lucien with Proveau, $150"; to a Mr. Joyall, $236.30; Louis Denoye, $30; and to James Daugherty, $72. These papers are in the Chouteau-Papin Collection, Mo. Hist. Soc.

[34] *First White Women,* 68 and 70.

[35] Letter in the Chouteau-Papin Collection, Mo. Hist. Soc. In another letter of the same date and addressed to the same company, Milton says that if an expedition comes to the Rocky Mountains in the spring he wants two mowing scythes sent out.

clined to send out more goods to the fort on the Laramie is not clear. Milton was suffering with his diseased leg, which could have put him in a disgruntled mood. The leg worsened, and on April 5, 1837, he died at the fort.[36]

The trade caravan that came out to the mountains in 1837 was captained by Fitzpatrick. With the company came Captain Stewart and his personal party, among whom was the capable artist, Alfred Jacob Miller. No diary of this trip has come to light, but the numerous Miller paintings and the accompanying written explanations by the artist give an important record of the journey. Some of the paintings show the train en route. One of Miller's texts tells of "about 30 wagons and 'charettes' (two-wheeled carts) crossing the Kansas River."[37] This indicates not only the size of the train but its place of departure — the earlier starting place of Independence, or Westport, instead of the Council Bluffs region. The veteran trapper Etienne Provost was with the train. Miller referred to him as "Monsieur Proveau, subleader, with a corpus round as a porpoise (no. 76), and his picture of Provost well illustrates this description.

The wagons must have been unloaded and left at the Laramie fort, as in the preceding summer, but the carts came on to rendezvous. Osborne Russell, waiting anxiously on the Green River, gives us the specific report: "The cavalcade consisting of 45 men and 20 Carts drawn by Mules under the direction of Mr. Thomas Fitzpatrick accompanied by Capt. Wm Stewart on another tour of the

---

[36] Sunder, 149.

[37] *The West of Alfred Jacob Miller* (Norman, 1951), 101. For other paintings showing the vehicles, see numbers 76, 132, 133, 139, 142, 147, 155, 162, 163, 177, 181, 197, and 198. Some pictures show the carts drawn by two horses or mules hitched tandem.

Rocky Mountains."[38] Russell writes of the enthusiastic greeting of the trappers, and the anxiety for letters or news and for supplies. Prices were high, he says, about 2,000 per cent on first cost: "Sugar 2$ pr pint Coffee the same Blankets 20$ each Tobacco 2$ pr pound alcohol 4$ per pint and Common Cotton Shirts 5$ each etc And in return paid 4 or 5$ pr pound for Beaver."[39]

William H. Gray, the missionary who accompanied the Whitmans and Spaldings to Oregon in 1836, was at rendezvous on his return eastward to get a wife and other missionaries. (He would be back at rendezvous 1838.) Coming from Oregon with some white and Flathead companions he reached Green River on July 2, 1837. He reports Drips and his trapper band as encamped near the mouth of Horse Creek. Gray describes a scalp dance conducted by 25 Delaware Indians:

> The men are mostly naked all holding some implements of war. Their dance consists in jumping first on one and then on the other foot, and passing and repassing each other in every direction, and going and jumping round in a ring. Their musical instrument, which is the same as the Flat Head's, is so managed as to change the time, beating slow, then quick with a double beat; at every change of their music, they give the yell and jump in a different position, placing their bodies in a different position, erect, stooping forward, and on both sides stooping down as if to look through the bushes, or the ring for their enemies, and stepping from one side to the other, keeping time with their music, and yelling at intervals, and firing their guns; their scalps, perhaps three whole ones, were cut into nine or ten pieces, pretending to be as many scalps, all strung on one pole. Their dance continued for about four hours, when they all retired.[40]

---

[38] A. L. Haines (Ed.), *Osborne Russell's Journal of a Trapper* (Portland, 1955), 60.

[39] *Ibid.*, 60.

[40] "Journal of W. H. Gray," in *Whitman College Quarterly* (June 1913), 55.

Gray was shocked at the buying and selling of Indian wives by the white trappers; and at the drinking and carousing. "No tongue can tell," he says, "the extent that blasphemy is carried at this place." On July 10 a band of Snakes arrived at Drips' camp and gave a scalp dance. Other diversions continued until the eighteenth, when the supply caravan arrived. The next day Gray entertained Capt. Fontenelle and Artist Miller at meals, and was visited by Capt. Stewart and Mr. Thing (British factor from Fort Hall). The Snake Indians gave a demonstration "all mounted on their best war horses, about two hundred and fifty. They proceeded upon the gallop, singing, yelling, and firing their guns, some naked some dressed in various ways to suit their fancy."[41]

After the rendezvous the trapper bands departed for their appointed fields. Fontenelle and Bridger with 110 men set out for the Blackfoot country of the upper Missouri. Russell with a small party headed for the Bighorn and Yellowstone.[42] Doc. Newell and others went into the Crow country of the Powder and Tongue rivers of Wyoming. About Christmas time Fontenelle went with 25 men to the fort on the Laramie, still generally called Fort William, for supplies, while his company, 80 strong, holed up on Powder River to await his return. He must have obtained little, for at the fort conditions were bad. Mr. B. Woods, chief trader, had few goods, and other traders on the North and South Platte were luring away his Indians.[43] Back in camp on the Powder River Bob Newell writes in

[41] *Ibid.*, 59–61.

[42] Haines' *Russell, op. cit.*, 60–61.

[43] J. A. Hamilton's letter to P. Chouteau, Jr., of Dec. 22, 1837; in the Chouteau-Maffitt Collection, Mo. Hist. Soc.

his journal: "times is getting hard all over this part of the Country beaver Scarce and low all peltries are on the decline."[44]

And this refrain was general throughout the country. The Panic of 1837 hit business in every quarter. Conditions were reflected in the American Fur Company Papers. At St. Louis Pratte Chouteau & Co. wrote in May that times are exceedingly tight, with many financial failures.[45] The press of the year was full of gloomy pictures.

It is well nigh impossible, from presently available records, to follow Thomas Fitzpatrick through the next year or so. He appears to have taken the train with the furs back to the States following rendezvous 1837; then disappears from the documents. He may have gone to the South Platte region, where he is seen in 1839, as will be mentioned shortly. It is even speculated that he may have made a visit back to his home in old Ireland, as Robert Campbell did in 1832.

Fontenelle, Bridger, and Drips, his former partners, continue to conduct trapping parties and supply trains for three more years. But no word about Fitzpatrick. Not until September 1839 do we catch a brief glimpse of him in the records. Then another void, until he comes again into clear light, now in the new profession of Guide, leading the first emigrant train headed for Oregon.

But we cannot leave the fur trade, with which he has been so prominently identified from the very beginning in the central Rockies, without a brief summary of events to

---

[44] Newell, *op. cit.*, 36.
[45] Calendar of American Fur Company Papers, in *Annual Report*, American Historical Association (1944), May 12 and 22, 1837.

the terminal year 1840, when the last rendezvous was held.

For the 1838 rendezvous Andrew Drips led the supply caravan, setting out from Westport on April 23. With him went a Swiss traveler destined for fame, August Johann Sutter. Capt. Stewart and party are again westbound for a hunting excursion and with the party are two sons of William Clark of Northwest exploration fame. An important contingent is the missionary party of William H. Gray, Elkhanah Walker, Cushing Eells, and A. B. Smith and their brides. In the diaries of these dedicated but quarreling missionaries a full and fascinating record of the trek is preserved. Myra Eells writes of the caravan: "The Company have about 200 horses and Mules; we have twenty-one horses and mules. They [have] 17 carts and wagons, we have one. We have 12 horned cattle. The waggons are all covered with black or dark cloth. They move first, one directly after the other, then the packed animals and cattle."[46]

Up the valley of the Platte the supply train moved without important incident and reached the vicinity of Fort William at the end of May. Here they found Fontenelle and Woods. Writes Mrs. Eells, "Three Indian women, wives of Capts. Drips, Fontinelle, and Wood, with their children call on us. The children are quite white and can read a little."[47]

At the fort wagons are left, but carts are retained. Fontenelle and his son join the party and Drips takes along his Indian wife. They reach rendezvous, this year near the junction of the Popo Agie and Wind River (not far from

---

[46] *First White Women*, II, 75.
[47] *Ibid.*, 87–88.

present Riverton, Wyoming), on June 23 and are to remain here about two weeks. On June 25 Joe Walker comes in "with a large company, perhaps 200 or 300 horses." On July 5 "Capt. Bridger's company comes in about 10 o'clock with drums and firing — an apology for a scalp dance. After they had given Capt. Drip's company a shout, 15 or 20 mountain men and Indians came to our tent with drumming, firing and dancing. If I might make the comparison, I should say that they looked like the emissaries of the Devil worshiping their own master."[48]

On June 8 some H.B.C. traders arrived at the rendezvous, and with them Jason Lee and P. L. Edwards on their way east. Lee is taking along some Indian boys to enliven his campaign in the East for support of the Oregon missions. After the breakup of the rendezvous Drips and Bridger remained in the mountains at the head of trapping brigades.

The fur trade caravan of 1839 was much smaller than heretofore. The beaver trade was decidedly on the decline, the rendezvous about to be abandoned. The fur company had but four two-wheeled carts, each drawn by mules and carrying 800 to 900 pounds each. In charge of these goods was the veteran Mountain Man, "Black" Harris, assisted by eight company employes. Missionaries and independent travelers increased the party to twenty-seven. Among these was a German physician from St. Louis, Dr. Adolph Wislizenus, on a tour of recreation and adventure to the mountains. His account of the expedition, published in German

---

[48] Mrs. Eells' diary, *ibid.*, 97, 100.

the following year, gives interesting observations and information on the journey to the rendezvous.[49]

Dr. Wislizenus gives a good description of wooden Fort William and says, "The whole garrison of the fort consists of only five men; four Frenchmen and a German. Some of them were married to Indian women, . . ." The fur-trade caravan pushed on westward, passed Independence Rock, "The Rocky Mountain Album," and over South Pass. Drips and Joe Walker came out to meet the train, which reached the rendezvous on Green River July 5.

What first struck our eye [says Wislizenus], was several long rows of Indian tents [lodges], extending along the Green River for at least a mile. Indians and whites were mingled here in varied groups. Of the Indians there had come chiefly Snakes, Flatheads and Nez Perces, peaceful tribes, living beyond the Rocky Mountains. Of the whites the agents of the different trading companies and a quantity of trappers had found their way here, visiting this fair of the wilderness to buy and to sell, to renew old contracts and to make new ones, to make arrangements for future meetings, to meet old friends, to tell of adventures they had been through, and to spend for once a jolly day. . . .

At the yearly rendezvous the trappers seek to indemnify themselves for the sufferings and privations of a year spent in the wilderness. With their hairy bank notes, the beaver skins, they can obtain all the luxuries of the mountains, and live for a few days like lords. . . . Formerly single trappers on such occasions have often wasted a thousand dollars. But the days of their glory seem to be past, for constant hunting has very much reduced the number of beavers. This diminution in the beaver catch made itself noticeable at this year's [1839] rendezvous in the quieter behavior of the trappers. There was little drinking of spirits, and almost no gambling.[50]

On his return trip to Missouri Dr. Wislizenus, to see

---

[49] Adolph Wislizenus, *Ein Ausflug nach den Felsen-gebirgen im Jahre 1839;* an English translation by the Doctor's son and published at St. Louis in 1912, is cited here, 28–29.
[50] *Ibid.,* 86–90.

more of the West, took a different route home. He went by way of Fort Davy Crockett in Brown's Hole on Green River, then to the forts on the South Platte, and thence to Bent's Fort and down the Arkansas. In September, at Fort Vasquez on the South Platte (about 40 miles north of present Denver), he wrote: "I met the well-known Fitzpatrick, who passed through many an adventure during his life in the mountains. He has a spare, bony figure, a face full of expression, and white hair; his whole demeanor reveals strong passions."[51] Nothing is reported as to why or in what capacity Fitzpatrick was there; but it is likely that he was attending to company business. Then he drops from sight in the records for another year or more.

In 1840 the last fur-trade caravan set out for a mountain rendezvous. It left Westport on April 30, under the leadership of Andrew Drips, with goods piled in carts and on pack animals.[52] Again there were Protestant missionaries bound for Oregon,[53] and now the outstanding Catholic Father, Pierre Jean De Smet was in the company. Also there was an avowed emigrant settler, Joel P. Walker (brother of famous Mountain Man, Joe) with his wife and five children.[54]

The route was again up the Platte; the story is told by Father De Smet. At Independence Rock, De Smet's "great register of the desert," the good Father added his name to the many already scratched or painted upon this famous

---

[51] *Ibid.*, 137.

[52] H. M. Chittenden and A. T. Richardson, *Life, Letters and Travels of Father Pierre Jean de Smet, S.J.* (New York, 1905), 201. Robert Newell, *op. cit.*, 39, says Bridger and Fraeb were with Drips.

[53] These were Harvey Clark, A. T. Smith, and P. B. Littlejohn and their wives.

[54] Joel P. Walker's "Narrative" (ms.), in the Bancroft Library, University of California, Berkeley.

landmark — the huge granite turtle resting beside the Sweetwater.

When the supply train reached Green River on June 30, Shoshones in great numbers were there to greet the traders and missionaries. Writes De Smet:

Three hundred of their warriors came up in good order and at full gallop into the midst of our camp. They were hideously painted, armed with clubs, and covered all over with feathers, pearls, wolves' tails, teeth and claws of animals, outlandish adornments, with which each one had decked himself out according to his fancy. Those who had wounds received in war, and those who had killed the enemies of their tribe, displayed their scars ostentatiously and waved the scalps they had taken on the ends of poles, after the manner of standards.[55]

But to veteran trapper Doc Newell the rendezvous was a tame affair — "times were certainly hard   no beaver and every thing dull."[56]

This was the last fur-trade rendezvous (1840), the finale to those spectacular mountain assemblages that for sixteen years had been the outstanding annual event, the unique institution of the Rocky Mountain West. To grizzled trappers who had seen the rise and the fall of the beaver skin business, this final gathering brought bewilderment and regret.

Men who had become attached to this fascinating, dangerous life were loath to leave it. But there was no choice left them. A livelihood no longer could be made by trapping beaver; and no fur company would agree to bring trade goods to the Green River Valley to barter for beaver pelts. The rendezvous was dead. Trappers must look for employ-

---

[55] De Smet, *op. cit.*, 217.
[56] Newell, 39.

ment elsewhere. Some would go to Santa Fe, some to California or Oregon, others would return to Missouri.

·Come [said Doc. Newell to Joe Meek], we are done with this life in the mountains — done with wading in beaver-dams, and freezing or starving alternately — done with Indian trading and Indian fighting. The fur-trade is dead in the Rocky Mountains, and it is no place for us now, if ever it was. We are young yet, and have life before us. We cannot waste it here; we cannot or will not return to the states. Let us go down to the Wallamet [in Oregon] and take farms.[57]

Fur forts on the North and South Platte, the Arkansas, the Green River, the Uinta, and the Gunnison had been established. And these were concerned primarily with the buffalo robe trade. The high-top silk hat had replaced beaver head gear in the style centers of the world and the beaver skin market was gone. The buffalo robe trade would pick up the broken fragments of the Western fur business and continue a halting traffic. The rendezvous gave way to the trading post; the beaver skin was supplanted by the buffalo robe. This was the end of a short but distinctive period in the history of the West.

Fitzpatrick had seen it come and go. He had been a discoverer of beaver streams of the central Rockies, and of the mountain passes that led to those clear, beaver-splashed waters. He had escorted the early missionaries to the West of the Rockies. He had watched their numbers increase since Jason Lee led the way in 1834. Now he was to witness the natural sequence to that penetration. A covered wagon company of westwardbound homeseekers was forming on the border of Missouri. The fertile soil of a potential empire beckoned on the Pacific Coast. But between the fron-

---

[57] Victor, *River of the West, op. cit.,* 264.

tier settlements and that distant goal lay a wide prairie, high plains, mountain ranges, and barren deserts. A seasoned Mountain Man and trusted leader was needed to pilot the enthusiastic but green homeseekers. Thomas Fitzpatrick, now ready to launch into a new career, was the man of the hour — of the period — to guide and safeguard these pioneer fulfillers of Manifest Destiny.

Chapter 9

Piloting the First Emigrants

THE MOVING TIDE of American emigration ran irresistably westward. Temporarily it had stopped on the western border of Missouri. Beyond lay the Great American Desert, which Major Stephen H. Long had described and labeled as a barrier Divine Providence had placed "to prevent too great an extension of our population westward." But there were Americans who did not accept the Major as a Prophet. Word had been brought back by hardy Mountain Men of a Promised Land beyond the desert. They spoke of California and Oregon, and these magic words stirred the blood for conquest of a new land of Canaan.

Poised on the bank of the mighty Missouri, above its abrupt northward bend, were pioneers with restlessness in their veins. For two or three generations they had been on the move, and they were not about to prosaically settle quiet.

At Weston, on the frontier's far edge, where pioneers

watched the sun set in a land of grandeur, a group of the unsatisfied gathered to consider a farther move. They called in Antoine Robidoux, who had been to Santa Fe nearly twenty years before, had trapped on the Green and Colorado, and had visited distant California. He could advise and would answer questions. He described a land of perennial spring, of fertile soil. Oranges, grapes, and olive trees demonstrated the climate. Large bands of horses and cattle ran wild in the boundless pastures of grass and sweet clover.

There were many points on which they wanted information, and when that was given there yet remained — to people afflicted as were the early settlers, with chills, fever, and ague—an all-important one: "Do they have fever and ague out there?"

I remember his answer distinctly [writes John Bidwell, a prominent member of the potential emigrants]. He said there was but one man in California that ever had a chill there, and it was a matter of so much wonderment to the people of Monterey that they went eighteen miles into the country to see him shake.[1]

This was enough. The Western Emigration Society was formed; a pledge was drawn up under which the signers agreed to equip themselves and to rendezvous for the start at Sapling Grove, west of Independence, on May 9, 1841. The plan of the society was announced in the newspapers, and prospective emigrants wrote from places in Missouri, Illinois, and Arkansas. Within a month a roll of five hundred names was listed. But just as everything looked most promising, a letter that put the Pacific Coast in a decidedly unattractive light appeared in the press. It was by Thomas J. Farnham, who had gone out in 1839, had had an un-

---

[1] John Bidwell, *Echoes of the Past about California* (Chicago, 1928), 14.

fortunate experience, and now saw fit to warn his com-
patriots against settling there. The reaction was immediate
and extreme. Enthusiasm waned, and members dropped
out. The more resolute, however, including four or five
from Weston, assembled with their families, to the number
of some sixty men, women, and children.

The men organized, electing John Bartleson, who lived in
the neighborhood, as captain. But as the time for starting
approached, it was found that no one knew the way. Bidwell had some maps, which turned out to be worthless, and
many of the men had heard reports of one kind or another;
but of definite information there was none. At this juncture
appeared a man who reported the approach of a missionary
party led by Father Pierre Jean De Smet, and headed for
the Oregon country.

This party had left St. Louis April 30, going by boat to
Westport, where the land journey began. With De Smet
were Nicholas Point and Gregory Mengarini as assistants,
five teamsters, and two trappers.[2] "They had with them
as guide," writes George R. Stewart, "one of the half-dozen
people in the world best qualified for that work. He
was no less a one than Thomas 'Broken Hand' Fitzpatrick,
among the most notable of the mountain men."[3] The Bartleson party decided to wait and propose that both bodies
travel together.

And it was well that we did [writes Bidwell], for otherwise

[2] H. M. Chittenden and A. D. Richardson (eds.), *Life, Letters and Travels of
Father Pierre Jean De Smet,* etc. 4 vols. (New York, 1905), 275–307. Hereafter cited as De Smet. See also *Wilderness Kingdom; Indian Life in the Rocky
Mountains: 1840–1847. Journals & Paintings of Nicolas Point, S.J.* Translated
and introduced by Joseph P. Donnelly, S.J. (New York, 1967). Hereafter
cited as Point's *Journal.*

[3] George R. Stewart, *The California Trail* (New York, 1962), 12.

probably not one of us would ever have reached California, because of our inexperience. Afterwards when we came in contact with the Indians, our people were so easily excited that if we had not had with us an old mountaineer the result would certainly have been disastrous.

The name of the guide was Captain Fitzpatrick; he had been at the head of trapping parties in the Rocky Mountains for many years.[4]

So on May 10, the first emigrant wagon train to set out from the settlements for the Pacific Coast, started in company with the party of De Smet. It had thirteen wagons, some drawn by mules, others by horses or oxen, while the missionaries, who rode mounted, had five two-wheeled carts, drawn by mules hitched tandem. Four days beyond the Kansas crossing the caravan was overtaken by Joseph B. Chiles,[5] with a wagon and five men, and on May 26 the eccentric Methodist preacher, Rev. Joseph Williams, caught up. He had ridden from the Kansas crossing alone and unarmed.[6] The total membership of the combined parties was about eighty.[7]

Along the trappers' route soon to be known as the Oregon Trail they journeyed.

In these immense solitudes [wrote Father Point] it was necessary to have an experienced guide. The choice fell not on the colonel [Bartleson], who had never crossed the mountains, but on the captain Father De Smet had engaged. He was a courageous Irishman, known to most of the Indian tribes as Tet Blanch (White Head) [or Broken Hand]. He had spent fully two thirds of his life crossing the plains.

---

[4] Bidwell, *op. cit.*, 23–24.

[5] For a biographical sketch of Chiles and a brief account of this trip, see *History of Napa and Lake Counties, California* (San Francisco, 1881), 444–46. Stewart gives a valuable appraisal of Chiles and his contribution.

[6] Joseph Williams' biography and his account of an extraordinary tour is presented in LeRoy R. and Ann W. Hafen (eds.), *To the Rockies and Oregon, 1839–1842* (Glendale, Calif., 1955), 199–287. Hereafter cited as Williams.

[7] *Ibid.*, 219, Williams says ". . . the company consisted of about fifty."

The missionaries and their party were regarded as the first body of the vanguard. Each day the captain gave the signal to rise and depart, ordered the march and the stops, chose the spot in which to camp, and maintained discipline. Whenever possible, camp was pitched on the wooded bank of some river that there would be no lack either of drinking water or of wood for cooking. First, the captain would mark a spot for our tent; then the vehicles would be arranged one beside the other in a circle or in a square, more or less according to the nature of the terraine, but always in such a maner as to provide the pack animals a secure enclosure for the night. . . . all the travelers, including the priests, stood watch according to roster, in order to guard against a surprise attack.[8]

A warm friendship sprang up between De Smet and Fitzpatrick. "I had the pleasure and happiness to travel in his [Fitzpatrick's] company during the whole summer of 1842 [1841]," wrote De Smet eight years later, "this being my second expedition to the mountains, and every day I learned to appreciate him more and more."[9] But straight-laced Preacher Williams saw the guide in a poorer light. "Our leader, Fitzpatrick," he writes, "is a wicked, worldly man, and is much opposed to missionaries going among the Indians. He has some intelligence, but is deistical in his principles."[10] In just what ways the wickedness of the guide was manifested we do not know; but as he was then guiding a missionary party to the Flatheads, and was held in the highest estimation by them, the statement may be classed as amusing rather than important.

Near the Platte the party had its first Indian scare. A young tenderfoot, Nicholas Dawson, who had been out hunting, ran madly into camp minus his mule, gun, pistol, and most of his clothes, with the report that he had been

---

[8] Point's *Journal*, 26.
[9] De Smet, 1465.
[10] Williams, 221.

attacked by a horde of Indians, robbed and maltreated. Most of the men became so excited that Fitzpatrick, despite his experience, lost control. Each driver started his team on the run, but Fitzpatrick spurred ahead, and as fast as the wagons and carts reached the river formed them into a hollow square. Presently some fifty Indians came in sight, but instead of showing hostility they calmly pitched their tepees nearby. Fitzpatrick and John Gray visited them, learned that they were Cheyennes (of a tribe at that time friendly) and that they had no intention of hurting the young man, but had been compelled to disarm him because in his terror at meeting Indians he seemed likely to fire at them. They readily surrendered his mule, gun, and pistol, and the incident was amicably closed. But the young hunter was a long time in hearing the last of it, for thereafter he was called "Cheyenne" Dawson.[11]

They reached the buffalo country, and from then on for many days they had ample stores of meat. On some days, however, the buffalo appeared in such enormous numbers that they constituted a menace. One night on the South Platte there was a buffalo stampede which threatened the annihilation of the camp. But Fitzpatrick led out from camp a company of riflemen, who kept up so constant a fire into the herd that the animals were forced to turn aside. "We could hear them thundering all night long," writes Bidwell, "the ground fairly trembled with vast approaching bands, and if they had not been diverted, wagons, animals and emigrants would have been trodden under foot" (pp. 14–15).

---

[11] Nicholas Dawson, *Narrative of Nicholas "Cheyenne" Dawson*, etc. (San Francisco, 1933).

At what later came to be known as Old (or Lower) California Crossing, near Brule, Nebraska, they forded the South Platte. The water was high, and great care had to be taken to prevent the wagons from being swept away by the current. They went on to the south bank of the North Platte, following it past the noted landmarks of Chimney Rock and Scott's Bluff, and on June 22 reached Fort Laramie, renowned western trading post.

Westward they went on to the crossing of the North Platte near present Casper, Wyoming. The stream was at flood, and again there was difficulty and danger in crossing. The missionaries, though much frightened, were persuaded to cross on horseback. "We were induced to do so," writes De Smet, "on seeing our hunter [Gray] drive before him a horse on which his wife was mounted, whilst at the same time he was pulling a colt that carried a little girl but one year old. To hold back under such circumstances would have been a disgrace for Indian missionaries. We therefore resolved to go forward."[12] One wagon was tipped over, the bed of another was carried some distance down the stream, and one mule was drowned, but otherwise the crossing was safely made.

Along the Sweetwater they journeyed, passed Independence Rock, crossed South Pass, and descended to Green River. Here Fitzpatrick met for the last time his oldtime partner, Henry Fraeb, still with a few followers making a meager living in the mountains. A month later Fraeb, with four of his men, was to be killed in a fight with Cheyennes and Sioux on what is now known as Battle Creek,

---

[12] De Smet, 309.

on the Colorado-Wyoming boundary.[13] From the Green the party continued to Ham's Fork, and thence on to Soda Springs, in present Idaho. Here the emigrant party divided, about half going to California, the remainder keeping on to Fort Hall and thence to Oregon. At Fort Hall the missionaries, here joined by friendly Flatheads, started northward, still led by Fitzpatrick.

They had not gone far up the Snake River before they encountered a band of fifty Bannock warriors. Writes Father Mengarini:

> At the first intimation of danger, our captain [Fitzpatrick] had ordered the wagons to be drawn up in a circle, and had seen that each man was at his post.
>
> None of the Indians of our party advanced to meet the Bannacks, for they had been engaged in a fight with them the previous year; neither did any of their party come over to us. Our captain advanced a little and told them by signs that they were Blackrobes, that we spoke of the Great Spirit, and that we were peaceable. They sat there with countenances perfectly impassive and answered neither by word nor by sign. I had put on my cassock and had persuaded Fr. DeSmet to do the same; and when the Canadians asked me where my gun was, I pointed to my reliquary.
>
> As evening approached, our visitors drew off and camped at a short distance.[14]

It is probable that Fitzpatrick spent the winter with the Flatheads.[15]

---

[13] See LeRoy R. Hafen, "Fraeb's Last Fight and How Battle Creek Got its Name," in the *Colorado Magazine,* VII (1930), 97–101. Also see Nolie Mumey, *The Life of Jim Baker, 1818–1898* (Denver, 1931), 22–23.

[14] Albert J. Partoll (ed.), "Mengarini's Narrative of the Rockies," in *Frontier Omnibus,* edited by John W. Hakola (Missoula, 1962), 143.

[15] Long afterwards De Smet, writing of these days, tells of "our dear Flatheads" and of one of their chiefs, Michael Insula, or Red Feather, also known as the Little Chief, and says: "A keen discerner of the characters of men, he loves to speak especially of those whites, distinguished for their fine qualities, that have visited him, and often mentions with pleasure the sojourn among them of Colonel Robert Campbell, of St. Louis, and of Major Fitzpatrick, whom he adopted, in accordance with Indian ideas of chilavry, as his brother."

In the spring or summer of 1842 Fitzpatrick was back again in the Green River Valley, where he had picked up his old partner, Bridger. Together, with some packs of furs they had garnered, they proceeded toward Fort Laramie. At or near this fort, on July 3, they met an emigrant train journeying to Oregon. It was the party organized by Dr. Elijah White (formerly a missionary with Jason Lee, but now Indian sub-agent for Oregon), which had left Independence on May 16. It was the second emigrant train to travel the Oregon Trail, and it numbered about 110 persons, with eighteen wagons and large herds of cattle.

Soon after setting out, says L. W. Hastings, a member of the company, "the 'American character' was fully exhibited. All appeared to be determined to govern, but not to be governed."[16]

Dissensions split the company into factions, and as separate units they reached the Laramie. Here, on learning that hostile Indians were about, the factions came together, and White now engaged Fitzpatrick as guide. "I am now in the Indian country," the Doctor writes from the fort, "with foes on every hand, subtle as the devil himself; but our party is large and strong, and I have been able to obtain the services of Mr. Fitzpatrick, one of the ablest and most suitable men in the country, in conducting us to Fort Hall, beyond the point of danger from savages."[17]

---

[16] L. W. Hastings, *The Emigrants' Guide to Oregon and California* (1932 edition), 6.

[17] A. J. Allen, *Ten Years in Oregon: Travels and Adventures of Doctor E. White and Lady West of the Rocky Mountains* (Ithaca, 1848), 114. The "Journal of Medorem Crawford," in the *Sources of the History of Oregon*, I, no. 1, also gives an account of this expedition. Doctor White promised Fitzpatrick $250 to pilot him from Fort Laramie to Fort Hall. — Letter of White in National Archives; Indian Affairs, Oregon, 1842. Also Supt. of Ind. Affairs. Letterbooks

All went well as they journeyed up the North Platte, crossed at the Casper ford and proceeded to the Sweetwater. But at Independence Rock, the "Great Register of the Desert," they were to have an experience with Indians that must for a time have threatened the most disastrous consequences. As the train, after a brief halt, moved on, Hastings and A. L. Lovejoy (a few months later to be the companion of Marcus Whitman on his midwinter ride from Oregon to the settlements), remained behind to carve their names on the Rock. While thus engaged, a band of several hundred Sioux suddenly appeared and seized and stripped them, making demonstrations as though to kill Lovejoy. The prisoners were held captive for two hours, while Fitzpatrick, surmising the situation prepared the camp for battle. The Indians then started toward camp.

> Mr. Fitzpatrick [says White] went forward to meet them, making demonstrations of peace, and a desire that they should stop. His repeated signs were disregarded, and they rode steadily onward till nearly within gunshot, when they suddenly halted, apparently intimidated by the array. After a short pause Hastings and Lovejoy were liberated, and ran joyfully to their friends, the tears rolling down their cheeks as they recounted their escape.[18]

The emigrants halted for a few days to lay in a supply of buffalo meat, and passing on soon found themselves in the neighborhood of a large village of Indians, to which those already encountered belonged. There were again some signs of hostility, and the emigrants therefore halted and prepared for defense. Fitzpatrick with three other men

---

in Kansas State Historical Society, volume 8, 177: Letter of Fitzpatrick to T. H. Harvey, Aug. 16, 1844, demanding balance due him as Dr. White's assistant and interpreter.

[18] Allen, *op. cit.*, 156. Lovejoy's account of the episode is found in *Oregon Historical Quarterly*, XXXI, 244 et seq.

went forward to meet the chiefs, who, after some conversation, were induced to visit the emigrants' camp. Here they were entertained, and some presents were given them, after which they peaceably departed.

No one had in greater degree than Fitzpatrick that prime quality of a good mountain man—the ability to avoid a fight with the Indians when a fight was not wanted. It was an ability, or an art, that required supreme courage, for the red man must see no sign of weakness or fear; consumate tact, for the red man held firmly to his standards of etiquette; a knowledge of the workings of the red man's mind, insofar as that knowledge could be gained by any white man; and lastly, a masterful coolness. Whenever there was a chance for a "palaver," Fitzpatrick could usually convince the red man that peace was more desirable than war.

These Indians were in a bad humor. Some of them had been in the fight with Fraeb's men a year before, and were still smarting over the severe punishment received by them in that bloody encounter. How far they would have gone toward the plunder and slaughter of the emigrants can only be surmised. White and another member of the party, Medorem Crawford, made light of the episode. Frémont, on the other hand, in the report of his first expedition, says that the situation was serious:

Long residence and familiar acquaintance had given to Mr. Fitzpatrick great personal influence among them [the Indians], and a portion of them were disposed to let him pass quietly; but by far the greater number were inclined to hostile measures; and the chiefs spent the whole of one night, during which they kept the little party in the midst of them, in council, debating the question of attacking the next day; but the influence of "the Broken Hand," as they called Mr. Fitzpatrick (one of his hands having been shattered by the bursting of a gun), at length prevailed, and obtained for them an unmolested passage; but they sternly assured him that his path was no longer open, and that any party of whites which should hereafter be found upon it would meet with certain destruction. From all that I have been able to learn, I have no doubt that the emigrants owe their lives to Mr. Fitzpatrick.[19]

This view is supported by a statement appearing in the St. Louis *Weekly Reveille* of September 14, 1846, which reads:

To his [Fitzpatrick's] presence, alone, one of the Oregon emigrating parties was indebted for safety from a war parrty of 300 Indians, who had followed them several days for the purpose of attacking and robbing them.

Hastings, in his characteristic way, gave himself, in his book, *The Emigrant's Guide*, the whole credit, but it is likely that, whatever the degree of danger, he exerted not the slightest influence.

Crossing South Pass, the emigrants reached the Little Sandy, where they had another split, some of them abandoning their wagons and making pack saddles. Stephen H. Meek piloted one section, Fitzpatrick the other,[20] and both arrived about the same time, August 15, at Fort Hall. Here Fitzpatrick left them, and again splitting into two parties they proceeded to Oregon.

Carrying some letters from the emigrants and official reports from Dr. White, Fitzpatrick started with a single companion, one Van Dusen, for the East. Turning southward from the Oregon Trail, the two struck the South Platte where that stream turns abruptly to the east, and ascending it past the present site of Denver, they crossed

---

[19] J. C. Frémont, *Report of an Exploring Expedition*, etc., *op. cit.*, 41.
[20] Stephen Hall Meek, *The Autobiography of a Mountain Man*, introduction and notes by Arthur Woodward (Pasadena, 1948), 7–8.

the watershed of the Arkansas in mid-September. Here they came upon the camp of Rufus Sage and his party and after a short stop went on to the Arkansas.

While descending the river they encountered a war party of Pawnees. Fortunately we have an account of the adventure from Fitzpatrick himself, in a letter written to D. D. Mitchell, Superintendent of Indian Affairs at St. Louis:

> St. Louis, November 28, 1842
>
> Sir: I take the liberty of laying before you a case of robbery committed on me by the Pawnee Indians, on the 28th ult., about three hundred miles from Independence on the Arkansas river. I left Fort Hall (Columbia river) August 20th in company with one man for the U.S. and thot I might more easily avoid the Sioux and Chiennes (who are now considered hostile). I left the usual route and came by Messrs Bent & St. Vrain's trading post on the Arkansas from which to the settlements I anticipated little or no danger; however about half way between that place and Independence I met with a war party of the Pawnee coming from the South. They at first appeared friendly, but our attempting to leave them and continue our route, they showed symptoms of hostility and in a scuffle which ensued they got possession of my gun, in the meantime my travelling companion fled and I have not since heard from him. I was therefore left at the entire mercy of the savages and they made good use of their power they then possessed as they rifled me of all my travelling equipage, save my horses which they politely returned to me. They did not leave me wherewith to make a fire, which you know it very inconvenient and one of the greatest privations. I will herein enclose a bill of the articles they robbed me of. In order that I may obtain redress according to the laws existing on that subject. The loss I have sustained is very trifling, but the insult is very great to have accurred as it were on the very borders of the settlements.
>
> I have appeared before a magistrate of the city, as you will perceive, and have sworn to the correctness of thè enclosed bill, however I will make some remarks on the different articles for your satisfaction. They are all priced and set down at what I believe they cost me except the spy glass which would be worth here about fifteen dollars, but in the Indian country I could at any time get a good horse or forty dollars for it. There were many other articles

amongst my losses which I could make no estimate of and therefore left out altogether, such as Indian curiosities, many curios,
petrifactions, mineral specimums, etc.[21]

In January 1843, Fitzpatrick was being considered in the
national capital for a position in the federal service. A
letter from Senator Thomas H. Benton, of Missouri, dated
at Washington on January 30 to W. L. Sublette indicates
that Fitzpatrick, as well as a brother of Sublette's, was
being urged for some suitable place in the federal service
in the West. But the Senator could ask no favors of the
Administration of John Tyler. He writes in part:

It will give me great pleasure to assist your brother to get a
suitable place, where I have no doubt he would be servicable to
the Government as well as to himself. The same of Mr. Fitzpatrick;
but I apprehend we shall have to wait for a change of administration which cannot now be far off. Two years will bring the democ-
racy into power and then qualifications for office will be a recommendation; at present favoritism and personal qualifications are
the only rule of action.[22]

But though the Senator did not at this time aid Fitzpatrick toward a federal appointment, he may have recommended the man to his son-in-law, Frémont, as the guide
for the Pathmarker's second expedition, which in a few
months was to set out for Oregon and California. No recommendation from Benton was, however, needed. Frémont
must often have heard of Fitzpatrick from Kit Carson, the
guide of his first expedition, as well as from many others.
As Fitzpatrick was now available and was widely regarded
as the most intelligent and capable of the mountain men,
the choice would appear to have been almost inevitable.

---

[21] William Clark Papers, no. 8, p. 110; Kansas State Historical Society. Rufus
Sage gave a secondhand account of the episode, apparently as reported by
Van Dusen: L. R. and A. W. Hafen (eds.), *Far West and the Rockies*, V, 73.
[22] This letter is in the Missouri Historical Society Library, St. Louis.

Chapter 10

Guide and Adjutant

BY THE MIDDLE OF MAY 1843, John Charles Frémont had assembled at Kansas Landing (site of present Kansas City, Missouri) the party for his longest and most important western exploring expedition.

"My party," he wrote, "consisted principally of Creole and Canadian French and Americans, amounting in all to 39 men; . . . Mr. Thomas Fitzpatrick, whom many years of hardship and exposure in the western territories had rendered familiar with a portion of the country it was designed to explore, had been selected as our guide.[1]

---

[1] J. C. Frémont, *Report of the Exploring Expedition to the Rocky Mountains in the year 1842, and to Oregon and North California in the Years 1843–44* (Washington, 1845), 105. Hereafter cited as Frémont, *Report*. This report, along with numerous related documents, all enriched with explanatory notes, are reproduced in Donald Jackson and Mary Lee Spence (eds.), *The Expeditions of John Charles Frémont; Volume I, Travels from 1838 to 1844* (Urbana, Ill., 1970). Other important records of the expedition are Charles H. Carey (ed.), *The Journals of Theodore Talbot, 1843 and 1849–52, with the Frémont Expedition of 1843* . . . (Portland, Oregon, 1931); and Charles Preuss, *Exploring with Frémont, translated from the German and edited by E. G. and E. K. Gudde* (Norman, Okla., 1958).

Although technically the guide, Fitzpatrick was in effect quartermaster, and of one section of the party he was to become the commander. The thirty-nine men of the party were armed with carbines and pistols, and a twelve-pound brass howitzer added a show of force. Provisions were loaded in twelve two-mule carts, while special instruments and equipment were to be carried in a light spring wagon.[2]

The Landing and the nearby towns of Westport and Independence were thronged with emigrants for Oregon. This was the year of what is known as the Great Emigration, guided by Captain John Gantt and accompanied by Marcus Whitman, who from his home on the distant Walla Walla had made a heroic horseback ride to the settlements, had then gone on to the East and was now returning. Never before had the country about the Bend of the Missouri witnessed such a scene — so many men, with their wives and children, making ready for the long journey; such lines of covered wagons, such herds of cattle and droves of horses, mules, and oxen. The streets and stores were crowded, and the countryside was dotted with camps. From time to time small trains of wagons moved out to assemble with others farther on, horsemen galloped here and there, herds were shifted about, and clouds of dust arose; while the busy hammering on blacksmiths' anvils, the braying of mules, and the bellowing of cattle combined in a pandemonium of noise.

To vary his route from the Oregon Trail taken the previous year, Frémont now followed up the valley of Kansas River and its affluents. Eager to reach the trading post of

[2] Frémont, *Report,* 106.

Fort St. Vrain on the South Platte,[3] Frémont divided the party, and on June 16, with fifteen men, the howitzer and a light wagon, forged ahead.

Fitzpatrick, with twenty-five men, Talbot among them, and the carts of heavy baggage, was left to follow at what pace he could. The streams ran out on the high dry plains, and Fitzpatrick was soon in trouble. By the first of July the men were experiencing much discomfort from the heat at midday, and the cold at night. In this arid region, they were soon suffering from thirst. On July 5 Fitzpatrick went ahead to look for water, but evidently found nothing deemed drinkable. A day later the men, almost maddened with thirst, were less squeamish.

About 8 o'clock [writes Talbot] we found some ponds in which the water was not quite so nauseaus, and there we camped. These ponds or wallows are formed by the buffalo wallowing, an amusement they are very fond of. When the rain falls it is collected in these places and here the buffalo come to drink and stand during the heat of the day; adding their own excremnts to the already putrescent waters. This compound warmed for weeks in a blazing sun alive with animalcules, make a drink *palatable* to one suffering from intense thirst. O, that some over-dainty conoisseur might taste it![4]

On July 8, to their great relief, near the present Fort Morgan, Colorado, the men struck the South Platte. Ascending the stream, they discovered, at the noon halt four days later, three Indians who hovered about as if wanting to make friends and who finally came up to the party. They proved to be Blackfeet living with the Arapahoes, and one was an old friend of Broken Hand's. In the evening, forty

---

[3] LeRoy R. Hafen, "Fort St. Vrain," in the *Colorado Magazine*, XXIX (Oct. 1954), 241–55.

[4] Talbot, *Journal*, 17.

or fifty Arapaho warriors visited the camp and brought meat. They had just given a band of Pawnees a good beating and had proof of their triumph in the fresh scalps dangling from their belts. Among the warriors, Fitzpatrick was delighted to greet Friday, his former protégé, whom he had not seen for several years.[5] When they reached the Arapaho village, whites and reds smoked the peace pipe. Three days later Friday said goodbye to his benefactor, and the white party went on to Fort St. Vrain.

Frémont had arrived there on July 4, and wanting to buy mules and provisions but finding none, had gone on toward Bent's Fort[6] by way of the Pueblo, on the site of the present city of that name. At this nondescript village, as the men were later to learn — a settlement made in the previous year by a number of trappers and their Indian wives — Frémont found Kit Carson and at once reengaged him. They met "accidentally," as Carson humorously said, but doubtless he knew, when he left his five-month bride back in Taos, that it would be many long months before he should see her again.[7] He at once told Frémont that he could get mules and provisions at Bent's Fort, and Frémont, sending him on the quest, slowly retraced his steps.

Meanwhile, Fitzpatrick had moved his party upstream to the neighborhood of a new trading post, Fort Lancaster (or Fort Lupton), built by Lancaster P. Lupton, a former lieutenant in the army, and located near the site of present

---

[5] *Ibid.*, 20–21.

[6] For a history of the fort see David Lavender, *Bent's Fort* (Garden City, N.Y., 1954).

[7] For a biography of Carson see Harvey L. Carter, *'Dear Old Kit,' the Historical Christopher Carson* (Norman, Okla., 1968).

189

Fort Lupton, Colorado.[8] On July 21, Fitzpatrick, with a companion, went in to the post, and to his joyful surprise found Carson, who had just come in from Bent's Fort with nine mules and a good stock of foodstuffs. The unknown youth whom Fitzpatrick had picked up at Taos and taken into his company twelve years before had now become famous. Frémont's report of the first expedtion, with its many references to Carson, had been printed as a public document in March; it had attained an immediate popularity, and parts of it had been reprinted all over the United States. There is nothing to show that his sudden leap into fame had affected him in the slightest way. Like his preceptor, he was a modest man, and he bore his honors meekly.

Fitzpatrick and Carson returned to camp, where, two days later, Frémont, with the remainder of the party, joined them. Failing in his own hunt for supplies and animals, he was gratified to learn that Carson had been successful and that Fitzpatrick had carefully husbanded the original store.

Mr. Fitzpatrick [writes Frémont], who had often endured every extremity of want during the course of his mountain life, and knew well the value of provisions in this country, had watched over our stock with jealous vigilance, and there was an abundance of flour, rice, sugar and coffee, in the camp; and again we fared luxuriously.[9]

During the week preceding Frémont's return Fitzpatrick had enjoyed a visit with Marcelline St. Vrain and the employes at his post, most of whom he knew intimately through months or years of association in the West. He

[8] LeRoy R. Hafen, "Old Fort Lupton and its Founder," in the *Colorado Magazine*, VI (1929), 220–27.
[9] Frémont, *Report*, 119.

observed that the trade had now become almost entirely a traffic in buffalo robes, the fall in the price of beaver skins and the depletion of the supply having made beaver trapping unprofitable. The trade in pelts had become a matter of merchandising with the Indians and had lost much of the glamour that had characterized it in the days of the trapper band and the rendezvous. Fort Jackson and Fort Vasquez,[10] a few miles up the river from Fort St. Vrain, were already deserted, and Frémont had noted their crumbling adobe walls as he journeyed to and from the Arkansas. Lieutenant Lupton was maintaining his post by supplementing his trading operations with a little agricultural and livestock activity, while the Bent and St. Vrain Company, with Fort Bent on the Arkansas and Fort St. Vrain on the South Platte, was dominating the regional trade through efficient management and good will.

Frémont was bent upon forcing a way through the Colorado Rockies. It is likely that Fitzpatrick tried to dissuade him, but if so, the effort was in vain. On July 25 he again divided the party, and with thirteen men, a Shoshone widow[11] and her two children, eager to get to Fort Bridger, started up the Cache la Poudre, not again to be seen by the others for nearly two months. He took with him the camp cook, Courteau, since Fitzpatrick, as Talbot writes, had become "tired of French cooking."

Fitzpatrick's party followed the trapper trail to Fort Laramie and reached the post on August 5. On the following

---

10 LeRoy R. Hafen, "Fort Jackson and the Early Fur Trade on the South Platte," in the *Colorado Magazine*, V (1928), 9–18; and Hafen, "Fort Vasquez," *ibid.*, XLI (1964), 198–212.

11 For identification of this woman, who became the wife of Mountain Man Barney Ward, see Hafen, *Mountain Men*, VII, 345.

day it set out westward along the Oregon Trail, Talbot noting how clear a pathway had been made by the wagons of the Great Emigration. On August 12 it crossed the North Platte and turned towards Independence Rock and the Sweetwater. The going was hard, with many discomforts; but the grim business of plodding on was occasionally lightened by diverting episodes.

A rather good-for-nothing member of the party, often in trouble, was Sam Neal, appropriately assigned to a horse and a pack mule of about the same rating as himself. On a torrid day, as the column was passing through a stretch of well-baked desert, he saw, a short distance away, what appeared to be a limpid stream. Mounted on "his charger, Old John," and leading "his big-headed mule, Jane," the thirsty adventurer turned aside, but on reaching its marge, man, horse, and mule immediately sank almost out of sight in the milky ooze of what proved to be an alkali pool. Shouting for help, Neal managed to scramble to solid ground, and his companions rushed up and with ropes extricated the animals to find, when the three were safe, that they were thickly coated with a slime that in the open air rapidly hardened into a stony armor. Amid jeers and laughter Neal resumed his place in the column.

This little incident [writes Talbot], together with Fitzpatrick's heartfelt regrets that the trio, mule, horse and man, alike worthless, hadn't gone to ---- in a family party, afforded much amusement to the rest of the men.[12]

At Independence Rock, which they reached on August 15, they must have heard from Fitzpatrick the story of the Indian scare of the previous summer, for Talbot found the

---

[12] Talbot, 37.

MEN FOR WHOM FITZPATRICK ACTED AS GUIDE

Upper left: John Bidwell (from Royce's *John Bidwell*)
Upper right: Father Pierre Jean De Smet (courtesy of the Missouri Historical
    Society)
Lower left: John C. Frémont (from Frémont's *Memoirs*)
Lower right: Stephen W. Kearny (courtesy of Thomas Kearny)

inscriptions of Hastings and Lovejoy. "Here are the names of two travelers," he writes, "who were taken prisoners by Indians while in the very act of inscribing them."

On the Sweetwater they had an Indian scare of their own. A band of perhaps forty or fifty mounted Sioux came rushing down on them, shouting, "We are Oglalas! We are good friends of the whites!" Fitzpatrick ordered them to halt, and threatened to fire upon them if they came farther. Thereupon they stopped, and a man who could speak Sioux was sent to confer with them. Finding that they were Minniconjous, who had professed to be Oglalas only because at the time the latter were supposed to be held in greater esteem by the whites, he called them dogs and liars for their attempted deceit, and then returned. Nothing happened, and both parties proceeded amicably on their way.

Somewhere toward the eastern entrance of South Pass the men saw a trail which they thought might be Frémont's. They were later to find that it was; for the "Pathfinder," baffled in his efforts to scale the Rockies, had turned north, reached the valley of the Sweetwater, where he found the emigrant trail, and followed it through South Pass and on to Soda Springs, in present Idaho.

Fitzpatrick's party crossed South Pass on August 22, reached the Green on August 25, and moved on southward to Black's Fork (probably in the neighborhood of the present Granger, Wyoming). In the earlier years the Trail had run westerly from about this point, but this year the emigrant train had dipped down to Fort Bridger, the new trading post of Jim Bridger and Louis Vasquez.[13] Fitzpatrick

---

[13] The first Bridger Fort appears to have been built on Green River. It was moved a time or two before finding a permanent location on Black's Fork, near the present town of Fort Bridger, Wyoming.

and his men passed by the old fort on August 30, but found the crude cabins, which were "built of logs, plastered with mud," deserted and dismantled.[14] Neither Frémont nor Fitzpatrick appear to have visited the new Fort Bridger.

Soon after Fitzpatrick camped near Black's Fork, Vasquez, with his "gallant party of mountaineers" and a band of Indians, came galloping up. They were soon followed by fifteen or twenty lodges of Utes, and all camped together. Vasquez had just returned from a hunting trip, and Bridger had recently started out with forty men to trap on Wind River. Evidently there were still beaver in the mountains, and because of this fact Fitzpatrick missed a meeting with his old companion and partner.

He learned that the Cheyennes had been on a rampage recently, had raided the post and run off the horses of the trappers and also of a band of Snakes camped in the valley. Pursuit was made, and the Indians were overtaken. The trappers had an eye for picturesque effect, even when they suffered losses.

They say it was a beautiful sight [writes Talbot] to see the Sheyennes, formed in the shape of a crescent driving the stolen horses at full speed before them. A party of skirmishers following closely behind zig-zagging, or as it is called, "making snake" along the line, which they endeavored to prevent the pursuers from breaking.[15]

Though the trappers recovered most of their horses, they lost several men killed. The Cheyennes managed to get away with but one fatality.

Fitzpatrick's men left the fort on the following day, and proceeded toward Fort Hall. On September 8, near Bear

---

[14] Talbot, 41. This was apparently one of the temporary posts of Bridger and Vasquez.

[15] *Ibid.*, 42.

Lake, they met "a great many Shoshones, who had all of them much to say to their old friend, Fitzpatrick." The Shoshones were usually in high favor with the whites. Though the gentle Peter Skene Ogden, angered by the thieving and treachery of many of those with whom he came in contact in the '20s, wanted to see the whole nation exterminated, the testimony of most Americans who knew them is strongly commendatory. Dragoon Percival Lowe, as we shall see later on, praises them in the warmest terms; and Bridger, who had an exceedingly poor opinion of Indians generally, made signal exception of the Shoshones. Talbot found their horses, as well as their men, a subject of the trappers' praise. "The trappers," he writes, "prefer Snake Indians and Snake horses before any race of men or horses in the world."[16]

On September 13 the party arrived at Fort Hall. At a distance of twelve miles from the fort Fitzpatrick had received a letter from Frémont saying that he had reached this point on September 6, had then turned down to explore Great Salt Lake and was now returning, but was in great need of provisions. Fitzpatrick, with a small escort and some foodstuffs, had accordingly moved forward to meet his chief. About a week later the whole party was reunited at Fort Hall.

This noted trading post, established by Wyeth in 1834, had passed into the hands of the Hudson's Bay Company in 1837, and was now in charge of Richard Grant. The whole of the Oregon country, it should be remembered — a vast region comprising present Washington, Oregon, Idaho,

---

[16] *Ibid.*, 45.

and parts of Montana and Wyoming — was in dispute and was dominated by the Hudson's Bay Company. Grant, as a servant faithful to his company, was not friendly to American settlement or exploration. Still, he sold Frémont several horses, which were poor, and five oxen, which were fat. What Frémont thought of the situation we know from his report. He favored the establishment at this point of a strong military post at which the emigrants could refit themselves for the farther journey.[17] It was deplorable, he thought, that the emigrants, exhausted by the long journey from Independence, should have to depend on aid furnished by a none-too-friendly British post.

What Fitzpatrick thought of it we can readily surmise. He was an Irish Catholic and thus born to a certain animosity toward the British Government; he was a follower of Andrew Jackson and thus a supporter of the doctrine of "manifest destiny"; and he was a trapper who had struggled with the intruding trappers from the North in the keen competition for furs. It can hardly be doubted that he viewed with a fiery resentment the continuing domination of this vast region by an alien company.

Cold weather was coming on. Snow fell, and ice formed. Frémont called his men together, told them what hardships were to be faced on the farther journey and offered to release those who did not care to continue. Eleven men withdrew. On September 23, facing a chill drizzle, the party set out for the Hudson's Bay Company post of Fort Boisé, on the way to Oregon. Four days later Frémont again divided the party and went forward, leaving Fitz-

---

17 Frémont, 162, 163.

patrick with the baggage carts. It was a rough, volcanic terrain that the men followed along the Snake. The food supply was low, but from time to time they were able to get fish from the river. They met many Digger Shoshones, all very poor and hungry and possessing few horses. One of them, who knew Broken Hand and who had once, in the Indian way, been rich and powerful, told a long story of his many reverses.

On October 6 the men crossed the Snake and headed for the Boisé River. While eating their evening meal on the following day they were approached by a little family of Diggers, consisting of an old man, a middle-aged, care-worn mother, with an infant at her back, a handsome boy of eight or ten years, and a girl just coming into woman-hood. They were all extremely poor and ravenously hungry, and intently they watched the men eat. The girl, according to Talbot, was strikingly beautiful, with a delicate, slender form, oval face, black eyes, a Grecian nose, and finely chis-eled lips; but the touch of famine was in her brilliant eyes and her flushed cheeks. The kindly voyagers gave them food and talked with them. Fitzpatrick was much taken with the boy and offered to adopt him. But though the mother knew how desperate was the struggle for life, re-peated pleas would not move her. "Paleface, I *love* my child," she answered, as with tearful eyes she drew her son closer to her bosom.[18] The next day the party passed on, never more to see their guests or to learn what became of them.

A few days later a large hunting party of Nez Percés and

---

[18] Talbot, 57.

Cayuses came in from a successful hunt on the upper Missouri. They were happy; they sang and danced, and to the white men's questions about the country they gave intelligent answers. Moving on, Fitzpatrick's men struck the Boisé River, followed it to its mouth and reached Fort Boisé.[19] Frémont, it was learned, was five days ahead. About this time Talbot ended his diary, and we have no further word from him.

Frémont, following the Emigrant Trail, reached Whitman's Mission, where he hoped to get flour or corn meal, but found that some of the Cayuse Indians had burned the mill during Whitman's absence in the East. Keeping on, he arrived at the Methodist Mission at the Dalles on November 5. From here he sent back word to Fitzpatrick to abandon the carts at Whitman's Mission and to come on with the pack animals; and leaving his party in charge of Carson he went down the river to Fort Vancouver, where the good-hearted chief factor, Dr. John McLoughlin, sold him a liberal supply of flour, peas, and tallow.

Back at the Dalles on November 18, and with his party reunited by Fitzpatrick's arrival on November 21, Frémont prepared for a new adventure. He had finished what he was authorized to do: he had made a reconnaissance as far as the Columbia. But for the present he had no notion of returning. He wanted to see the Klamath Lakes, the region west of Great Salt Lake, Mary's Lake, the fabled Buenaventura River, and already he had dreamed of a visit to sunny California.

A small drove of beef cattle had been bought, and the

---

[19] Fort Boise was established by the Hudson's Bay Company in 1834.

number of pack animals had been increased to 104. The carts and then the wagon had been abandoned, and the only contrivance on wheels was the howitzer. With a party of twenty-five men, including a Chinook guide, he set out for the south on November 25, in nipping cold weather, amid flurries of snow. A foreboding of what was to come prompted him to give thought to his mounts. "In anticipation of coming hardships, and to spare our horses," he writes of the second day's travel, "there was much walking done today; and Mr. Fitzpatrick and myself made the day's journey on foot."[20]

Lower Klamath Lake (the more northern one) was reached on December 10, and here the party spent two days. The Indians had been reported hostile, but a discharge of the howitzer seems to have convinced them of the virtues of peace. From here the party moved east and then south to Warner Lake, where Christmas was celebrated. Then it moved on, south and southeast, into the present northwestern Nevada. The going was rough, the weather cold, and a snowfall obstructed their way. The food supply was growing scantier, and but one of their cattle was left to feed the hungry men, when on January 10, 1844, they came to a large lake, well stocked with salmon trout. From the high rock rising from its waters Frémont named it Pyramid Lake. Onward to the south they went, and on January 18 arrived at what has since been known as the Carson River.

The men were hungry, for the last steer had been killed five days before; their equipment was in a sorry state; fif-

---

[20] Frémont, 198. Subsequent quotations in this chapter are from Frémont's *Report*.

teen of the pack aimals had died or disappeared, while the remainder were footsore, and the country to the south and east did not invite adventure. Frémont decided that there was but one thing to do — scale the snowy Sierra and recoup his party at Fort Sutter. He had no business on the other side of the range, for a Mexican decree early in the previous year had closed the Santa Fé Trail and barred Americans from entering California. The project, moreover, was one of appalling danger.

Neither political nor physical obstacle, however, dismayed him. From a point a day's march east of the present Virginia City the party started on January 19. Five days later it met an old Indian of the Washo tribe who volunteered to lead it to a good pass, but two days later he quit. The way grew rougher and steeper. On January 27 and 28 Frémont and Fitzpatrick forged ahead to one of the first passes, and the party was brought through, but the howitzer was abandoned. A young Washo was now hired as guide, and on January 30 he led the men to the head of Antelope Valley, but becoming cold and discouraged, left them. Some other Indians who were met advised the whites not to go farther or they would all perish. They kept on, however, and on January 31 saw before them the towering peaks of the central chain.

There for a day and a half they halted, while they repaired their clothing and made ready for the great climb. The temperature was at zero, and the snow lay in places three and four feet deep. Food was scarce; pea soup was the main ration, though one of the messes banqueted on a fat dog. If among the men any faltered, we have no word of the fact. Frémont exhorted them to be resolute; he pictured to them the smiling plenty that awaited them in the valley of the Sacramento, only seventy miles away, as his instruments showed; and though some of them remained "unusually silent" as he spoke, there was no talk of retreat.

On February 2, led by a new Indian guide, they began to break paths. Each man of a party of ten, mounted on one of the strongest horses, worked forward until he was tired, when another took his place; and over this trodden path the remainder of the company made its way. Sixteen miles were scored the first day, but less than half of that the second, and on the third progress was brought to a stop. Two more Indians came up, haranguing the whites of the dangers ahead. For the first time some of the men began to despair. The Chinook guide wept, and on the morning of February 5 the local guide deserted them.

February 6. — Accompanied by Mr. Fitzpatrick, I sat out to-day with a reconnoitring party, on snow shoes. We marched all in single file, trampling the snow as heavily as we could. Crossing the open basin, in a march of about ten miles we reached the top of one of the peaks, to the left of the pass indicated by our guide. Far below us, dimmed by the distance, was a large snowless valley, bounded on the western side, at the distance of about a hundred miles, by a low range of mountains, which Carson recognized with delight as the mountains bordering the coast.

They had seen the promised land, and greatly encouraged, they struggled back through the increasing cold toward the point where the party awaited them.

It was late in the day [writes Frémont] when we turned towards camp; and it grew rapidly cold as it drew towards the night. One of the men became fatigued, and his feet began to freeze, and, building a fire in the trunk of a dry old cedar, Mr. Fitzpatrick remained with him until his clothes could be dried, and he was in a condition to come on.[21]

21 *Ibid.*, 232.

A little thing, perhaps; but one that reveals the innate nobility of Broken Hand.

On February 9 began the great effort. The path had filled with snow, and a new path was beaten out. But Fitzpatrick, attempting to follow with the pack mules, found that the packed snow would not support their weight — that some plunged about in the drifts, while others sunk below the surface. The entire force was now turned out with mauls and shovels to make a trail and to strengthen it with pine boughs. Hungry, weak, and almost blinded from the glare of the snow, they kept to their task as foot by foot and day by day they advanced.

On February 20, to the inexpressible joy of all, the whole company was brought to the summit of the main pass, 9,338 feet above the sea. Fifty-seven animals had survived the ordeal, and though the howitzer had been sacrificed, all the baggage had been saved. Now the weather cleared, and under promising skies the party began its winding descent. February 24: "Another horse was killed tonight for food."

Farther on Frémont, with a small escort, hurried ahead, reaching Fort Sutter on March 6, and then starting back with provisions. A sorry looking sight were the men of the rear section. "They were all on foot," he writes, "each man, weak and emaciated, leading a horse or mule as weak and emaciated as themselves." A few days later, as well fed, reclothed, and reequipped they leisurely strolled about the fort, they could laugh at the recollection of what they had suffered in crossing the snow-bound Sierra.

Fitzpatrick may have met Captain Sutter, now lord of a domain, when the latter accompanied the missionary party of 1838 to the Columbia. This adventurous Swiss, who had landed at New York in 1834, had expansive dreams and boundless energy. From Oregon he had sailed to the Hawaiian Islands and thence back to San Francisco bay. In California he had obtained a large land grant on the Sacramento River, and in five years had carved out an inland empire. His adobe-walled fort was mounted with brass cannon from the Russian Fort Ross, which he had purchased, and an ample guard made the fortress safe from any likely attack. American overseers were already assisting him in managing his estate and dealing with the hundreds of Indians and Kanakas employed on his vast acres and in his varied industries.

Sutter was hospitable; all the facilities of his establishment were turned over to Frémont. Fresh horses and cattle were provided; the mill furnished flour and the blacksmith shop was kept busy making shoes and bridle bits for the animals. The little company was soon transformed. With 130 horses and mules, plenty of equipment and supplies, and thirty head of cattle, including five milk cows, it was ready to resume its journey.

The party broke camp on March 22, lingered for two days at a location a few miles farther on, and then set out southward. The valley was green with a grassy carpet, dotted with gold patches of waxen poppies. Along the San Joaquin River the party marched, with the snow-capped Sierra on its left, for some 300 miles, when they turned east and crossed the range at Oak Creek Pass. Turning southeast again, they wound through the northwestern border of the Mojave Desert.

On April 20, "after a difficult march of 18 miles, a general shout announced that we had struck the object of our search — the Spanish Trail." This famous route, "deviously traced from one watering place to another," had been broken through from New Mexico, the land of sheep, to California, the land of horses and cattle. Opened in 1830–31, it had become a well-beaten path carrying traffic between Santa Fe and Los Angeles.[22]

On April 24, while the men were in camp, a Mexican man and boy, dazed and well-nigh exhausted, came running up, crying out their pitiful story. The man, Andreas Fuentes, and an eleven-year-old boy, Pablo Hernandez, were the survivors of a party of six, including two women, who with thirty horses had been traveling from Los Angeles when a band of Indians fell upon them. The man and boy were somewhat apart from the others, guarding the horses; and starting the herd ahead they had ridden at break-neck speed back along the trail where they met the Frémont party. The explorer added the two to his band and pushed on to Resting Spring, where the attack had occurred. The women were gone, but the naked bodies of two men were there, pierced with arrows.

There happened here a feat of daredevil courage seldom matched in the annals of the West. Kit Carson and Alexander Godey volunteered to pursue the savages and recover the horses; and Frémont halted the expedition and let them go. The two men followed the hoofprints of the captured horses till late at night, when the trail was lost. They lay down and slept for a time, but at dawn were again in their saddles. At sunrise they discovered the marauders'

---

[22] See LeRoy R. and Ann W. Hafen, *The Old Spanish Trail* (Glendale, Calif., 1954).

camp, and creeping forward saw the campfires and the boiling kettles of a band of thirty Indians gathered for breakfast. The two men carefully studied the scene. A frightened horse betrayed their presence, and only an act of the utmost daring could save them. With a warwhoop they charged the camp, firing their rifles as they ran. Two Indians fell, and the rest, evidently thinking the attackers the advance party of a large force, fled in panic. Both Indians were scalped; however, one was found to be still living, and was at once dispatched. Rounding up the horse-herd, Carson and Godey hurried back, and amid the shouts and congratulations of their comrades, rejoined the command.

On April 29, the party reached the scene of the attack on the travelers. A little lap dog that had belonged to Pablo's mother ran up and with frantic joy welcomed the sobbing boy. The horribly multilated bodies of the two men were found, but there was no trace of the women, who no doubt had been carried off captive.

When we beheld this pitiable sight [writes Frémont] and pictured to ourselves the fate of the two women carried off by savages so brutal and so loathsome, all compunctions for the scalped-alive Indian ceased; and we rejoiced that Carson and Godey had been able to give so useful a lesson to these American Arabs, who lie in wait to murder and plunder the innocent traveler.

On May 3 the party came to the springs and little creek of Las Vegas (the meadow) where now is the glamorous Nevada city of that name. Here the worn and half-famished animals found plenty of grass. Early the following morning the journey was resumed. Now came the dreaded *jornado,* an arid journey of fifty miles. The men and animals struggled on over the hot and glaring sand and gravel.

Darkness came, and they kept on. About midnight the mules, scenting water, began frantically to push ahead, and within a short time the party reached the Rio de los Angeles, now known as Muddy River.

Here, in the Moapa Valley, troubled and threatened somewhat by Digger Indians, the men rested for a day. Then they crossed a mesa to the Virgin River, which they followed north, and on May 9 reached the springs at present Littlefield, in the extreme northwestern corner of Arizona. From the camp here, one of the most popular men in the party, Baptiste Tabeau, disappeared; and Frémont, Fitzpatrick, and a few others, searching for him, found evidence that he had been slain by Indians. Though the men wanted to pursue the murderers, Frémont felt that the broken-down condition of the animals forbade such an attempt, and the march was resumed.

On May 12 they finished the crossing of the desert and reached the travelers' paradise, the Mountain Meadows — later the scene of the terrible massacre of emigrants in September 1857. Keeping to the north, they approached the Wasatch Range. Joseph R. Walker, following from Los Angeles with the regular California caravan, and guessing from their traces who they were, hurried ahead and overtook Frémont. The region now to be traveled being well known to Walker but unknown to Fitzpatrick, the latter gladly relinquished the guidance to Walker's capable direction.

After reaching Utah Lake, they crossed the Wasatch Range and came to Antoine Robidous's Fort Uinta, where Frémont obtained some supplies. Now again they were in country well known to both Fitzpatrick and Carson. Keeping on to the east and north, the party came to that corner of Utah that abuts on Wyoming and Colorado and entered Brown's Hole, in the old days a famous gathering place for trappers. The trading post on the east bank of the Green, Fort Davy Crockett, was already in ruins — an eloquent reminder of the brief span of the active period of the fur trade. There were still trappers in the mountains, but they lived a precarious life, gleaning small returns and because of their weak numbers, facing great dangers. Very likely Fitzpatrick and Carson congratulated themselves on having gotten out when they did.

They went on to the North Platte, whence a few days' journey would have taken them to the well-marked Oregon Trail. But Frémont must have one more fling at the unknown. So they turned south, up into the beautiful mountain park region of what is now Colorado, through regions which, as Frémont says, "although well known to hunters and trappers, were unkown to science and history." Crossing South Park, they reached the waters of the Arkansas, and followed the river to the plains, reaching Pueblo on June 28 and Bent's Fort on July 1.

At this fort, Carson and Walker left the company. The others, including Fitzpatrick, continued on and arrived at Kansas Landing on July 31. A steamboat took them to St. Louis, where they were disbanded on August 7.

Chapter 11

With Kearny and Abert

IN 1845 MEN TALKED EXCITEDLY of an impending conflict with Mexico. Two years earlier the Mexican Minister to Washington, Juan Almonte, had notified President Tyler that the annexation of Texas would be regarded by his government as an act of war. And now Congress had passed a joint resolution admitting the infant republic to the Union, and on March 1 it had been signed by the President. Almonte thereupon demanded his passports and left the country; the American minister to Mexico, Wilson Shannon, was dismissed; the Mexican consulates in the United States were closed; Mexican ministers in Europe were informed that war would soon begin; and an army of 6,000 men, under General Juan Mariano Paredas, was ordered to the Rio Grande.

James K. Polk, who succeeded Tyler three days after the signing of the resolution, at first hesitantly watched and waited, but within a few months was to dispatch a force of Regulars, under General Zachary Taylor, to the Texas Coast. The force was, to be sure, an insignificant one — only about 1,500 men; it was poorly equipped; it was commanded by an officer whose inefficiency was matched only by his amazing luck; it set up its camp a long way east of the Rio Grande; and it was specifically ordered to avoid any act of aggression. But the strained situation on both sides of the Rio Grande portended war, and few men believed that it could be prevented.

The clash might come at any time, and the Government must needs prepare. In the West was a vast territory that would certainly be involved in the struggle. There was California, a plum ripe for the hand that would take it, with England closely watching for a favorable opportunity. There was New Mexico, with its back country of Arizona, eagerly desired by American expansionists for the rounding out of the continental domain. There was the No Man's Land of the Texas Panhandle and Western Oklahoma, to which Mexico had never relinquished her claim, and which might serve as a path of approach to an army headed for Santa Fé. And finally there was the great plains country from the Arkansas to far beyond the Platte, inhabited by thousands of red warriors who were growing restless and turbulent because of the increasing tide of emigrants to the Pacific. Should an army move toward New Mexico, a backfire of savage warfare on the plains would be disastrous.

The Government decided to send out three small expeditions — one of them military, two semi-military. Captain John Charles Frémont, with sixty well-armed men, was to put himself where he could watch developments in California and be ready to act should action seem warranted.

Lieutenant James William Abert, with thirty-two men, was to make a reconnaissance through No Man's Land. Colonel Stephen Watts Kearny, with a force of Dragoons, was to march to South Pass and back, warning the Indians on the way that any violence would be promptly and severely punished. It fell to the lot of Fitzpatrick to guide two of these precautionary expeditions and to win from the commanding officer of each the highest praise for his efficient service.

Fitzpatrick probably spent the winter of 1844–45 in St. Louis. Early in the spring he went to Ft. Leavenworth, where the South Pass expedition was being fitted out. Primarily this expedition was intended as a warning to the Indians against molesting the emigrants; but it was further intended as a field study of a problem that men were then hotly debating. Would the safety of the emigrants be better assured by establishing a chain of forts from the Missouri to the Columbia, or by occasionally sending out a force of troopers as an evidence of the white man's power to punish? Frémont had officially recommended the forts; Kearny, as we shall later see, was against the forts.

On May 18, with five companies of the First Dragoons, a total of about 250 men, well mounted, armed with sabre, carbine, and pistol, and with two howitzers, Kearny set forth.[1] Their appearance and general order of march are thus described by Lieutenant J. H. Carleton, in charge of the commissary:

First the guide [Fitzpatrick], is seen by himself, some quarter of a mile ahead of all: then the commanding officer, followed by his

[1] S. W. Kearny's "Report of a Summer Campaign to the Rocky Mountains," etc., in *Sen. Ex. Doc.* 1, 29th Cong. 1st Sess., pp. 210–13.

orderly and the chief bugler: then the staff officers: then a division, mounted on black horses, marching by twos: then another on greys — another on bays — another on sorrels, and a fifth on blacks again, with an interval of one hundred paces between each division to avoid one another's dust: then the howitzers, followed by a party of dragoons to serve them under charge of the sergeant major: then the train of wagons, with a detail to assist in getting them over bad places, under the immediate command of the quartermaster-sergeant, who receives his directions from the quartermaster: then the drove of cattle and sheep, followed by their guard of nine men under the command of a corporal — and lastly, the main guard, under an officer to bring up the extreme rear. Each day the divisions alternate in taking the lead — as do the several wagons. Such is the usual order of march — though occasionally, where the ground admits of it, the command moves in two columns abreast.[2]

Moving northward and then westward, the command reached the Trail probably near the present Marysville, Marshall County, Kansas. The great emigration of the year, that was to total nearly five thousand men, women, and children, with hundreds of wagons and thousands of cattle, horses, and mules, was already on its way, and section after section was passed as the Dragoons kept up their steady march. Kearny saw to it that count was made of persons and animals, and from the figures given in his report it is evident that the command passed more than half of the year's emigration.

The Dragoons moved on to the Platte and then along its south bank to the ford of the South Platte. All about was familiar ground to Fitzpatrick. It was now more than twenty years since he had first followed the line of the river from the Missouri to the Sweetwater; and though most of his earlier journeys were along its north bank as far as

---

[2] Louis Pelzer (ed.), *Prairie Logbooks, Dragoon Campaigns to the Pawnee Villages in 1844, and to the Rocky Mountains in 1845,* 172.

Fort Laramie, he had come in later times to know well the shorter route that cut across country from the present Kearney to the Bend of the Missouri.

The command forded the South Platte, moved on to the south bank of the North Platte and kept on past the familiar landmarks of Chimney Rock, Court House Rock, and Scotts' Bluffs. At the mouth of Horse Creek it passed the place where a few years later Fitzpatrick, with his colleague, Colonel D. D. Mitchell, was to stage the greatest and most picturesque pageant of the early West — the Indian council of 1851. On June 14, twenty-seven days out, the Dragoons reached Fort Laramie, still a trading post of the American Fur Company.

The fort, writes Captain Philip St. George Cooke, of the Dragoons, "swarmed with women and children, whose language — like their complexions — is varied and mixed — Indian, French, English, and Spanish.[3] These were the wives and children of the traders, hunters, and trappers. But their red relatives and friends were also about. Some twelve hundred Sioux warriors, with their families, were camped in the vicinity, with a sprinkling of other tribes. The fort had become the main trading center of the plains Sioux, and was visited also by many Cheyennes and Arapahoes. There was still beaver to be bought; some two thou- and pounds a year came in, but the main trade was now in buffalo robes, of which more than nine thousand had but recently been sent to market.

The main business of the expedition — that of impressing the Indians — was not forgotten. On June 16 Kearny met

---

[3] P. St. George Cooke, *Scenes and Adventures in the Army* (Philadelphia, 1859), 335.

them on the plain between Fort Laramie and the Platte. From tall staffs three flags floated. Two were the Stars and Stripes, while the third was of Indian design, with two crossed bands (said to represent the winds), nine stars (possibly symbolic of nine plains tribes) above the bands and clasped hands beneath. Chairs and benches backed with elk skins had been provided for the council leaders, and the ground had been carpeted with buffalo robes. The warriors seated themselves in a large semicircle, with women and children, many deep, making up the rear.

The peace pipe was smoked, and Kearny arose to address the assembled braves. He assured them of the love and solicitude of the Great Father at Washington for his red children of the plains; he told them that the emigrant road must remain open and that those who traveled it must not be molested, and he gently admonished them against the trade in whisky brought up from Taos. Bull Tail, the principal chief, made a friendly response. Presents of scarlet and blue cloth, red and green blankets, tobacco, knives, looking glasses, beads, and such things were distributed, and for a final effect on the untutored mind a skyrocket was discharged and three shots from the howitzers were fired.

There was a considerable number of Arapaho braves present, according to Francis Parkman, who was at the fort a year later; and they seem to have been impressed to a degree beyond anything that could reasonably have been expected. In spite of the influence of one of their chiefs, Friday (Fitzpatrick's protégé), outrages had been committed by them, but they now saw and heard things that warned them to mend their ways. On the discharge of the howitzers, writes Parkman:

BENT'S FORT, 1845
(After the drawing by J. W. Abert)

FORT LARAMIE, 1842
(From the drawing accompanying J. C. Frémont's *Report*)

many of the Arapahos fell prostrate on the ground, while others ran away screaming with amazement and terror. On the following day they withdrew to their mountains, confounded with awe at the appearance of the Dragoons, at their big gun which went off twice at one shot [the howitzers threw a shell], and the fiery messenger they had sent up to the Great Spirit.[4]

But it was a lost lesson, Parkman laments, for the treacherous killing of the trappers Boot and May, some months later, by an unruly band of Arapahoes, had not been promptly punished by the military, and so the whole tribe, fearless of consequences, were again threatening and were reported to have "determined to kill the first of the white dogs whom they could lay hands on."

The Dragoons, Fitzpatrick showing the way, continued their march, without notable incident, to South Pass, where they arrived on the last of June. The Pass reached, they turned about and started back. At Fort Laramie they turned from the Oregon Trail and set out for Bent's Fort along the old trappers' and traders' trail leading southward. On the Chugwater branch of the Laramie they came to a village of Cheyennes, and here the second and last Indian council was held. Somewhere on the upper waters of Lodge Pole Creek, north of the present Cheyenne, they met four Arapaho braves, one of whom rushed forward to greet Fitzpatrick with the most extravagant demonstrations of joy. The brave man was of course Friday, whom Fitzpatrick may last have seen two years before while journeying with Frémont, though the two may have met in St. Louis in the summer of 1844. The soldiers, amazed at such a greeting between white man and red, learned the story of the guide's rescue and adoption of the Indian boy.

---

[4] Francis Parkman, *The California and Oregon Trail,* chapter XVI.

216

Keeping on to the south, the Dragoons came to the mouth of the Cache la Poudre and traveled past the four adobe trading posts, already abandoned, on the South Platte. Following Cherry Creek, they crossed the low watershed, descended to the Arkansas and after turning downstream arrived, on July 29, at Bent's Fort. The troopers had thus far made their journey of some 1,700 miles in seventy-two days — an excellent record for such an expedition, in which the horses had subsisted solely on grass.

Here Fitzpatrick remained, while Kearny with his Dragoons continued to Fort Leavenworth. In his official report the Colonel advised against the establishment of forts along the Oregon Trail. Maintenance would be expensive, he argued, and the small garrisons so stationed could do little in case of Indian disturbances. Much better, he thought, would be the sending out, from time to time, of just such an expedition as that he had commanded. At a minimum expense it would serve all the purposes, he believed, of persuading the Indian to keep the peace. But he thought the Oregon Trail too roundabout, and he believed that a survey by a competent explorer could find a shorter and better route. He had no hesitancy in naming the man he considered best for the work.

Should it be deemed advisable [he writes] to have that country explored, with a view to finding such a route as I have alluded to, I would respectfully recommend for the purpose Mr. Thomas Fitzpatrick, who was our guide during the late expedition, an excellent woodsman — one who has been much west of the mountains, and who has as good, if not a better, knowledge of that country than any other man in existence.[5]

Three days after the departure of the Dragoons, Frémont,

[5] Kearny's Report, *op. cit.*, 213.

at the head of his third expedition and accompanied by Lieutenant J. W. Abert and his party, arrived at the fort. He had with him several of his old followers, and there must have been a joyful reunion with Fitzpatrick. Godey was there and so was Basil Lajeunesse, this time going to his death in the far-off Klamath country; and Carson would be in within a few days. Kit was now trying his hand at farming and stock raising on the upper Cimarron; but he was at once sent for; and he would, as the speeding courier reined up in front of him and told him that his old commander wanted him again, drop everything, commit his young wife to the care of friends who would take her back to Taos, and come as swiftly as a good steed could carry him.

Fitzpatrick was not to remain with his old friends. He was assigned — very likely the assignment had been made some months before — to guide Abert's command. Whether or not he would have preferred to go on with Frémont none can say. Probably not, for his wish in the matter would have been almost law with the Pathfinder. Perhaps he preferred to keep within reach of an official communication from Washington, for he had been more than once proposed for a place in the Indian service, and he may have felt that the appointment might come at any time. And so Frémont went on without him.

Abert pitched his camp on the south bank of the Arkansas, at the mouth of the Purgatory, and here, on August 12, Fitzpatrick joined him. With Abert's thirty-two men was the second in command, Lieutenant J. J. Peck, and there were four wagons and sixty-three horses and mules. For a scientific party, supposed to make a survey, it was amusingly short of instruments, its sole stock consisting of a sextant and a chronometer for determining latitude and longitude. But it had arms and ammunition and a fair store of supplies, and (what was of prime importance) it was to be piloted through the hostile country by the man most capable of doing the job successfully.

Technically, Fitzpatrick was a mere guide. Actually he was the executive officer, under a nominal commander. Guidance was a small part of his manifold duties. For that matter, he was not acquainted with the country to be traversed. Fourteen years before, in that tragic journey on which Jedadiah Smith was slain, he had crossed it transversely along the Cimarron branch of the Santa Fé Trail, and that was all. But the skilled mountain man had knowledge not set down in books. He could sense the physical features of a region never before seen by him; could guess the height of ridges and the depth of depressions, the trend of slopes, and the course of streams. He knew every sign and portent that nature yields and every device by which to outwit the cunning of a prowling foe. He knew how best to care for the animals, how most skillfully to choose and prepare a camp and all else necessary to assure comfort and safety for those in his charge. Young Abert, but three years out of West Point, and wholly unfamiliar with the West, recognized the man's ability at once and gladly gave over to him the practical details.

I was at once delighted with the carefulness of our guide [Abert writes]. He directed one to loosen the noose, which, passing round the mule's nose and neck, held them so closely together as to prevent its eating; another, never to tie his mules in the bushes, for alarmed at every rustle they are constantly looking wildly around, expecting some enemy. These things may appear trifling, but those who have been upon the prairie know well how much depends upon the care and attention bestowed upon the animals.[6]

The party was to travel through the upper part of the Comanche country, and hourly danger was to be apprehended. There was always the threat of trouble with the Comanches, but at this time the situation was acute. A fight between a company of Texans and a band of these banditti had recently occurred and forty warriors had been dispatched to the happy hunting grounds. Their friends and relatives would probably take revenge on the first whites encountered. Abert wanted peace. He took along with him a trader well known to the Indians, John Hatcher, who at the isolated trading post later known as Adobe Walls would seek to bring the Comanches and the equally difficult Kiowas into council. But a peaceful bearing was no assurance of security, and Abert and Fitzpatrick would set forth determined to observe every precaution against surprise.

The command started south along a branch of the Santa Fé Trail, up the valley of the Purgatory. *Rio de las Animas Perdidas en Purgatorio* (River of Lost Souls in Purgatory) the Spaniards had named the stream; French trappers called it the *Purgatoire;* the first Americans called it sometimes the Las Animas, at other times the south fork of the Arkansas, or the Purgatory, and the more facetious of the latter ones twisted the name into Picketwire. Up the valley the men made their way toward those noted landmarks of the Southwest, the Spanish Peaks, known in one of the Indian tongues as Wah-to-yah, the Breasts of the World.

---

[6] "Journal of Lieutenant J. W. Abert, From Bent's Fort to St. Louis, 1845," *Sen. Ex. Doc.* 438, 29th Cong., 1st Sess., p. 6.

On the third day they met a moving Apache village. Horses and dogs were equipped with the travois — two trailing lodgepoles — and on these poles were packed the camp paraphernalia as well as many baskets laden with black-eyed children. The warriors were peaceably inclined. The village had met with ill success in its hunt for food, and one of the braves had killed a stray ox, found along the Trail. He expressed himself as sorry for the transgression, which only the dire need of food had prompted. He intended to pay for the ox, Abert reports, "and should retain the tail, which he showed us, as a remembrance of his indebtedness. . . . Mr. Fitzpatrick told him he had done perfectly right, that the white people would not be angry if, when forced by hunger they should commit such an act, provided they came bodly forth and acknowledged it, and offered remuneration."[7]

From the head of the valley they crossed Raton Pass and descended to the headwaters of the Canadian. Some called it (as some still call its upper course) the Red River, but it becomes the Canadian. After following this stream southward for several days, they noticed signal fires from various high points about them. The Comanches, as Fitzpatrick explained, were telegraphing the news that strangers were in the country. There followed an immediate tightening up of precautions against a surprise.

Mr. Fitzpatrick [writes Abert] directed the inclosure of a "kraal" [corral], which we formed by felling large trees, and arranging them in such a manner as to describe the arc of a circle, interlacing them with small branches and the remainder of the circle, completed by the wagons and tents, giving us a pretty strong position of defense. . . . These precautions were never afterward neglected

---

[7] *Ibid.*, 10.

while traveling through the Comanche country, when we were able to find the necessary timber. When wood could not be found we endeavored to make such a selection for the position of our camp as afforded some natural obstruction, such as a deep ravine, a bluff bank, with which our wagons could be so disposed as to render abortive any attempt to charge through the camp, which is the most usual mode of attack.[8]

In the southeastern part of the present San Miguel County, New Mexico, the Canadian turns sharply to the east. Here the party came upon a traders' trail leading into the Comanche country proper, and followed it, passing now and then broken bits of wooden-wheeled carts, discarded by Mexican travelers. The trail approximated that of Josiah Gregg's trading caravan from Fort Gibson to Santa Fé, six years earlier, a route that somewhat farther on had been broken by Major Stephen H. Long's expedition in 1820. Deer, antelope, and buffalo were found and made a welcome addition to the regular bill of fare. Some of the French *voyageurs*, less particular than their Anglo-Saxon companions, ate a skunk. It was hardly a dainty thing to do, according to the young West Pointer, and the odor, he reports, was "too pungent to suit every one's olfactories."

Many Comanches, Kiowas, and even Crows (the last-named, remote wanderers from their Wyoming-Montana home) were encountered, but they kept aloof; and as no least chance of taking the party unawares was offered, there was no clash. Through what is now the Texas Panhandle the party followed the windings of the Canadian until they came to some point in the present Hemphill County. Then they turned south to explore the headwaters

---

[8] *Ibid.*, 32.

of the Washita, or Buffalo Creek. They returned to the Canadian and toward the end of September reached the Cross Timbers, that well-known belt of woods extending north and south as far as the eye could see. Trees and shrubs had taken on a rich autumnal coloring. The landscape "was graceful, undulating, with long swells; the valley everywhere heavily timbered, and the prairie land covered with a luxuriant growth of grass. . . . Bands of buffaloes were feeding on every hillside, and deer and turkeys unusually abundant." The Lieutenant was thrilled and "Mr. Fitzpatrick appeared enraptured with the scene."

The command laid in a supply of buffalo meat and went on. The cold, drizzling rains of October set in, chilling the spirits as well as the bodies of the men. On October 10, near the present Purcell, Oklahoma, they came to the ruins of Fort Holmes, established in 1835, but abandoned after a few years. The lofty gatepost "leaned mournfully over the ruins," fragments of wagons were scattered about, and an empty fireplace dreamed of winter nights when merry Dragoons had clustered about its cheery fire. Eastward from the post a trail led through the dense forest of oak and hickory, but fallen trees had to be removed and deep gullies filled before the wagons could be pulled along.

A few days' travel brought the party to some Creek Indian settlements. It was a relief to find Indians who were civilized, who worked for a living and who kept the peace. They were dressed "most tastefully," writes Abert. "Handsome shawls were gracefully twisted around their heads. They also wore leggins and moccasins of buckskin, handsome calico shirts and beautiful pouch, with broad belt ornamented with massive beadwork."[9] It was this time the turn of Indians to be alarmed at the approach of whites; for the men of the Abert party were by now a wild-looking lot, and the peaceful Creeks doubtless supposed them to have been out "robbing Santa Fe traders or shooting Indians." Suspicion was natural enough, Abert concedes, "for we were dressed in buckskin trousers, with fringed seams; shirts of bright red flannel and calico of all colors; our hair long and wild; our faces sunburnt and unshaven; and with our rifles flung across the saddlebow we presented a formidable, not to say ferocious, appearance." Explanations, however, were soon made, and the party was well received.

The remainder of the journey was over well-known highways, along which many emigrant wagons were making their way to the wide expanse of Texas. On October 21 the party reached Fort Gibson and was warmly greeted by Colonel R. B. Mason and the soldiers of the post. For the first time in history wagons had made the journey from Bent's Fort to the settlements by way of the Canadian, a distance of some six hundred miles, and the feat had been performed without a battle and with no loss. Continuing through Arkansas and Missouri by way of Maysville and Springfield, the party on November 12 reached St. Louis, where it was disbanded.

Fitzpatrick spent the winter of 1845–46 in Missouri, while Lieutenant Abert continued on to Washington, where he began preparation of the formal account of his late expedition. In order to enrich the report he wrote to Fitzpatrick on January 22, posing a list of questions about

---

[9] *Ibid.*, 69.

Indian tribes and languages, etc. From St. Louis Fitzpatrick responded at some length, giving information and opinions that for the time are rather remarkable. From this letter of February 5, 1846, we quote some extracts:

I will give you my own opinions of the Indian languages of the northern and western portions of the Union together with all the territory east of the Rocky Mts., which is, that there is two great roots from which spring all the different tongues now spoken by the Indians, now and hitherto inhabiting that region, with the exception of a few tribes which have no resemblance of language whatever with the others and are the Pawnis, Arickaras, Mandan, Cheyenne and Kiowas, those tribes I think have originally belonged to the extreme southern part of the Union or far in the interior of Mexico. In order to inform you better in regard to the two roots spoken of I will here name some of the tribes belonging to each, of the first and most numerous are the Souix, Kanzas, Osages, Ottoes, Ioway, Mahas, Punkas, Sax & Foxes. And besides these there is numbers of others which have a close affinity to the above named, the other root is the Iroquois to which belongs the Shawnies, Delawares, Chippiways, Tuscorara, Mohawk, and indeed all the New York and Canadian Indians, together with those bordering on the lakes, the State of Ohio, and Indiana. But now that they have become so crowded and mixed together on the Western and Northern frontier they are fast losing their originality and it would be even now difficult to classify them.

The Crow or Upsaroka Indians live along the eastern base of the Rocky Mts., on the Yellowstone and its tributaries and is one of the most warlike and formidable tribes in all that country; their language is also a dialect of the Sioux and is very harmonious and agreeable to the ear.

I will now cross the Rocky Mts by way of the South Pass and in going over I would like to take with me the Comanches and place them where they properly belong, amongst the Shoshone or Snake Indians, as I found their language exactly the same, and with them I would also place the Ottawa, Ponacs, Sanpitch, Piutas, Timpana Utas, together with all the very numerous small tribes in the great desert west of the Salt Lake, and lying between the Columbia river on the north and the Colorado on the south, all of which belongs to the Shoshone or Snake Nation.

I next proceed to the north fork of the Columbia, all along which we find numerous tribes altogether differing in character, and language from any we have yet met with, and in naming them will begin above and descend the river, thus the Cotonays, Flathead, Cottespellum or Pond de reil, Spogan, Nez perce, Kiuse, Wallawalla, and many other smaller tribes, all of which speak a similar language, but so very harsh and gutteral that few of our people have ever made any progress in attaining it.

The Chinooks are the remnants of a once powerful tribe near the mouth of the Columbia, and more properly belong to the coast Indians who differ very much in language and appearance from those of the interior, and I believe might with greater propriety be arranged and placed with the Islanders of the Pacific, than with the inland tribes. The whites have never been able to learn the Chinook language, but in order to have some manner of communications, they have manufactured a sort of giberish out of English french and Chinook which all talk and understand.

In regard to cannibalism I think it has never been a custom of our Northern or Western tribes, more particularly those of the Rocky Mts., however the custom of offering human sacrifices pervailed I believe amongst many of them in former times, but has gradually ceased until it has finally been abandoned almost altogether, so much so that I have only known one instance of a ceremonial sacrifice in the whole of my experience. Nevertheless I have reason to believe it was once a custom of many tribes. And in conclusion of the great ceremony which always took place on those occasions, the medicine man and braves of distinction would eat of the victim, more perhaps for the purpose of perfecting the ceremonial than for any relish they had for human flesh

Those poor miserable wretches inhabiting the great desert west of the Salt Lake and which I have before noticed as belonging to the Snake nation, are no doubt canibals, for they will eat anything whatever either animal or vegetable that is not poisonous, and has been known in many instances to eat their own offspring. This occurs from desperate necessity, but they are fast decreasing and will in a short time become extinct.[10]

In replying to a second letter Fitzpatrick wrote from St. Louis on May 12:

---

[10] Fitzpatrick's letters to Lt. J. W. Abert, found in the National Archives, Washington, D.C., photostat in my possession.

I received yours of the 15th ulto today, and hasten to acknowledge the receipt thereof, in doing so I will first request you not to accuse me of negligence for not replying at an earlier day. I have just returned from the southern portion of this state, where I have been attending a democratic Convention for the purpose of nominating a candidate to represent this distict in the next congress, which was done by a unanimous vote in favor of the Hon. J. B. Nowlin now in Washington City. Mr. Campbell was also absent on a tour up the Missouri river and only returned two days before me, this I hope will be a sufficient apology for the seeming inatention on our part.

I was gratified to learn that my former letter was of so much importance as you represent it, indeed I only wish it had been filled with more interesting matter, as there were other subjects in your inquiries and perhaps more interesting but was afraid to meddle or write on such subjects: Birds, plants, etc. of the different sections of country would be altogether too delicate a subject for me to attempt, without specimens to produce, and as you had no means whatever of procuring or if procured, of preserving those specimens it cannot be expected of you to render much information on those subjects, further than a few general remarks. However I will here observe that in no other wild and uncultivated country in the world are there a greater variety of plants and grasses to be found than the eastern slope and along the base of the R. Mts. perhaps on our late trip we met with a greater variety of plants and even also of a more luxuriant groth than they are found further north more particular the cactus were of greater variety and more abundant than I have seen it elsewhere.

I have no news from the Indian Country that would in the least interest you though we had arrivals here from Laramie, Bents Fort and Santa Fe but brought nothing of interest.

The emigration to Oregon and California will be very large this year, and I presume has left West port ere this.

I have had many offers to accept the leadership of the different emigrating parties but declined all, waiting for the final decision of Congress on the Oregon question, but their deliberations have been so slow and tardy that we of the West have lost all patience and I might say interest in that very important question.

I noticed in a late number of the Washington Union the arrival of Capt. Fremont at Mr. Suters on the Sacramento, and that he discovered a new and better route to Oregon. This I think is a mistake, not made by Capt. F. but by some other person not at all acquainted with the geography of the country. Therefore when we hear from Capt. F. himself the new route discovered will be to California and not to Oregon. These remarks are only confined to the date of his arrival at Suters, for I have no doubt whatever but that on his homeward trip he will greatly improve and shorten the distance to Oregon also, and I here take it upon me to say that there is no land route to Oregon more direct or easy than the present one, from this place to Fort Hall and South fork of the Columbia. But from Fort H. to the Walamatte Settlements there is great room for shortening and improving the route. . . .

Great excitement prevails in our city today in organising Volunteers etc. for the Rio Grande and to aid Genrl Taylor who seems to have blundered into a bad scrape, but the Missouri boys will soon relieve him, and thrash the Mexicans into the bargain. . . .

In his official report Abert gives high tribute to the Guide on his expedition:

Mr. Fitzpatrick is a gentleman eminently qualified in every respect to fill the arduous and responsible station assigned him. Having spent many of the best years of his life exposed to the toils and vicissitutes of the mountain and the prairies, he has acquired an intimate knowledge of the Indian character, which enabled him to conduct our little party safely and successfully through a country inhabited by numerous and powerful hordes of people, long notorious for their faithlessness and treachery. . . . The preservation of our party was due to his vigilance and discretion.[11]

---

[11] Abert's Journal, *op. cit.*, 8.

Chapter 12

The Army of the West

THE TROUBLE WITH MEXICO soon culminated in the clash of arms. In March 1846, General Taylor advanced from Corpus Christi to the Rio Grande, and on April 25 a detachment of sixty-three troops under Captain S. B. Thornton was ambushed, and after sustaining severe losses, captured.

President Polk received the news on May 9. Two days later he addressed a message to Congress, declaring that "war exists, and notwithstanding all our efforts to avoid it, exists by the act of Mexico herself." Congress immediately responded — the House of Representatives on the same day and the Senate on the following day — by authorizing the President to employ the army, navy, and militia, to enlist 50,000 volunteers and to expend $10,000,000 in the prosecution of the war.

This news, flashed by the newly-invented telegraph to the western frontier, was greeted with enthusiasm. Merchants and freighters and all who were interested, directly or indirectly, in the trade with New Mexico, welcomed the conflict that promised to remove barriers and to end the exhorbitant import taxes levied at Santa Fe. Colonel Kearny (soon to be made a brigadier general) was ordered to prepare for an invasion of New Mexico, and the Governor of Missouri was called upon to raise eight companies of mounted troops and two of light artillery to accompany the First Dragoons.

Prior to the outbreak of the war, moves had been made to procure for Fitzpatrick a position in the government service. On April 9, 1846, Thomas H. Benton, the distinguished senator from Missouri, had written to William Medill, U.S. Commissioner of Indian Affairs, proposing the establishment of an Agency on the Upper Arkansas and the Platte. For Agent, wrote the Senator, "I am recommending Thos. Fitzpatrick of St. Louis, Mri., a man of character and experience, who has been above twenty years acquainted with those Indians, and the guide to Capt. Fremont in his two first expeditions, and also of the last expedition as far as the Upper Arkansas, where he became the guide of Lieutenants Abert and Peck on their return through the Comanches."[1]

The appointment was proposed by the President and on August 3, 1846, was approved by the U.S. Senate.[2] At the suggestion of Senator Benton, the Commission and Instructions to Mr. Fitzpatrick were sent to Robert Campbell at St. Louis for delivery, Fitzpatrick having already departed

---

[1] National Archives, Records of the Office of Indian Affairs, Letters Received, Upper Platte, B-2757/1846.

[2] Office of Indian Affairs, Letters Received, Upper Platte, S-4048/1846.

for service with Kearny's Army of the West. In the letter Benton states that Frémont has "by letters on file in the War Dept. urged the establishment of this Agency and the appointment of Mr. Fitzpatrick."[3]

Robert Campbell received at St. Louis Fitzpatrick's Commission as Indian Agent and forwarded it to Santa Fe. In his letter of September 12, 1846, to the Commissioner of Indian Affairs Campbell stated: "The appointment has given satisfaction here, where Mr. Fitzpatrick is best known, and I can speak myself from an acquaintance with him of twenty years duration, and a better man could not be found for the situation."[4]

In the meantime the war had commenced and Fitzpatrick had been drawn into service with the military. Several caravans of Santa Fe traders had departed for New Mexico in the spring of 1846. One of them, that of Albert Speyers, was alleged to be carrying arms and munitions to be sold to the Mexicans. To stop these trains Kearny, early in June, dispatched Captain Benjamin Moore (later killed in the battle of San Pascual, California) with two companies of Dragoons, and Fitzpatrick was chosen as guide.[5] From Fort Leavenworth this command hastened over the Santa Fe Trail and met an incoming train, with buffalo robes and furs, and with the news that hostile Indians were hovering about Pawnee Fork. As the command pushed on, it passed

---

[3] *Ibid.*, Letters Received, Upper Platte, B–2747/1846.

[4] *Ibid.*, C–2579/1846. The *St. Louis Republican* of September 11, 1846, in announcing the appointment of Fitzpatrick wrote: "This is one of the few appointments of the present Administration to which we can subscribe with pleasure. Mr. Fitzpatrick has been for years engaged in the Indian country, and probably knows as much as any other man of their habits, character, wants, and necessities. He speaks many of their languages, and has within himself the means of making an efficient and vigilant agent."

[5] J. T. Hughes, *Doniphan's Expedition* (Cincinnati, 1848), 19, 26.

various westbound parties, all of which were ordered not to cross the Arkansas ahead of the army. But it failed to overtake Speyers' party, and at Bent's Fort it encamped to await the arrival of Kearny. One by one the trading companies came up until there were assembled near the fort more than 400 wagons, with more than a million dollars worth of merchandise.[6]

The main army, part of it from Fort Leavenworth and part from Independence — all of it to be known as the Army of the West — was on the way. A total of 1,600 men, including infantry, cavalry, and artillery, with 1,556 wagons and nearly 20,000 oxen, mules and horses, followed the Trail. There had been inadequate preparation: food supplies and forage ran short, and worn-out shoes and clothing could not be replaced. The season was dry, water was scarce, the heat was often terrific, and mosquitoes and buffalo gnats were constant pests, yet resolutely the men kept on.

The companies of infantry kept pace with the mounted men [writes John T. Hughes, a private soldier and later the author of *Doniphan's Expedition*]. Their feet were blistered by their long and almost incredible marches. The ground was often marked with blood in their footprints; yet with Roman fortitude they endured the toils of the campaign. Their courage could neither be abated by distance, nor their resolution relaxed by difficulties, nor their spirits subdued by privations, nor their ardor cooled by length of time.[7]

Fitzpatrick, still with Captain Moore's battalion at Bent's Fort, left on July 29 with a message for Kearny. He had not far to go, since the army was already within eight miles of the fort. Here, in the bottom lands of the Arkansas River, camp was made, and for a few days the army rested. Kearny, with Fitzpatrick, went on to the fort.

---

[6] Justin H. Smith, *The War with Mexico* (New York, 1919), I, 289.
[7] Hughes, *op. cit.*, 29.

And now this old fortified trading post, built in 1833 and for so many years an isolated fortress on the plains, took on the liveliest aspect of its long history. Traders and freighters, officers and men of the army, mounted or afoot, surged through its gates and crowded its interiors, and its wonted calm was broken by clang and clatter and uproar. Mrs. Susan Shelby Magoffin, who was with her hsuband in one of the halted caravans, paints a lively picture of the scene:

The Fort is crowded to overflowing. Col. Kearny has arrived, and it seems the world is coming with him. . . . There is the greatest possible noise in the *patio*. The shoeing of horses, neighing, and braying of mules, the crying of children, the scolding and fighting of men, are all enough to turn my head. . . . The servants are all quarreling and fighting among themselves, running to us to settle their difficulties; they are gambling off their cloths till some of them are next to nudity, and though each of them are in debt to *mi alma* [my soul — in other words, her husband] for advancement of their wages, they are coming to him to get them out of their scrapes.[8]

At Bent's Fort Fitzpatrick received word that his appointment as Indian Agent would be made, but that he would be permitted to continue with Kearny throughout the campaign. From the fort, on July 31, he wrote to his friend, Andrew Sublette:

Late news which we received from Santa fee would indicate that we shall have no fighting, and indeed it has always been my opinion that there would not be a blow struck at Santa fee, whatever may be the case elsewhere. I know not, but from what I can learn the campaign will not end in New Mexico.[9]

On August 1 the Army of the West, with Fitzpatrick as guide, and with William Bent added as an additional pilot, left the vicinity of the fort, following the general course

[8] Susan S. Magoffin, *Down the Santa Fe Trail and into Mexico*, edited by Stella M. Drumm (New Haven, 1926), 66–67.
[9] Sublette Collection, Mo. Hist. Soc.

of the "Mountain division" of the Santa Fe Trail. The days were hot, grass was scant, and water scarce, but the "long-legged infantry" kept pace with the cavalry and moved steadily on. Three days later Bent and six men were sent ahead to reconnoiter the mountain passes. They met and captured a Mexican squad of five men, who had been sent out to gain knowledge of the American approach and to detain persons attempting to pass out of New Mexico. A wretched looking lot were these captives, and when brought to the American camp were the objects of a great deal of derisive mirth. "They were mounted on diminutive assess," write Lieutenant William H. Emory, "and presented a ludicrous contrast by the side of the big men and horses of the First Dragoons. Fitzpatrick, our guide, who seldom laughs, became almost convulsed whenever he turned his practised eye in their direction."[10]

Over the difficult Raton Pass the army marched, and down into the Valley of the Mora. At the town of Las Vegas Kearny (now a brigadier general, for his new commission had just arrived), climbed a ladder to a flat-roofed house, and before the *alcalde* and citizens read his proclamation absolving them from allegiance to the Mexican Government, promising them protection and warning them against taking up arms.

Those who remain peaceably at home, attending to their crops and their herds [he declared], shall be protected by me in their property, their persons, and their religion; not a pepper, nor an onion, shall be disturbed or taken by my troops without pay, or by

---

[10] W. H. Emory, "Notes of a Military Reconnoisance," in *H. Ex. Doc.* 41, 30th Cong., 1 Sess., 21.

the consent of the owner. But listen! he who promises to be quiet, and is found in arms against me, I will hang.[11]

Descending, he and his officers mounted their horses, and the army went on. At the little red-adobe town of San Miguel, southeast of Santa Fe, the Las Vegas performance was repeated. The *alcalde*, however, was somewhat hesitant about recognizing the new authority and indicated that he preferred to wait and see who should win the forthcoming battle. "It is enough for you to know, sir," replied the General, "that I have captured your town." There was nothing more to be said. "Doubtless, in their muddled way," as Justin H. Smith, the historian of the Mexican War, remarks, "the people wondered at this first illustration of liberty; but with characteristic politeness, timidity and guile they wrinkled their faces as if pleased."[12]

For a time it looked as if a stiff resistance would be made. The swashbuckling Governor, General Manuel Armijo, issued a proclamation defying the Americans to enter Santa Fe, and assembled several thousand troops at Apache Canyon. It was an admirable place for defense, and the troops might, if well led, have beaten back the invaders. But in the meantime, James Magoffin, the trader-ambassador, had been skillfully negotiating with the Mexican leaders, most of them eager enough to get rid of their Governor, with the result that Armijo lost heart. It was useless, he decided, to oppose the Americans, so he fled, and his following dispersed, leaving the way open.

On August 17, as the army approached the ancient town of Pecos, its fat *alcalde* rode his little mule at full speed

---

11 *Ibid.*, 27.
12 Smith, *op. cit.*, I, 292.

toward the troops and amid a roar of laughter shouted to General Kearny: "Armijo and his troops have gone to hell, and the canyon is all clear."[13]

Unopposed, the army marched into Santa Fe, and with a formal salute of guns the Stars and Stripes were raised over the Governor's Palace. The next day the General addressed the people, proclaiming himself Governor and declaring the inhabitants subject to the control and entitled to the protection of the United States. Several of the officials were retained in office, and to these was administered the oath of allegiance.

Fitzpatrick's account of events and appraisal of the military situation are described in his letter from Santa Fe of August 24, 1846:

Genl Kearney arrived here on the 18th Instant with his Army in fine condition and took possession of the town without meeting with any resistance, notwithstanding no country in the world affords better opportunities for an inferior force to stop, or, indeed defeat an army than the one we just passed through; for sixty miles before we arrived here we were continually passing through the most intricate and narrow defiles where seemingly an army of Ten Thousand men might easily be defeated by one thousand or perhaps less.

Previous to our arrival great preparations were in progress to accomplish our defeat and Gov Armijo had collected a large force in order to "chastise the invaders and drive them from the Sacred Soil of Mexico," but on the near approach of our little Army the brave and Magnanimous Mexicans with their General fled without striking a single blow, and now we are all here enjoying very peacably the pleasures and luxuries of Santa Fe — we are not as yet "reveling in the Halls of the Montezumas," but in those of Armijo as the General has taken up his headquarters in the *Palacio*.

The Army are all quartered in and about the city with the exception of a small detachment sent off about 20 miles for the purpose of grazing and taking care of the stock as there is little or no

---

[13] Emory, 29.

grain in the Country for feed — indeed the Keeping of Horses at this place will be very difficult and is a much greater obstacle in the way of conquering this Country than Mexican Valor.

I can hardly at present venture an opinion in regard to the sincerity of the people or their fidelity to the United States although the Alcalde and other functionaries together with many of the most influential citizens have taken the Oath of Alegiance to our government. Still I have my doubts. — The country is only adapted for a population such as now inhabit it and the acquisition so far as the country acquired is concerned is of but little value.

We have had no late intelligence from Col Price but expect him in about three weeks when Genl Kearney will again resume his march for California where he also intends to plant the Star Spangled Banner.

The troops dislike the expectation in prospect for California as they apprehend much difficulty and suffering in getting there by land, and indeed my own opinion is that it would have been better to have sent the troops for that Country by sea, but the General has determined that your humble servant will accompany him as I presume you are aware that I am the last person that would desert the Cause whilst I can be useful to it.

A few days since Genl Kearney gave me permission to return to the United States and enter upon the duties of the office which is said to be in contemplation for me, but the General has changed his mind on that subject and desires that I should go with him and I have determined on remaining so long as he considers my Services of importance to my Country, no matter what may be the fatigues or sufferings.[14]

On September 3 Fitzpatrick wrote a second letter from Santa Fe:

The inhabitants of this place who fled on the approach of the army are now returning, and, apparently, becoming reconciled with the new order of things. Indeed, one would think from the present aspect that the conquest of New Mexico was now complete; however, much remains yet to be done, and General Kearney is using all his exertions to prevent any occurrence which might be prejudicial to the interests of the United States in this quarter.

---

[14] This letter was written to Robert Campbell and by him major extracts were copied and forwarded to Commissioner Medill. — Records of the Office of Indian Affairs, Letters Received, Upper Platte, C–2583/1846.

Ex-Governor Armijo is yet in the province, and is said to be prowling about in the mountains with a band of two hundred men; and, strange to say, the inhabitants of that vicinity where he is said to be are more in dread of him and his band of guerillas than they are of the American army; and well they may be, as they have nothing at all to fear from us should they conform to the laws — on the contrary they have a great deal to fear from a guerilla war, which Armijo is disposed to wage, not only against us, but against all the inhabitants of New Mexico. Indeed, his dastardly conduct and his inglorious flight has not left him a single partizan, save those with him, in all New Mexico. This, together with his already having been an outlaw in some of the lower provinces, leaves the poor wretch hardly a hole by which to escape; all this will have a tendency, no doubt, to make him desperate.

Had Armijo acted as a brave and patriotic man should have done in the defense of his country and the Government which supported him, with the advantages that the nature of the country afforded, together with the exhaustion of our troops and horses after so long a march, he could have certainly given us very hard work to perform, and he would now have held a very different position in the opinion of mankind. But he has fallen, never to rise.

Gen. Kearney left here yesterday morning, with about eight hundred men, for the purpose of visiting the most important settlements of this province, in the south, and to manufacture the inhabitants thereof into good *American citizens*, which, I fear, will be a difficult process, at least for the present. I have frequently witnessed the process, and it apparently is all palatable enough until the *oath* is being administered; then comes the bitter pill which few have swallowed with good grace. However, should Gen. Kearney be able to capture Armijo and his band (as I think it is his intention to make an effort to that effect, and he has kept it secret the better to accomplish it), no doubt it would tend greatly to quiet the fears of the people, for they yet hold him in great dread lest he should again get the upper hand, and resume with double force his usual tyrannical sway. These views are absurd, and are only to be found amongst the ignorant (unfortunately a large portion of the population), who are accustomed to consider their rulers invincible; therefore, if the tyrant is caught, it will greatly allay their foolish fears.

There is little or no change taken place in the Government as yet. The native functionaries have still their places, notwithstanding there are aspirants here as well as with you — men who are ready to fill *any* office in the gift of General Kearney or the Government, from Governor down; and, what is most extraordinary, the very men who are so full of patriotism and so eager to fight the battles of their country, would *now* lay down their arms in order to fill a petty office in Santa Fe. Indeed, I have had myself not less than three applications to intercede for men, some of whom you well know, and would be astonished were I to name them; but you know that I am very modest in matters of this kind, and even if I had any influence I would be very particular in the manner of its disposal.

Gen. Kearney will be absent about fifteen days, at the expiration of which we may expect to depart for California. But much is yet to be done before that is undertaken; and let it be conducted as it may, its accomplishment will be attended with great difficulty, and its performance, *by an army*, will be a feat such as has never been done before. But I will not dwell longer on this subject, as those unacquainted with the nature of the country would suspect me of seeking an excuse to back out from so arduous an undertaking. Far from it. On the contrary, I am anxious for it, so far as my individual comforts are concerned; moreover, I hold it a high honor to belong to the advance guard of that American army which will have the glory of planting the stars and srtipes on the shores of the Pacific.

The traders have all arrived here, and, together with the army, make Santa Fe a crowded as well as a lively place. But very few important sales have been made here this year, and, as they have a very heavy stock of goods on hand, I know not what they will do with them unless they can go south; but as we have learned nothing of Gen. Wool's movements it is considered too much risk to go in that direction, until there is some certainty of protection. I think many of them now wish they had stayed at home, for, with the immense number of stock and men, with everything double what it was before, their outlay is necessarily much more than they can afford from the profits of any sales which they are likely to make this trip.[15]

On a height overlooking the city the building of Fort Marcy was begun. More troops arrived, and yet more were on the way. In the main, the citizens had welcomed the

---

[15] *Ibid.*, C–2591/1846. This letter was also given by Campbell to the *St. Louis Reveille* and was published therein on October 26, 1846. There are minor variations in the two versions.

new regime. Kearny, feeling that all was safe, prepared to move on to California. Doniphan was dispatched westward to give the troublesome Navajos a needed lesson, then to turn back and proceed to Chihuahua; and on September 25 Kearny set out. He had with him 300 Dragoons, with Fitzpatrick as guide and Antoine Robidoux as interpreter.

Without noteworthy incident the march was made down the Rio Grande to the neighborhood of the town of Socorro. Here the column met Kit Carson, with an escort of fifteen men, carrying dispatches from Stockton and Frémont in Los Angeles. Carson, who had heard nothing of the revolt that broke out immediately after his departure, reported that everything was quiet in California and that American authority was supreme. Kearny thereupon decided to retain but 100 of his Dragoons and to send the others back to Santa Fe. As Carson had just traveled the Gila River route, and as Fitzpatrick had never been upon it, Kearny ordered the former to return toward the west as guide to the expedition. Against this unwelcome order Carson protested. For more than a year he had been absent from his home in Taos; and now, when only a few days' ride would take him there for a brief halt on his long way, he must set forth on a journey that would mean another year's absence. But with sullen resignation he turned again to the west.

The dispatches carried thus far by Carson were turned over to Fitzpatrick, with orders to take them to Washington. In company with 200 Dragoons he reached Santa Fe. Here he reported to Colonel Sterling Price, who with the Second Regiment of Missouri Mounted Infantry had arrived only three days after Kearny's departure and was now in command of the military district. On October 14

Fitzpatrick set out from Santa Fe and in mid-November reached St. Louis. He departed for Washington on November 22 with the distpatches.[16] These he delivered to the War Department; and then reported to the Commissioner of Indian Affairs, received his Commission as Indian Agent, and began service December 1, 1846.[17]

Fitzpatrick was now to enter upon the third great period of his life's work. His years of experience in the West, his many contacts with the Indians of the mountains and plains were in a sense but the training school for this last great service. He was now to be the representative of his government to the untutored natives of the Upper Platte and Arkansas. In the hands of this first ambassador to the nations of the far western plains was placed the fate of hundreds of his pioneer countrymen.

---

[16] St. Louis Reveille, November 23, 1846.

[17] Fitzpatrick's letter to T. H. Harvey, Commissioner of Indian Affairs, February 4, 1847. — In Commissioner of Indian Affairs, files, St. Louis Superintendency, H. 75.

Chapter 13

Ambassador to the Plains Tribes

FOR YEARS THERE HAD BEEN Government agencies among the tribes along the Missouri, the lower Platte and the lower Kansas, as well as among the five civilized tribes and the Osages in the present Oklahoma. In 1842 a sub-agent had been appointed for far-away Oregon. But until the creation of the Upper Platte and Arkansas agency the wild tribes of the plains had been ignored. Some of these Indians had themselves recognized the need of an agent. Andrew Drips, who had forsaken the American Fur Company to become agent for the Upper Missouri region, reported in 1845 that he had met Cheyennes who said that their Great Father, the President, must have forgotten them entirely, or an agent would have been sent to them. Senator Benton's letter already referred to, is an expression of the current feeling that the plains tribes should have a Government representative.

So the agency of the Upper Platte and Arkansas was

established. Its headquarters were to be at Bent's Fort, but this designation was impracticable, as Fitzpatrick was later to learn. He was to meet his Indians where he could find them — sometimes at Bent's, in other times at Fort Laramie, or at the Big Timbers, or at Fort Mann, or Fort Atkinson. Cheyennes, Arapahoes, and certain bands of Oglala, Brulé, and Minniconjou Sioux were the Indians with whom he was primarily to deal; but he would be expected also to see what could be done with those more turbulent peoples, the Comanches, the Kiowas, and the plains Apaches, who as a rule kept below the Arkansas. Some 3,300 warriors, together with their women and children, as he was to estimate a year later, were to come under his charge — the Cheyennes with 500, the Arapahoes with 800, and the Sioux with 2,000.

Indian tribes were recognized as nations, and agreements with them were made by treaty. But they were not foreign nations, and could thus make no treaties with a government other than that of the United States. Chief Justice John Marshall had settled that little matter away back in the early '30s. They were to be regarded, he ruled, as "domestic dependent nations," with a relation to the United States which "resembles that of a ward to its guardian." An Indian agent was thus in a certain sense an ambassador; but he was also a counselor, and in the last analysis a representative of the authority of the Great White Father. He could not only advise and warn, but if the need arose could also command.

The appointment of Fitzpatrick, as already mentioned, was warmly acclaimed. "A better selection could not have been made," wrote T. P. Moore, agent of the Upper Missouri.[1] The St. Louis *Weekly Reveille* of September 14, 1846, gave him high praise:

Thomas Fitzpatrick, Esq., the well-known mountain guide, has been appointed, by the President, Indian Agent for the tribes on the head of the Arkansas, Platte and Kansas Rivers. Mr. Fitzpatrick is the well-known "chief of the withered hand," as the Indians style him. He was Captain Frémont's guide during two trips [actually but one] among the mountains — he returned with the engineers by way of the Arkansas [Canadian], and is now guiding the California expedition under General Kearny. This appointment will give general satisfaction; for among both the whites and the Indians upon the frontier and the plains, Mr. Fitzpatrick is deservedly held in high respect — the latter indeed, reverence his person, and, from this fact, he has more power to control and restrain them than even the presence of armed forces.

With dispatches for Santa Fe he left Washington in December. At St. Louis he was joined by Solomon Sublette, and the two proceeded to Fort Leavenworth, which they reached on January 3, 1847. Sublette engaged to carry the dispatches to Santa Fe,[2] and Fitzpatrick remained at the fort. The question of how the emigrants on the Oregon Trail might best be protected was still being discussed — Kearny's word on the matter not having been accepted as final — and Fitzpatrick was asked by Lieutenant Colonel Clifton Wharton, commander of the post, to give his views.

My opinion [Fitzpatrick replied] is that a post at or in the vicinity of Laramie is much wanted. It would be nearly in the vicinity of the buffalo range, where all the most formidable Indian tribes

---

[1] Annual Report of the Commissioner of Indian Affairs for 1848, 296.

[2] Sublette set out forthwith on his midwinter journey. He fed his mules on cottonwood bark and such other food as could be found along the Santa Fe Trail, and made the trip without mishap, reaching Bent's Fort Feb. 6 and Santa Fe on Feb. 21. The old mountaineer, Joe Walker accompanied him back from New Mexico, the party arriving at the Missouri on April 21. Sublette was paid $500 for the round trip. — Sublette Collections, Mo. Hist. Soc. Letter dated at St. Louis, May 1, 1847.

are fast approaching, and near where there will eventually (as the game decreases) be a great struggle for the ascendancy. Three hundred mounted men at that post would be necessary. . . . Another post at or near Fort Hall with a force of 100 or 150 men would be advisable, not more on account of the protection it would afford travelers than to have it as a place for resting and recruiting men and animals, for the further prosecution of the journey to and from the Pacific. The next and last of that line I would place as near as practicable to the mouth of the Columbia River, where it would serve many purposes not necessary to relate.[3]

It was the advice of Fitzpatrick, and not that of Kearny, that the Government was to follow. A year later it established Fort Kearny, on the lower Platte, and two years later it bought Fort Laramie, and established a post, Camp Loring, near Fort Hall.

The question of protecting the Santa Fe Trail also came up, and Fitzpatrick was again asked his opinion. He advised the establishment of an adobe fort at the Big Bend of the Arkansas and another near the mouth of the Purgatory, and the abandonment of the Cimarron division of the Trail because of the hostility of the Comanches and the Apaches. It may be, as tradition affirms, that the Government sought within the next two years to buy Bent's Fort. Later it established Fort Mann and Fort Atkinson near the Cimarron crossing of the Arkansas, Fort Larned at the Big Bend, Fort Wise (later known as old Fort Lyon) at the Big Timbers, and finally the new Fort Lyon not far from the ruins of Bent's Fort.

It was nearly summer before Fitzpatrick was enabled to begin his first official tour. Lieutenant John Love, of the First Dragoons, was to set out for Santa Fe and Fitzpatrick

---

[3] This report, dated Jan. 11, 1847, is in the Indian Bureau archives at Washington, D.C.

was asked to accompany him. On June 8 the command left Fort Leavenworth. "We traveled along happily and with much expedition," writes Fitzpatrick in his first report of September 18, 1847, "until we arrived at Pawnee Fork, a tributary of the Arkansas River, 300 miles from Fort Leavenworth."[4] Then things began to happen.

The Pawnee was in flood, and a cluster of Government and traders' wagons crowded both its banks. Impatient wagonmasters paced back and forth, and indolent bull-whackers watched the roaring waters and made their positive predictions as to the time and date of subsidence. Two days earlier a large band of Comanches had attacked the camp on the west bank. A hundred and fifty oxen, worth about $4,000 had been run off, a loss that necessitated the abandonment of twenty-five wagons and the *caching* of several thousands of dollars worth of goods.[5]

Lieutenant Love swore vengeance on the Comanches, but apparently nothing was done. On the following day the flood subsided and the Fork was crossed. For safety the two west-bound Government trains were ordered to travel and camp as near as possible to the Dragoons. This eminently sensible order was, however, rejected by the commander of one of the trains, a bumptious person named Hayden, who let it be known to all concerned that he had received his orders at Fort Leavenworth. He was soon to

---

[4] This first Annual Report, written from Bent's Fort, Sept. 18, 1847, is listed in the contents of the Commissioner of Indian Affairs Annual Report for 1847 as document 9½, but is not included in the separately-bound volume. However, it is found in *Sen. Ex. Doc.* 1, 30th Cong., 1st Sess. (Serial 503), Appendix, 238–49. It is the chief source for information given in this chapter on Fitzpatrick's movements as agent up to the date of its writing.

[5] An account of this affair is found in the spritely pages of Lewis H. Garrard, *Wah-To-Yah and the Taos Trail*, edited by R. P. Bieber (Glendale, Calif., 1938).

learn a much-needed lesson. At the end of the first day's travel Hayden camped his train out on a level plain a mile from the Arkansas, while the Dragoons and the other train camped on the river bank. Early the following morning, after Hayden's oxen had been turned out to graze, Comanches raided the herd and ran off the whole of it. Lieutenant Love, watching the distant scene with a spyglass, ordered "boots and saddles," but just as he was ready to rush to the rescue a large force of warriors made a demonstration near his own camp. So circumstanced, he could spare but twenty-five men for the pursuit. They made a gallant charge against overwhelming numbers, but were beaten back with a loss of five killed and six severely wounded.

After this needless loss of lives and property, the now humbled Hayden was content to obey Lieutenant Love's orders. By redistributing the remaining oxen between the two trains all the wagons could be moved. It was necessary, however, to remain in camp several days until the wounded became convalescent. Then the caravan proceeded to Fort Mann, twenty-five miles east of the Arkansas crossing. It was found to be a fort without soldiers, for the garrison, in dread of an Indian attack, had abandoned it only a few days before.

Bent's Fort was Fitzpatrick's destination, but the caravan was going to New Mexico by the Cimarron route. It would be madness to attempt the journey alone, and there was thus nothing for Fitzpatrick to do but to go with the caravan, which after an eventless journey arrived in Santa Fe on August 8, just two months out.

Fitzpatrick found conditions in New Mexico most deplorable. Much had happened since he left the southwest capital in the previous October. The Taos uprising of January 1847, in which Governor Charles Bent and other Americans had been murdered, had been rigorously suppressed, and the army, under Colonel Sterling Price, was in general control of the settlements. But drunkenness was common, vice and crime were rampant, and on the frontiers marauding Indians were exacting a heavy toll in life and property. "What seems very strange," wrote Fitzpatrick, "they carry their hostilities (except when they want presents, and then they are as gentle as lambs), almost within gunshot of the headquarters of the Army of the West."

He was disgusted with the life of the soldiers. "It has been a matter of surprise to many," he wrote, "that in a country so healthy and salubrious and with so gentle a climate as New Mexico, so many volunteers should die of disease. Let these wonderers pay a visit to Santa Fe, remain one week as I have done, and observe the life there led, day and night, and they will be still more astonished that so many have lived." Conditions were to get worse before they bettered; for two years later the veteran Cerán St. Vrain asserted that a worse state of things had not existed in the country since he came there; and Indian Agent James S. Calhoun, at Santa Fe, in reporting this statement, added that "the number of discontented Indians in this territory is not small, and I regret to add, they are not the only evil people in it. This whole country requires a thorough purging."[6]

Glad of the opportunity of getting away, Fitzpatrick, in

---

[6] Annie Heloise Abel, *The Official Correspondence of James S. Calhoun* (Washington, D.C., 1915), 42.

the company of a force of discharged soldiers, journeyed to Bent's Fort. With him went an old friend, John Smith, whom he had met in Santa Fe, and whom he had induced to act as interpreter for the Cheyennes and Arapahoes. Smith had been for some years a trader for Bent and St. Vrain and was highly respected among the Indians. He had married a sister of Chief Yellow Horse, of the Cheyennes, and the fruit of this union was little Jack, now a husky, dusky lad of four years. Mother and son, astride their horses, rode along in the little party as full-fledged horsemen. This boy was the Jack Smith who as a young man living with his mother's people was to be shot down by white soldiers in the famous (or, as some say, infamous) Battle of Sand Creek in 1864.

Bent's Fort was reached late in August. It was the main trading rendezvous of both the Cheyennes and the Arapahoes, and here they traded their furs and buffalo robes for scarlet cloth, beads, looking glasses, guns, and ammunition. William Bent was the resident owner. Twelve years before he had married a Cheyenne, Owl Woman, who had borne him four children, and on her death had married her sister, Yellow Woman. His relations with the tribesmen were close and intimate, and no white man exercised more influence among them.[7]

Fitzpatrick found a large camp of Cheyennes near the fort. They welcomed him, for they realized that he was their new agent, and they were acutely conscious that an agent of the Great Father should have presents to distribute. But the agent was not so provided. The stored

---

[7] See David Lavender, *Bent's Fort* (Garden City, N.Y., 1954).

Government goods on which he had counted had been carted off to Santa Fe and distributed to other Indians. Here he was, empty handed, about to have his first official meeting with his Indian friends. They were impatient, too, and already they had been asking the traders:

How is it that the Great Father has not sent us presents as a token of regard for our good behavior, while he sends presents to those who are in the habit of plundering the whites?

A recent unfortunate episode had put some strain upon the feelings of the Cheyennes. One of their chiefs, Cinemo, known as Old Tobacco, had been shot and fatally wounded by one of a party of whites who did not recognize him. Just before passing away the Chief had called his family about him and asked them not to avenge his death, for the act was due to a mistake and the men were his friends. Though no reprisals followed, it was too much to expect that the episode had not left some trace of resentment.

The situation was somewhat critical. But Fitzpatrick had credit with Bent, and he obtained a large supply of bread and coffee. If he could not give presents he could at least give a banquet. The chiefs and braves were assembled, the bread and coffee were served, and then Fitzpatrick addressed them. He was his own reporter and what he said is included in his first annual report. He explained the object of his visit and the kind intentions of the Government towards peaceful Indians.

I also told them [he writes] that I was particularly instructed by their Great Father to ascertain what Indians were engaged in plundering and robbing travellers on the Santa Fé road, and throughout the country, in order that when he sent his soldiers into the country, the innocent should not suffer equally with the guilty. In fact, I explained to them the policy and intention of the Government towards Indians generally, and that their Great Father was disposed to treat them more like his children than like enemies; but that there were some things which he could not overlook, and these were, the murdering and plundering his people — the perpetrators of which would be speedily and severely punished. I reminded them of the great diminution and continual decrease of all game, and advised them to turn their attention to agriculture, it being the only means to save them from destruction. I pointed out and enumerated the many evils arising from the use of spirituous liquors, and advised them to abandon altogether so degrading and abominable a practice (pp. 241–42).

Yellow Wolf, one of the principal chiefs, arose and in a dramatic manner responded:

My father: your words are very good; the Chyennes all hear and cherish them, and those that are absent shall hear and remember them also. My father, we are very poor and ignorant, even like the wolves in the prairie; we are not endowed with the wisdom of the white people. Father, this day we rejoice; we are no more poor or wretched; our Great Father has at length condescended to notice us, poor and wretched as we are; we now know we shall live and prosper, therefore we rejoice.

My father, we have not been warring against your people; why should we? On the contrary, if our Great Father wishes our aid, the Chyenne warriors shall be ready at a moment's warning to assist in punishing those bad people, the Camanches. . . . Tell our Great Father that the Chyennes are ready and willing to obey him in everything; but in settling down and raising corn, that is a thing we know nothing about, and if he will send some of his people to learn us, we will at once commence, and make every effort to live like the whites. We have long since noted the decrease of the buffalo, and are well aware it cannot last much longer. Tell him also that the white people, a short time ago, killed one of our wisest and best chiefs; that the tears of the orphans and relatives of the deceased chief are not yet dried up; yet we still remain the friends of the whites (p. 242).

The language is of course that of John Smith, improved by the literary touch of Thomas Fitzpatrick, who in his youth had evidently been fed on classical oratory. No one can say how much our familiar examples of Indian oratory have been helped by the white man's sense of form and logic. Some of them, indeed, like the celebrated speech of Logan — have been made up, phrase and substance, out of the whole cloth. This speech of Yellow Wolf's, however, has the ring of genuineness.

There were some Arapahoes present, and they joined in the expressions of good will made by the Cheyennes. They told the agent that though some of their tribe were among the Comanches attacking the whites, these warriors would be sent for and brought back. It seemed like a successful council. There had been as yet no talk of a formal treaty, but only an effort to promote friendship. Fitzpatrick distributed a supply of tobacco and the council closed.

From Bent's Fort Fitzpatrick had written his first annual report on September 18, 1847, previously mentioned; and he followed it with a special report on October 19.[8] In both documents he gives his opinions on a variety of matters connected with his office. He writes as one who has thought deeply on these subjects and has waited a long time for an opportunity to express himself. No man of his time and place wrote so well. Carson could then not even read, and Bridger was never to learn. What has come down to us

---

[8] This special report we found in the Indian Bureau archives in Washington. A portion of it was written in reply to printed inquiries sent out by Henry Schoolcraft. Fitzpatrick's response is incorporated in Schoolcraft, *Historical and Statistical Information Respecting the History, Condition and Prospects of the Indian Tribes of the United States*, etc., Part I, 259–64 (1851).

This report of Oct. 19, 1847, is reprinted by Alvin Josephy, "A Letter from 'Broken Hand,'" in the New York posse *Westerners Brand Book*, X, no. 2 (New York, 1963), 25–27, 41–46, and is there mistakenly called Fitzpatrick's "first official report to his superior" (p. 26). It is also stated in the editor's introduction that it "has not before been published in its entirety." But this is incorrect. It was edited by me and published in full in *New Spain and the American West, Historical Contributions Presented to Herbert Eugene Bolton* (Lancaster, Pa., 1932), II, 124–37.

from Jedediah Smith, William Sublette, Robert Campbell, William and Charles Bent, and Cerán St. Vrain are in most respects inferior to what we have from Fitzpatrick. Nothing much in literary achievement is rightly to be expected of one who leaves school at sixteen and spends the next thirty years on the frontier and in the wilderness. But Fitzpatricks' early lessons had sunk deep. He retained what he had been taught, and he added to the store by constant thought and observation. He writes with precision and force, with a sense of form and not seldom a feeling for the inevitable word. In his letters there is sometimes an awkward phrase, or a slip in syntax, just as there is in the writings of more cultivated men. There is sometimes a word too much, for he wrote in a day when prolixity was a virtue, and the florid verbosity of a Benton was by many esteemed a model. But the marvel is that, writing under the difficult conditions that beset him, apart from contact with books and the society of bookish men, he could do so well.

Many matters concerned him. There was, for instance, this question of the nomad Indian's readiness for civilization. Fitzpatrick had been studying Indians for upwards of thirty years, and he knew them from the ground up. He wanted to see justice done to them, and he wanted all the well-meant experiments tried, but he had no easy optimism regarding a solution of the Indian problem. To him the nomad savage was a being hundreds of years behind the settled, industrious white, and could be brought to civilization only by a long cultural process of aid and encouragement, with swift and rigorous punishment for his acts of violence.

I do not wish [he writes] to be understood as placing much

confidence in the professions of the Indians of this country; neither do I in those of any other. Circumstances and necessity may seem to change their disposition; but ingratitude, low, mean cunning, cowardice, selfishness and treachery, are the characteristics of the whole race [Doubtless he would, on being closely questioned, have excepted the Flatheads, the Nez Percés, and some of the Shoshones from this sweeping indictment]. Yet I believe the Chyennes are serious in their professions of friendship; they plainly see what must befall them on the extinction of game, and therefore wish to court the favor of the United States Government, hoping to obtain assistance. Many of them appear very desirous to commence raising corn, but I fear that effort will be found too laborious for them, unless they are encouraged and assisted (p. 243).

He reverts to the subject in his special report (of October 19, 1847):

I am well aware of the great advantage and importance of securing the good will and friendship of the Indians of this agency, as it is through their country the two great thoroughfares to the West pass. And I believe the duties of this agency properly and judiciously executed of more importance at this time than any other under the Indian Department. I have used my best endeavor to keep quiet and reconcile the Indians hereabout, and I flatter myself that in a manner I have succeeded. Yet I am still apprehensive of a union between them and the Comanches, notwithstanding the Cheyennes have offered their service to fight in our behalf; but I have made a rule, in all my intercourse with Indians, whenever I found them very officious and professing great friendship, to double the guard and become more vigilant in guarding against surprises.

And again:

I am not one of those who expect and look for the immediate improvement and civilization of the Indian tribes; by the means generally recommended, as I am well aware they will have to pass through a long and protracted ordeal before they can even attain at [to] the first step to civilization, and I have yet to learn and decide whether the full-blooded Indian is capable of such a change.

He had met but few Indians, he continued, who seemed to him prepared to receive instruction in civilization and

Christianity. These were in the region of the Columbia River and its tributaries [doubtless Nez Percés, Flatheads, and some of the Shoshones], and the improvement of these Indians he attributed to the "severe but just administration of the Hudson's Bay Company."

The eccentric Methodist preacher, the Reverend Joseph Williams, who accompanied the Bidwell-Bartleson emigrant train guided by Fitzpatrick in 1841, had said, as will be remembered, that Fitzpatrick was opposed to the missionaries. It is better to trust what Fitzpatrick himself says:

Although I disapprove much of the conduct of the missionaries, yet I believe that their introduction amongst these tribes at this time would have very beneficial and satisfactory results — not at all in a religious point of view, but the improvement of their physical condition, which together with their morals ought to be the first thing that a missionary undertakes.

In brief, the Indian should be taught hygiene, industry, and good conduct and spared instruction in theological doctrine and the practice of religious rites. He continues:

But instead the missionary begins at the very place where he ought to give the last touch; nearly the first thing the missionary performs is to baptise the subject. The Indian, thinking the ceremony some great "medicine" which will render him invulnerable or produce some good luck, will submit to the ceremony with a good grace until he finds that those who have passed through all the ceremonies of religion have no better luck in hunting and war than they had before, and comes to the conclusion that the white man's "medicine" is not so strong as his own and therefore loses all faith in it.

The missionary, he adds, should begin with the Indian as with a child, by instilling moral principles and explaining how the Great Spirit wishes his children to conduct themselves. It would be time enough later to teach him the doctrines of Christianity. If by education he could be taught to be an honest, moral, and generous being, the result would "certainly be a great achievement, and what is considered by many impossible."

Always he speaks strongly for the abolition of the liquor traffic among the red men. The larger organizations, such as the American Fur Company and the Bent and St. Vrain Company, would gladly lend their support to the achievement of this purpose, for they had long since learned the inexpedience of the trade in whiskey. The petty independent traders "whose whole stock in trade amounted to only a few trinkets and three or four hundred gallons of liquor" were the traffickers who debauched the natives.

About seventy-five miles above this place [Bent's Fort] and immediately on the Arkansas river [Fitzpatrick continues in his report of September 18], there is a small settlement, the principal part of which is composed of old trappers and hunters; the male part of which is composed mostly of Americans, Missouri French, Canadians and Mexicans. They have a tolerable supply of cattle, horses, mules, etc.; and I am informed that this year they have raised a good crop of wheat, corn, beans, pumpkins and other vegetables. They number about 150 souls, and of this number there are about 60 men, nearly all having wives and some have two. These wives are of various Indian tribes, . . . Mexicans and Americans. The American women are Mormons; a party of Mormons having wintered there and on their departure for California, left behind two families. These people are living in two separate establishments near each other; one called "Pumble" [Pueblo] and the other "Hardscrabble"; both villages are fortified by a wall 12 feet high, composed of *adobe* (sun-dried brick). Those villages are becoming depots for the smugglers of liquor from New Mexico into this country; therefore they must be watched.

Alexander Barklay, the prominent Englishman who built Fort Barkley and carried on trade in northeastern New Mexico, was a friend of Fitzpatrick and had written to him making certain inquiries. To these Fitzpatrick responded in a letter from Bent's Fort on December 18, 1847:

I received your favor of the 10th inst. per Mr. Lupton and regret that I am not able to send you a more satisfactory reply in regard to your enquiries.

In regard to the Government waggons at this place I have no authority whatever to dispose of them, nor neither do I know what disposition the government intends making of them. I have written to the QreMaster at Santa Fe in regard to their ruinous and failing condition; and expect some instructions by the first arrival about them, and should they be ordered for sale will notify you of the same in due time.

The Battalion of men under the command of Colonel Gilpin, and lately arrived on this river, were certainly raised and organized expressly for the purpose of the subjugation of the hostile tribes, as well as the protection of travellers and people of this country, besides I know it to be the intention of the government to establish Military posts, at different points throughout the Indian country, amongst which some point on this river will be the most conspicuous. This you may rely on, as the very nature of things, as well as our late Territorial acquisitions demands such a course.

I regret to learn of your late indisposition which seems to be something similar to my own, but I am now recovering and hope soon to be able to give myself the pleasure of accepting your kind invitation, and enjoying your society.

I should be happy to receive frequent communications from you and any information which I can give you will be always ready and willing to communicate. I could write you many little particulars but you will be better able to obtain from the gentlemen of your town.

Your Obt Servt

Alexr Barkley   Thos. Fitzpatrick[9]

On December 18, 1847, Fitzpatrick also wrote an official report from Bent's Fort.[10] He says that Major William Gil-

---

[9] This letter was called to my attention by Mr. Fred Rosenstock and was located for me at the Bancroft Library, University of California by my friend George P. Hammond. It is published here by permission of the Director of the Bancroft Library.

[10] This was found in the Upper Platte Agency File, 1846–1851, Social and Economic Branch, Office of Civil Archives, the National Archives, Washington. It was edited by Alvin M. Josephy, Jr. and published in the New York posse's *Westerners Brand Book* (1963), X, 75–76 and 87–91, from which I quote.

pin had arrived on November 21 with two companies of mounted troops to deal with Indians on the Santa Fe Trail and had left three companies of infantry at Fort Mann near the Cimarron Crossing of the Arkansas. These infantrymen were largely Germans, who knew nothing of Indian character and warfare. They were soon embroiled with Pawnees who visited the fort, and in the fight the soldiers "killed four of them and wounded many more, some of which made their escape, with a knife or bayonet yet sticking in them." This latter information was brought to Bent's Fort by General Sterling Price, who was on his way to Santa Fe.

Fitzpatrick was much concerned about the incident at Fort Mann and anticipated more trouble, especially in view of what had happened some months before. He writes:

Last summer a party of Camanche Indians, 30 in number, killed and scalped 8 men, and then marched off with shouts and exultations, and with the utmost impunity. Show one instance of this sort occuring in the last twenty years amongst the trapers. Traders or hunters (there are none). On the contrary, the trapers, traders and hunters have always beat the Indians of this country, three to one, and often ten to one against them, and which gained them a reputation amongst the Indians which I regret to see on the decline. In short I mean to say that the country is at present in a far less state of security, and tranquility, than before the commencement of the Mexican war, or before the marching and countermarching of United States troops, to and from New Mexico. . . .

I respectfully solicit the War Department to withdraw the force which have just arrived in this country for its tranquilization as I am very certain that this force will only excite ridicule and be instrumental of doing more mischief to the cause than can be remedied perhaps in five years to come.[11]

During the winter of 1847–48 Fitzpatrick and Gilpin got

---

[11] *Ibid.*, 87, 90.

into a controversial clash over dealings with the hostile Indians. Five years earlier both had accompanied Frémont to Oregon, and in 1846, one as major and the other as guide, had marched with Kearny's Army of the West to Santa Fe. But now each was in independent authority in the same region, and as neither was much given to reconciliation, their differences in views brought about a sharp exchange of verbal gunfire.

It was this way. In the summer of 1847 the Comanches and Kiowas had been committing depredations along the Santa Fe Trail. It was estimated that forty-seven Americans had been killed, 330 wagons destroyed, and 6,500 cattle stolen.[12] Gilpin, just returned from the Doniphan campaign, had been called upon by Governor Edwards, of Missouri, to lead a punitive expedition against the hostiles. With five companies he had left Fort Leavenworth in September and moved as far as Fort Mann, where he put his three infantry companies in garrison, as already mentioned, with orders to repair and enlarge the fort. With his two cavalry companies he had then advanced to Bent's Fort. So far no Indians had been met and punished. At the fort the two men must soon have found themselves at loggerheads, for the first we hear of them they are addressing each other by letter.

On February 8 Gilpin wrote Fitzpatrick suggesting that the Cheyennes and the Arapahoes be settled on the Arkansas to begin farming and also to act as a buffer against the hostile Indians to the south. Two days later Fitzpatrick replied, agreeing that a settlement of the peaceful Indians

---

[12] Major Gilpin's report from Fort Mann Aug. 1, 1847, in *House Ex. Doc.* 1, 30th Cong., 2nd Sess., 136–40.

was desirable, but asserting that he had no authorization to act. He did not, however, think that Indians should be used in an effort to tranquilize the country, because they could not be trusted.

To Superintendent T. H. Harvey, at St. Louis, a few days later, he wrote of Gilpin's plan of settling the Cheyennes and the Arapahoes as "visionary," since neither he nor Gilpin had any means for accomplishing this project. He also complained that Gilpin had refused to furnish him an escort of ten men for a journey to the South Platte to suppress the liquor trade with the Indians and to capture a refugee who had murdered a man at the Pueblo. Gilpin may have suspected that Fitzpatrick had lodged a complaint against him, since on the following day he wrote a letter in which he said that the agent had refused to cooperate with him.[13]

Soon, however, their ways parted — Gilpin journeying with his troops to the New Mexico settlements to obtain supplies for a spring campaign and Fitzpatrick leaving to visit his wards on the Platte River. But before leaving, Fitzpatrick met some of the Kiowa chiefs who had formerly been allied with the Comanches. They promised to quit marauding and to join the Cheyennes and the Arapahoes on the Arkansas.

On February 27, 1848, with an escort, Fitzpatrick set out from Bent's Fort.[14] In and around the Pueblo he remained for about six weeks, studying the situation. The arrival of a party of traders bound northward gave him the

---

[13] This Fitzpatrick-Gilpin correspondence is in the Indian Office archives in Washington.

[14] The account of his doings is given in his report of June 24, 1848, which is found in the Upper Platte File, Indian Office archives, in Washington.

opportunity to continue his journey. From a band of Arapahoes he learned of large encampments of Sioux on the
South Platte, and on proceeding he found villages at intervals over a stretch of eighty miles. At all of them he was
well received, and by making presents of tobacco and
trinkets he was able to promote friendship. The Sioux
promised not to disturb the emigrants, but the chiefs admitted they had little power over the braves, especially
regarding liquor. To what extent Fitzpatrick was able to
control the liquor trade we do not know, but he mentions
the confiscation from a trader of two kegs of whiskey which
he dumped into the muddy waters of the Platte.

The valley of the South Platte appealed to him as the
most suitable location for his agency headquarters, and he
recommended it in his report (June 24, 1848): "It is also,"
he wrote, "the best agricultural district in the country, as
well as excellent for the raising of stock. The establishment
of an agency house occupied by one or two men alone in
the wilderness is seemingly a wild project, but it may
shortly become a nucleus for the Indians to resort to, and
may be the means of inducing many of them to settle
around the vicinity and in that case be brought and taught
to begin agricultural pursuits."[15]

Evidently he had met all of his Sioux wards, for he did
not go on to Fort Laramie. Instead, he went down the
river. East of the forks he met the emigrant trains making
for Oregon and California. With characteristic pains he
counted the wagons and asked the men their destination.
The wagons numbered 364; the homeseekers bound for
Oregon about 1,700 and those for California about 150.

---

15 *Ibid.*

These figures, which seem never to have been used by historians, more than double the emigration usually estimated for 1848. Other emigrants, whom he did not meet because he left the Oregon Trail, were said to be behind. As for the Mormons, who in still larger numbers journeyed to the Salt Lake Valley that summer, he could give no estimate, since they followed the route on the north bank of the Platte, and he did not contact them.

Fitzpatrick arrived at Westport and from there probably took the steamboat to St. Louis, which he reached before the middle of June. The St. Louis *Reveille* of June 15, 1848, reported his arrival and commented that his opinion upon Indian matters "is worth more than the combined expression of a dozen political theorists."

On June 24 he made his report to Superintendent Harvey. One week earlier his old friend, Robert Campbell, had written to Senator Benton suggesting that Fitzpatrick, inasmuch as he had information that would prove of value to the Government, should be called to the capital to report in person. The letter was endorsed by Benton and forwarded to the Commissioner of Indian Affairs.

Doubltess it resulted in the suggested order, since Fitzpatrick went to Washington. Of his doings in the capital, however, the record is scant. We know only that in Washington on August 11 he submitted a supplemental report to Indian Commissioner Medill. He recommended the immediate establishment of a fort on the Oregon Trail and one on the Santa Fe Trail, each to be garrisoned by 500 mounted troops, with a few howitzers. The commanders, he emphasized, should be men well acquainted with Indian character, habits, and mode of warfare. It was lack of such leaders, he contended, that accounted for the failure of recent Indian campaigns. There was no way to stop the Indians from robbing and killing except by rigorously punishing them. The troops should be continually on the move and ever ready for battle.

He further proposed — and in this matter he was many years ahead of his time — a winter campaign against the Comanches. All the hostiles, no matter what they had done, imagined themselves secure in their winter retreats. The white soldiers, they believed, could not endure the cold and hardships incident to such a campaign; and some of them persisted in this delusion a generation later, after the whites had given many signal instances to the contrary. "The soldiers," tauntingly said the Sioux chief, The Crow, to Major Guido Ilges, in January 1881, "are cowards and afraid to fight. They cry in winter and cannot handle a gun." Fifteen years after Fitzpatrick's recommendation — in January 1863 — Colonel Patrick E. Connor was to march against a band of thieving Bannocks, near present Franklin, Idaho, and in spite of the terrible sufferings of his men, administer a crushing defeat. Custer, in late November 1868, was to destroy Black Kettle's village on the Washita, and Miles and Mackenzie, in the winter of 1876–77, were to teach Lame Deer and Dull Knife that the whites could follow wherever the Indians chose to secrete themselves. But in 1848 this far-sighted recommendation of Fitzpatrick's must have seemed an absurdity.

From Washington Fitzpatrick returned to St. Louis, and there on October 6, 1848, wrote his second annual report.[16]

---

[16] Found in the "Commissioner of Indian Affairs Report of 1848," in *House Ex. Doc.* 1, 30th Cong., 2nd Sess.

He severely criticized the military operations along the Santa Fe Trail, on the ground that the troops acted almost wholly on the defensive. It had been a bad summer on the Trail, for the Comanches and Kiowas had been busy. From his camp in New Mexico Gilpin had fruitlessly ransacked the canyons of the Canadian and had then returned to the Arkansas. He had fought several minor engagements with the hostiles, but they had suffered little harm. To Fitzpatrick it seemed that his campaign had lacked in energy.

He recommended, however, as did Gilpin, more forts and more troops. The pillage, murder, and multilation of the whites could be stopped only by force, and the sooner it was applied the better. With the doctrine that Indian atrocities were due to the white man's provocation he had no patience; and for the sentimentalists who, remote from danger, made maudlin excuses for these atrocities, he had the heartiest contempt. He wanted justice done the Indians, and he was long to be remembered by the Indians with whom he dealt as their truest friend. He was kindhearted; he had adopted and put to school an Indian boy; and he would have adopted another had not the mother resisted his earnest pleas. But he knew, as few other white men knew, the Indian's passionate urges and he believed that these could be held in restraint only by the sternest retribution for acts of violence.

It has always appeared to me [he writes] that great error exists in the public mind, in regard to the relations between the white man and the Indian, inasmuch as whatever atrocities have ever been committed by the Indians are invariably attributed to the rascality and swindling operations of the white man. . . . I am aware that great violations of justice have been committed on both sides; but the Indians of whom I now speak (the wild tribes of the prairie) have always kept far ahead of the white man in the perpetration of rascality; and I believe it is only in order to keep pace and hold his own with the Indian, that the white man is often obliged to resort to many mean practices. With this the poor immigrants have nothing to do; all they want is a free and unmolested passage through to their destination; and, in my opinion they ought to have it, cost what it may (pp. 471–72).

He further recommended the extension of trade among the Indians. Trade, he writes, has been the great civilizer of mankind, and must have its beneficial effect upon the nomad Indians. It ought, however, to be protected from abuses; and he believed that the establishment of a sutler-ship for each tribe, with the sutler under strict control by the Government, would prevent the numerous frauds charged against Indian traders.

About this time Fitzpatrick acquired the courtesy title of major. Perhaps it dates from the beginning of his Indian service, since according to the custom of the time an Indian agent must have, in the public estimation, at least a major's rank. Most of the outstanding mountain men, whether or not they ever became Indian agents, received these honorary titles from the public, and no one disregarded them. "Captains" were as plentiful as huckleberries, and few were the factors or head men at the various trading posts who were not so called; Bridger, Andrew Drips, and others became "majors," Alexander Culbertson, William Bent, Louis Vasquez, and others became "colonels." Broken Hand is hereafter Major Fitzpatrick, and by no one is the title more cheerfully accorded him than by his immediate superior in the Indian service, Superintendent T. H. Harvey. In forwarding Fitzpatrick's report he writes (October 4, 1848):

I cannot too strongly recommend the views advanced by Agent

Fitzpatrick, which have been communicated to you at different times through this office. Major Fitzpatrick's experience and frequent intercourse with the troops on the plains, together with his close observation, directed by a strong, discriminating mind, entitle his opinions upon subjects of this kind to great weight.[17]

---

[17] *Ibid.*, 446.

Chapter 14

Peace Plans for the Frontier

FITZPATRICK LEFT ST. LOUIS early in October 1848, and joining a party of traders at Westport, set out for Bent's Fort. At Big Timbers, that welcome stretch of trees along the Arkansas so generally sought by the Indians for winter quarters, he found a large gathering. The Indians wanted a "big talk," and the Agent obliged them.

It was while he was encamped here that Frémont arrived with thirty-three men and a long pack-train, again westward bound. The adventurous Pathmaker was now on his fourth expedition, this time a private enterprise. He was looking for a transcontinental railroad route, and he expected to find it through the San Juan Mountains, that formidable rampart that was tragically to baffle and defeat him. As he chatted with his former guide on that sunny November day, little did he divine that before two months had passed all of his 120 pack animals and a third of his gallant company would lie dead beneath the powdery, shifting snows of the Colorado Rockies.

Frémont, overjoyed to meet his oldtime companion, learned from Fitzpatrick the story of his labors in this new field. It was, we may believe, with deep satisfaction for the opportunity of paying tribute to a man's worth, that Frémont, on November 17, at Bent's Fort, wrote to Senator Benton:

We found our friend, Major Fitzpatrick, in full exercise of his functions at a point about thirty miles below this, in what is called the Big Timber, and surrounded by about 600 lodges of different nations — Apaches, Camanches, Kioways and Arapahoes. He is a most admirable agent, entirely educated for such a post, and possessing the ability and courage necessary to make his education available. He has succeeded in drawing out from among the Camanches the whole Kioway nation, with the exception of six lodges, and brought over among them a considerable number of lodges of the Apaches and Camanches. When we arrived he was holding a talk with them, making a feast and giving them a few presents. We found them all on their good behavior, and were treated in the most friendly manner; were neither annoyed by them, nor had anything stolen from us. I hope you will be able to give him some support. He will be able to save lives and money for the government, and knowing how difficult this Indian question may become I am particular in bringing Fitzpatrick's operations to your notice. In a few years he might have them all farming here on the Arkansas.[1]

Upon arriving at Bent's Fort on November 7 Fitzpatrick found large bands of Indians in the neighborhood. These he met in council, one tribe at a time, gave them some presents, and counseled peace. Major Benjamin L. Beall, who came up from New Mexico to obtain the release of Mexican prisoners held by the Indians, had meager success. Some of the more recently captured prisoners were eager to return home, and were released, but those who for years had lived among the Indians and who had Indian

---

[1] John Bigelow, *Memoir of the Life and Public Services of John Charles Frémont* (New York, 1856), 359.

wives or husbands, had no wish to return, nor would their captors surrender them.

On January 3, 1849, Fitzpatrick wrote from Bent's Fort a letter to Mrs. Jessie B. Frémont to give latest news about her husband:[2]

Madam: You will learn, from the pen of your husband, of the particulars of his journey, welfare, and progress, up to the time of his arrival at and departure from this place. But I have received intelligence of the Colonel twelve days later. I am sure it will be pleasing to you, even if but one day later than his own letters. The Colonel left this place in fine health and spirits, and ascended the Arkansas to a small settlement called Pueblo, seventy-five miles higher up, at which place he procured a sufficient supply of forage to support his animals in crossing the mountain which lies between the Arkansas river and the Rio del Norte. Two days after his departure from the Pueblo he was followed by two men who wished to join his party; but Col. Fremont being in no want of their services they returned. From these men I learned that they came up with the party ascending the mountain through very deep snow, Col. Fremont being in advance, with a few of his ablest men, breaking a road for the horses and mules to follow. They were then within six miles of the summit of the [Sangre de Cristo] mountain, which, when gained, the most difficult part is accomplished, as the descent would be much more easy and rapid. On crossing the mountain, Col. Fremont will fall immediately on the Rio del Norte, and a considerable distance north of the New Mexico settlements; from which place I believe it is his intention to steer directly for California, leaving the two hitherto traveled routes, one north and the other south of him, and passing midway between the two; and which, if he is able to find a practicable route, will be much more direct and shorter than any hitherto traveled.[3]

For some time Fitzpatrick had been planning a general

[2] This letter was published in the *Daily Missouri Republican* of March 7, 1849, and reprinted in LeRoy R. and Ann W. Hafen, *Frémont's Fourth Expedition* (Glendale, Calif., 1960), 286–87.

[3] This description of Frémont's intended route indicates that he planned to take a course up the Rio Grande and between the better known routes by way of Cochetopa Pass, to the north, and via Abiquiu and the Old Spanish Trail, to the south. This has definite bearing on the controversy as to the responsibility of Frémont and of Old Bill Williams for their subsequent disaster.

and all-inclusive treaty with the more or less friendly tribes of the plains. He wanted to provide against capricious outbreaks by obtaining the pledged word of the Indians that they would keep the peace; and he wanted the Government to make some compensation to the Indians for the rapidly diminishing supply of game. He would have the Indians gather in a general assembly, there to be met by agents of the Great Father, who would talk with them about their problems and over the solemn ceremony of the peace pipe reach with them a binding agreement. Before making his first endeavors, however, he must have authority from Washington, and this he determined to get on his next trip to the East.

After spending the winter with his wards, Broken Hand set out for St. Louis on March 11, 1849, accompanying William Bent and his trading party. The whole Indian trade on the two Plattes and the Arkansas, as he reported, was now confined principally to the one commodity of buffalo robes, and this year the trade had been unusually good. Two firms, with goods costing about $15,000 in St. Louis, had bartered in some 13,000 robes, which would sell for an average of $3 each and thus bring in a tidy profit.[4]

At the Big Bend of the Arkansas, he met a caravan for Santa Fe, in charge of Solomon Sublette. Fitzpatrick was evidently full of his project regarding the treaty, for he talked of it at some length to his friend. Sublette, however, was skeptical; the treaty "would not be worth the least consideration," he wrote to his wife. "As soon as they [the

---

[4] Fitzpatrick's report of May 22, 1849, written upon his return to St. Louis. A copy of this report was kindly supplied to me in October 1971, by my good friend Janet Lecompte of Colorado Springs, Colorado.

Indians] get the presents they would commence war."[5]

How sanguine Fitzpatrick was over the matter may be judged from the fact that he told Sublette that he expected to be back at Fort Mann in about six weeks and meet the Indians, with an official authorization for making the treaty. He was to learn that official matters do not move with such celerity nor always with a consideration for the greatest good to the greatest number.

He reached Westport on May 1 and soon thereafter arrived at St. Louis.[6] He found that Harvey was no longer at the head of the Central Superintendency, and that the former superintendent, Colonel David H. Mitchell, after a gallant service in the Mexican War, had returned and was back in his old place. Mitchell, though evidently friendly enough to the plan, declared that he had no power to act; but on August 1 he told Fitzpatrick to go to Washington and urge his plan in person. Accordingly, Fitzpatrick went, and on August 16 received instructions and promise of a preliminary $5,000 for the purchase of presents and with instructions to arrange for a great council during the summer of 1850.

Meantime, in the early summer of 1849, the keenly expectant red men and their families began to assemble around Fort Mann. Several thousand of them were there when James S. Calhoun, newly appointed Indian Agent for New Mexico, passed the place, about the middle of June. Arapahoes, Cheyennes, Kiowas, Comanches, Utes, and others had arrived, and their expectations "were so extravagant as to cause emigrants and others to have fearful appre-

---

[5] This letter is in the Sublette Collection, Mo. Hist. Soc.
[6] *St. Louis Reveille,* May 7, 1849.

hensions on account of those, who were expected to be on the plains after July 15, the day named by the Indians for the return of Mr. Fitzpatrick.[7] Those who had faith in the good Broken Hand were subjected to a severe strain. He had said that he would be there, but week after week passed and he had not come. They did not know that with fiery zeal and untiring industry he was doing what he could in their behalf. But as the days passed with no word of him they peacefully dispersed. In spite of Agent Calhoun's dismal apprehensions there were no reprisals.

With the $5,000 appropriated by Congress, Fitzpatrick purchased presents for the Indians, and in the early fall of 1849 had them freighted by wagons from Westport to Bent's Fort at six cents per pound. Here he distributed presents to the Indians. Regarding the great council and the treaty he could give them no greater assurance than that the matter was being carefully considered by the Great Father and his council of sachems.[8]

So weighty a matter as that of making treaties with these "domestic dependent nations" had to go before Congress. Both the Commissioner of Indian Affairs and the Secretary of the Interior recommended, in their annual reports for 1849, the making of a treaty. On March 18, 1850, Senator Atchison of Missouri was to introduce a bill authorizing the expenditure of $200,000 for the purpose. It would pass the Senate on April 29, 1850, but fail in the House,[9] and for the time, the project would rest.

Fitzpatrick makes no mention of that important episode,

---

[7] Annie H. Abel, *The Official Correspondence of James S. Calhoun* (Wash., D.C., 1915), 18.

[8] The general story is told in Fitzpatrick's Annual Report of Sept. 4, 1850.

[9] *Congressional Globe,* March–July 1850, pp. 547, 844, and 1482.

the abandonment and destruction of Bent's Fort. It is certain, however, that at the time of the distribution of presents to the Indians in the fall of 1849 the fort had been deserted and partially wrecked. William Bent had for some time, so the story runs, contemplated abandoning the old fort. It had come to be associated with many painful memories — the death of his young brother Robert, killed by Comanches in 1841; of another brother, George, a victim of consumption in 1847; of his brother and partner, Charles, killed in the Taos uprising in 1847, and of his first wife, Owl Woman, who passed away within its walls. He had in mind the erection of a new fort, thirty miles down the river, at a better location, the Big Timbers. This year 1849 was the year in which the Government bought Fort Laramie and established a post near Fort Hall. A quartermaster's agent, so the story continues, came to Bent with an offer of purchase. Negotiations followed, but the price finally offered was so low that Bent, in indignation, removed his stores and blew up the structure in August 1849.[10]

Fitzpatrick was now fifty years old. So far as we know he had thus far been impervious to the charms of women, white or red. Back in the trapping days most of his companions — some of them with white wives at home — had had Indian wives in the wilderness. "For however it may

---

[10] The *Missouri Republican* of Oct. 2, 1849, carries correspondence from Independence of Sept. 27 which tells of the abandonment of the fort. Messrs. Palady and Riley brought in the word. They visited the dismantled fort on Aug. 22, when the rubbish was still smoking. J. S. Calhoun, Indian Agent in New Mexico, reported in his letter of Oct. 5, 1849 (*House Ex. Doc.* 17, 31st Cong., 1st Sess., 213): "One of the owners of Bent's Fort has removed all property from it and caused the fort to be burnt." No annual report from Fitzpatrick in the fall of 1849 has been found, and his annual report of 1850, dated at St. Louis, Sept. 24, makes no mention of the occurrence. For the general story see David Lavender, *Bent's Fort* (Garden City, New York, 1954), 301–16.

be considered as a reproach on his character," wrote the good Montford Stokes, agent of the Western Cherokees, in explaining the tangled affairs of the recently deceased Colonel August Pierre Chouteau, "almost all traders who continue long in an Indian country have Indian wives." Fitzpatrick had been a seeming exception; there is no word to indicate that at any time he followed the custom of the time and the region. Nor is there any word to indicate an attachment to one of the daughters of his own race.

But about this time — very likely in November 1849 — he took a wife. The marriage was formal, as we learn from his will, written two years later, wherein the woman is designated as his lawful wife and the devisee of a part of his property. She was Margaret, the daughter of John Poisal and Snake Woman, the sister of Chief Left Hand.[11] Poisal was a French-Canadian trapper who had probably accompanied the Bents when they journeyed into Colorado and began the building of their fort. As early, perhaps, as 1830 he had become a trader among the Arapahoes, had married and made his home with them. We do not know when Margaret was born, but she may at this time have been sixteen or seventeen years old. Probably she had received some schooling, back in Independence or in St. Louis, since it was not unusual for white men who took seriously their marriage with Indian women to educate their half-breed children; and we know that, sixteen years later, at one of the treaty councils, she served as Government interpreter. It is a poor and fragmentary record we have of her, and Fitzpatrick gives us little help. A reticent man, except when

---

[11] Dawson Scrapbooks, State Historical Society of Colorado, IV, 141; and *Colorado Magazine*, XII, 125.

FITZPATRICK'S WIFE AND CHILDREN

From left to right: Margaret Poisal Fitzpatrick, Andrew Jackson Fitzpatrick,
Virginia Thomasine Fitzpatrick
— Courtesy of Henry Meagher

he was writing to the Government what he thought should be done about this thing or that, he tells us nothing with which to fill out the story.

In mid-November 1849, with a team, wagon, and driver, Fitzpatrick started from the vicinity of Bent's Fort for the South Platte. It seems certain that his young wife accompanied him. Diverging from the beaten path, he met scattered bands of Cheyennes and Arapahoes, and then went on to Fort Laramie, which he reached on Christmas Eve. Among the many Indians gathered there he made a careful distribution of presents.

In the middle of February 1850, he again set out for the Arkansas. Passing the site of Bent's Fort, he arrived at the Big Timbers; but to the Indians assembled there he could say only that the Great Father had not yet spoken definitely on the matter of the great council.

While at Big Timbers Fitzpatrick was visited by William Quesenbury and a party of westbound emigrants. Quesenbury records in his diary of May 29, 1850, that the Major gave him much information about the country and advice about traveling.[12] On June 8, 1850, Quesenbury visited the Greenhorn settlement on Greenhorn Creek (a branch of the Arkansas) and gives a good description of the village. He writes: "We rode up to a man setting by a ditch. He said his name was Poisel [Fitzpatrick's father-in-law]. We had letters to him and others [probably from Fitzpatrick to his wife]. At his invitation we put up at his house. Staked our horse on the hill. Slept out of the house, by the front wall. Kinney couldn't be obtained for a guide.

---

[12] I went through Quesenbury's diary of 1845–61 at Duke University in February 1957.

Took supper with him. Maj. Fitzpatrick's wife or squaw looks sleepy and doesn't begin to come up to previous descriptions."

Fitzpatrick waited a month at Big Timbers, noting the Indians' "great interest and anxiety in regard to the contemplated treaty," and hoping for news. None came, and he went on to the trail crossing of the Arkansas, where again he waited. Here he found an assembly of Sioux, Cheyennes, Arapahoes, Kiowas, and Plains Apaches, all of whom he had invited to meet him. The Comanches sent word that they would not come; they had had an attack of cholera from too close contact with the whites, and their medicine man had told them they would have another if they risked contact again. They might further have told him, which they did not, that the comparative freedom of the Trail from outrages during the summer of 1849 was due to this epidemic and the Indian fears of coming within its range. Fitzpatrick, disappointed and angry at getting no word from the Government, set out from the Crossing on June 10 and arrived at St. Louis June 26, 1850.[13] In September he prepared his annual report of 1850, in which he said of the treaty project:

I regret exceedingly that the whole arrangement has not been completed the past summer, as I am confident that the Indians of that country will never be found in better training, or their disposition more pliable, or better suited to enter into amicable arrangements with the Government, than they are at the present time. And I can with confidence and perfect knowledge further state that delays and putting off matters of this kind with the Indians is a thing they can hardly brook, as they will invariably attribute such delays to a course of tampering and temporizing, in order to gain time for the purpose of maturing some plan or occasion for their

---

13 *St. Louis Republican,* June 27, 1850.

disadvantage or injury. Indians are exceedingly jealous and selfish, as well as full of deception; yet, strange to say, there is nothing they abhor more than to find such characterization in a white man.[14]

He also expressed regret over the failure of the plan to take some of the chiefs of the various tribes to Washington. The Indians, he said, "have not the slightest idea whatever of the strength and power of the United States, and all overtures made or favors extended them, even in the most liberal sense, will be construed as a sign of our weakness and inability (other than bribery) to protect our citizens traveling through the country." Could some of the influential ones be taken through the populous centers of the capital, they would get an impression of the numbers and resources of the whites that would persuade them to make treaties and to keep them. On the other hand, he asks that the Government do its duty in the matter of compensating the Indians for what they have lost. "The immense emigration traveling through that country [the region traversed by the Oregon Trail] for the past two years has desolated and impoverished it to an enormous extent." Yet the Indians there had been peaceful. "Under these circumstances," he concludes in his Report of 1850, "would it not be just, as well as economical policy, for the Government at this time to show some little liberality, if not justice, to their passive submission?"

On October 8, 1850, was born his first child, a son, whom he named Andrew Jackson.[15]

---

[14] In the *Annual Report of the Commissioner of Indian Affairs, 1850* (Wash., 1850), 52.

[15] The date of birth of the son is given in the baptismal records of Father De Smet, found at St. Louis. This datum was kindly furnished by Father G. J. Garraghan of St. Louis University, in his letter to me of July 16, 1929.

At some time during the winter of 1850–51 Thomas Fitz-patrick was removed from office. No record of his dismissal has been found, and the reasons for it are unknown. It may be that some one with a political "pull" wanted the office, or that Fitzpatrick's language in some of his reports was considered too aggressive for a subordinate. However that may be, he refused to be discharged. It was not much of an office in a pecuniary way; it paid but $1,500. But Fitz-patrick liked the work and believed that he was doing something worthwhile. Taking his case before the Missouri delegation in Congress, he scored a speedy victory. Repre-sentative Willard P. Hall, in speaking of the matter before the House on February 20, 1851,[16] said that the reappoint-ment had already been made. Perhaps so, but a notation in the Indian Office gives the date as March 12, and the representative may at the time have had only the promise of a reinstatement.

Victory came to him also in his cherished plan of bring-ing peace to the frontier by a treaty. The Deficiency Appro-priations Act, approved on February 27, included an item of $100,000 "For expenses of holding treaties with wild tribes of the prairie, and for bringing delegates on to the seat of Government."[17] Superintendent Mitchell and Agent Fitzpatrick were at once appointed Commissioners to treat with the Indians. They chose September 1 as the date and Fort Laramie as the place, and to Fitzpatrick was assigned the task of spreading the information to his Indian wards.

---

[16] Representative Hall said in part: "One of the most intelligent and efficient men in the United States, Mr. Fitzpatrick, is now stationed upon the frontiers. . . . I believe we cannot get any better gentleman this side of the Rocky Moun-tains than Mr. Fitzpatrick to fill the office to which he is assigned, as events have justified."

[17] U.S. Statutes at Large, IX, 572.

Purchasing some goods for presents, he left St. Louis by boat on April 22, 1851. From Kansas Landing he set out over the Santa Fe Trail, and in due time came to the Big Bend. No rain had fallen for weeks, and the bed of the Arkansas was dry except for two stagnant pools. For sixty miles the party ascended the river without finding water except at a considerable distance under ground.

On June 1 they reached the vicinity of Fort Mann. The fort was in ruins, but a mile distant another post had been started. It was to be called by various names during its first year, but after that it was to be known by the name of its historic predecessor on the middle Missouri, Fort Atkinson. It was an "insignificant station," as Fitzpatrick described it, "beneath the dignity of the United States, and at the mercy and forbearance of the Indians."

Small squads of red men, with their families, were scattered about the neighborhood. Fitzpatrick told them of the forthcoming council; sent out runners, and within two weeks both sides of the river were thronged with the tepees of Cheyennes, Arapahoes, Kiowas, Apaches, and Comanches. A feast of bread, pork, and coffee was served, some presents were distributed, and an explanation was made of the purposes intended at the council. The Cheyennes and the Arapahoes readily agreed to go, but the Comanches, Kiowas, and Apaches refused outright. "They had too many horses and mules," they said, "to risk on such a journey and among such notorious horse-thieves as the Sioux and the Crows."

Before the departure of the Indians, Colonel E. V. Sumner, with his command, bound for New Mexico, came up and camped a mile or so above the fort. During the two days he remained there the Indians were permitted free intercourse in and about the camp. Fitzpatrick had strong views on the matter and did not hesitate to express them:

Such free and unrestrained intercourse, carried on between officers, privates, squaws and Indians, not braves nor chiefs, but as the Indians themselves would term them, "dogs," was certainly a new thing to me, and what I have rarely seen allowed even by the traders. . . . I have frequently witnessed a want of self-respect exhibited by men in high positions on such occasions, thereby inviting the disrespectful and rude treatment of the untutored Indian; and I regret that the idea prevails, to a more or less extent, among many persons, that, to receive the respect and attention of Indians, one must cast off all the restraint of civilized society, and assume conduct and manners entirely the reverse; such, however, is a great error, and I do, without hesitation, assert, that there is no course more proper for a white man to pursue among Indians than an upright, virtuous, and moral one, both in conversation and conduct; and, moreover, that the very rules of decorum which govern a gentlemen in civilized society, are both suitable and applicable in his intercourse with the Indian race.[18]

The wisdom of his counsel was soon exemplified. A Cheyenne brave, presuming too far on the freedom of intercourse allowed, committed some act for which an officer ordered him punished. The penalty was flogging, an act regarded by all Indians as deeply humiliating. There was an uproar from the seething throng, and only by the tactful intervention of Fitzpatrick and the prompt military precautions taken by Sumner was a bloody conflict averted.

Fitzpatrick now set out for Fort Laramie and in crossing the South Platte made contact with some soldiers. Percival G. Lowe, a corporal in the First Dragoons, and the author, many years later, of an interesting book, *Five Years a Dragoon*, tells of meeting Fitzpatrick at the ford and of

---

[18] *Annual Report of the Commissioner of Indian Affairs, 1851* (Wash., 1851), 72.

his aid in enabling a party to cross safely. Lowe's memory as to details is sometimes at fault, but the story is probably founded on fact. The river was swollen from the melting snows in the mountains, and its bed, as was well known to the traders and trappers, was of quicksand. Lowe writes:

Now [said Major Fitzpatrick] if we should hitch up and start to cross with a load without beating down the quicksand, thereby making a firm roadbed, we would get mired in the sand; one side would settle and upset the wagon, or the whole wagon sink; in short, 'twould be impracticable to cross in that way. Now the way to pack the sand and make a firm roadbed is to travel over it with a lot of animals until it is well beaten down, and then cross your wagons; the more travel over it the better the road gets. Now in the morning we will have a lot of men mounted and drive all of our cattle over and back, keeping them as near together as possible, and then we will cross as fast as we can, giving the roadbed no rest, and a good way for you to do with your little outfit will be for you to follow us when we drive the cattle back.[19]

Lowe's "little outfit" followed this sage counsel and crossed without trouble. Lowe was then with a small escort accompanying the army paymaster on his way to Fort Laramie. He was to go all the way there, return to Fort Leavenworth and then again return to Laramie, this time as one of the escort under Major Robert H. Chilton that took Superintendent Mitchell and his party to the Great Council. It is well for us that he did so, for we have from his pen a recital of the most dramatic episode of that highly dramatic gathering (see following chapter).

Fitzpatrick arrived at Fort Laramie on July 25. Many Indians were about, but he wanted more, and so he had runners sent out to spread the tidings of the great assembly. From St. Louis Superintendent Mitchell had set out with

---

[19] P. G. Lowe, *Five Years a Dragoon* (Kansas City, 1906), 55. Lowe erroneously speaks of Fitzpatrick as one of the party of traders at the crossing.

an imposing party, which included Colonel Samuel Cooper, adjutant general of the army and later to be adjutant general of the Confederate forces; Colonel A. B. Chambers, editor of the *Missouri Republican*, who was to act as secretary of the council; Robert Campbell; and B. Gratz Brown, a young lawyer who was to report the proceedings for the *Republican*, as well as to serve in the capacity of assistant secretary, and who was later to be Governor of Missouri and vice-presidential candidate on the ticket with Horace Greeley. Father De Smet, with the Indian agent, Colonel Alexander Culbertson, was on the way.

And so, with the red clans gathering, and the paleface dignitaries daily nearing the scene, Fitzpatrick eagerly waited for the great event that was to fulfill or to shatter his long-cherished hopes.

Chapter 15

The Great Indian Council

INDIANS BEGAN TO GATHER about Fort Laramie as early
as July, and when all had arrived they formed a mighty
host. Lowe, of the Dragoons, writing from memory fifty-
four years after the event, gives for the number present the
impossible figure of 60,000. Probably it was not more than
10,000; but even so it was a native horde such as no white
man had ever seen before. The earliest to reach the scene
were the plains tribes — the Cheyennes, the Arapahoes, and
bands of Oglala and Brulé Sioux. Friendly with one another, they mingled freely. The real test would come when
the mountain tribes appeared, particularly the Shoshones
(or Snakes) and the Crows. Would it be possible, men
asked, for the small force of 195 soldiers to keep the peace?
Fitzpatrick, Bridger (who was to interpret for the Snakes),
Poisal, and Smith, already on the ground, had faith that
all would be well.

The Mitchell party, with seventy-five more Dragoons,

arrived on September 1, but it brought no wagon train of provisions and presents — a failure that endangered the success of the project. "Without these," writes Reporter Brown, "no man living — not even the President of the United States — would have any influence with them [the Indians], nor keep them together a day. . . . Provisions are the great and most important item. I have yet to see the first Indian, whether chief or notorious brave, that is not hungry and wanting something to eat."[1] Mitchell could only report to Fitzpatrick that at Kansas Landing, where he expected to learn that the train was already six or seven days out, he had found that some of the wagons were not even loaded. Neither cursing nor entreaty could make up for lost time. He could only urge the utmost haste and then proceed on his journey, hopeful that the train would appear before the end of the council. To the chiefs the delay was explained, and though they showed their keen disappointment, they decided to stand fast. They knew Broken Hand, and they had faith in his promise.

Word came that the Snakes, led by their beloved head-chief, Washakie, devoted friend of the whites, were near at hand, and a feeling of wild excitement spread throughout the Indian mass. Nor were the whites at ease; for the Snakes were age-long enemies of the people of the plains, and the slightest act of violence might precipitate a bloody conflict and bring the council to a tragic end. With great misgivings the Snakes must have made their journey from

---

[1] An excellent description of the treaty council was written by Mr. Brown and was published in the *Missouri Republican* in October and November 1851. This account is the chief source for the story in this chapter. Dr. Grace R. Hebard, of the University of Wyoming, years ago, kindly lent us her copy of the correspondence.

the Valley of the Green, since they had hardly set forth when a band of Cheyennes, in violation of the truce, attacked them; and though the attackers were driven off, two of the Snakes were killed and scalped. The party was now approaching the fort, and all eyes were alert and all nerves at highest tension for what might happen.

> About noon one bright day [writes Lowe], a long line of dust was seen from our camp, looking west towards Laramie Peak. Soon a long line of Indians came moving slowly down in battle array, arms ready for use and every man apparently expectant, the women and children and baggage bringing up the rear, well guarded. It turned out that Major Bridger, the interpreter, had reported to headquarters the approach of the Snakes, and he had been directed to lead them down near to our camp. All the head men of the Sioux and Cheyennes had given assurance that they should not be molested, so down they came, moving very slowly and cautiously, the chief alone a short distance in advance. They were dressed in their best, riding fine war horses, and made a grandly savage appearance. In the absence of Major Chilton down at the post, seeing all this caution on the part of the Snakes, Lieutenant Hastings had "boots and saddles." sounded so as to be ready whatever happened.[2]

The little force of Dragoons was camped far to the west of the fort, in the direct line of the Snakes' approach; and upon this body would rest the duty of dealing with any outbreak that might occur.

> Just below us [continues Lowe] was a large Sioux camp, and the people were showing great interest and some excitement at the approach of their hereditary enemies, and a few squaws howled in anguish for lost friends who had died in battle with these same cautiously moving warriors. When the Snakes reached the brow of the hill overlooking the beautiful Laramie, less than a mile away, and the chief commenced the descent, a Sioux sprang upon his horse, bow and arrows in hand, and rushed towards him. A Frenchman, an interpreter, had been watching this Sioux, expecting trouble, and he, too, mounted his horse and was instantly in pursuit. The

---

[2] P. G. Lowe, *Five Years a Dragoon* (Kansas City, 1906), 79–80.

Snake column stopped and sent up a wild shout of defiance, the chief moved a few steps farther and raised his gun ready to fire just as the intrepid Frenchman reached the reckless Sioux, pulled him from his horse, disarmed and stood over him.

Then ensued a harangue between interpreters and chiefs. The wild Sioux, who had sought to revenge himself on the Snake chief who had killed his father some time before, was led back to camp while the Snakes held their ground. Their position was a good one; every man had a good gun, plenty of ammunition, besides bows and arrows. Not one out of a hundred Sioux had guns, and the Snakes, though not one to five [actually not one to ten] of the Sioux, would have defended themselves successfully, and the battle would have been the most bloody ever known amongst the wild tribes.

From that tensely dramatic moment Lowe and his comrade Dragoons were partisans of the Snakes against all other tribes whatever.

The attitude of the Snakes [he continues], the cool, deliberate action of the chief, the staunch firmness of his warriors and the quiet demeanor of women and children, who were perfectly self-possessed — not a single outcry from that vast parade save the one cry of defiance that went up spontaneously as the chief raised his gun to take aim at the Sioux. The scene was impressive, as showing the faith that band of warriors had in each other; the entire confidence of their families in them; the self-reliance all through. It was a lesson for soldiers who might never again see such a grand display of soldierly manhood, and the lesson was not lost. Every Dragoon felt an interest in that tribe.

Bridger, exultant over the dauntless bearing of his friendly wards, afterward said to Lowe:

"Well, you seen that fool Sioux make the run, didn't you?"

"Yes, sir" [Lowe replied].

"Well, ———," referring to the brave interpreter, whom he knew well, "saved that fellow from hell; my chief would 'er killed him quick, and then the fool Sioux would 'er got their backs up, and there wouldn't have been room to camp 'round here for dead Sioux. You Dragoons acted nice, but you wouldn't have had no show if the fight had commenced — no making peace then. And I tell you another thing: the Sioux ain't goin' to try it again. They see how the

Snakes are armed. I got them guns for 'um, and they are good ones. It'll be a proud day for the Snakes if any of these prairie tribes pitch into 'um, and they are not a bit afraid. Uncle Sam told 'um to come down here and they'd be safe, but they ain't takin' his word for it altogether. They'll never be caught napping."[3]

The Shoshones pitched their tepees near the tents of the Dragoons, and an air of peace settled over the vast encampment. Some preliminary meetings were held by the Commissioners with the various chiefs. But the thousands of horses had close-cropped the grass for miles around the fort, and a new location must be found. At the mouth of Horse Creek, thirty-six miles down the Platte, were good forage and plenty of camping room, and there it was agreed that the great council should be held.

The large emigration of the year had long passed by, and the Trail was clear. But the removal would be no easy task. Not only must camp equipment and two or three weeks' provisions for the whites be transported, but also presents for the Indians. There must be tobacco, coffee and sugar, blankets, knives, beads, and trinkets. The wagon train was still lumbering along from the east, and so whatever could be spared from the stores at the post must be requisitioned. The main food supply of the Indians would make the journey on four feet. Some of the more provident of the savages had had the good sense to bring along stores of dried buffalo meat; but most of them had great numbers of dogs, and all of them (except the Snakes) held dogmeat in the highest favor.

With everything in readiness, on September 4 the migration began. Mounted troops led the way, and then (strange

---

[3] *Ibid.*, 82.

sight for a place 600 miles from the settlements) came carriages, in which were seated the paleface dignitaries. Behind were the creaking, laden wagons, and all about were Indian villages in motion. Sedately the elders rode in rank; hundred of young braves and boys galloping here and there, displaying their horsemanship and working off their surplus energy; women and girls with pack horses, other horses drawing large travois laden with camp equipage and small children, and dogs with smaller travois, lightly packed — all swept forward in a surging mass, enveloped in clouds of choking dust.

At 3 o'clock in the afternoon of September 5 the council ground was reached. The Platte, with its two affluents — Horse Creek on the south side and Spring Creek, three miles upstream on the north — afforded a broad area of bottom lands with good grazing. Superintendent Mitchell set up his headquarters tent in the triangle formed by Horse Creek and the river, while Fitzpatrick (with his wife and infant son) pitched his tent farther up the creek among the white traders and interpreters — Poisal, Smith, and others — with their half-breed families. All of the south bank of the river below Horse Creek was reserved for troops, wagons, parade and treaty grounds, the Snake Indians, and such other visiting tribes as should attend. To the Sioux, the Cheyennes, and the Arapahoes was given the north side of the river, with any unoccupied ground on the south side to the west of the creek. Lines of sentinels were maintained, and no one was permitted to pass them without permission.

The council would not formally open until Monday, September 8, and in the meantime the Indians would busy themselves with visiting, feasting, and dancing. A large part of one day was taken up by them in elaborate ceremonial calls on the Commissioners.

On Saturday [writes Brown] a large band of the Sioux chiefs, braves and men, nearly a thousand in number, well mounted, came down the Platte. They marched in solid column, about four abreast, shouting and singing. As they passed over the hill into the plain they presented an imposing and interesting sight. In the center rode their principal chiefs, who carried an old American flag, which they say was given them by General Clark, in the early days of his superintendency. They marched into camp. The chiefs and braves dismounted, and formed a circle. Colonel Mitchell gave them some tobacco and vermillion and informed them that he would expect them to meet him in council on Monday morning, at the firing of the cannon. Later in the day several hundred Cheyennes, also mounted, rode over the hill, in manner similar to the Sioux, came into camp and were treated with the same presents.

The seventh would be Sunday — as the Indians were diplomatically informed — "a big medicine day" with the whites, who would much prefer to be left to themselves. The intimation was duly honored. The Indian women, displaying a wonderful dexterity in their work, with their lodge skins and poles erected in the center of the encampment a kind of amphitheatre, with an arbor for the Commissioners, their staff, and their white friends. The warriors and chiefs spent the day in visiting one another. In the afternoon the Oglala Sioux were hosts to the Snakes, the Arapahoes, and the Cheyennes at a great feast, which was followed by dancing. Feasts and dances were given in most of the other villages and the drumming of tomtoms and the chanting of the revellers continued throughout the night. The din disturbed the slumbers of the whites, but buoyed them up with a great hope, for the revelry portended good will and a highly successful council.

Monday came, and at break of day the whole encampment was astir with eager preparation. At the center a flagstaff, made of three lodgepoles lashed end to end, had been set up, and from its peak the Stars and Stripes were unfurled. At 9 o'clock the cannon thundered the signal for assembling, and all the Indian nations started toward the circle.

When the whole body commenced moving to the common center [writes Brown] a sight was presented of most thrilling interest. Each nation approached with its own peculiar song or demonstration and such a combination of rude, wild and fantastic manners and dresses never was witnessed. It is not probable that an opporunity will again be presented of seeing so many tribes assembled together displaying all the peculiarities of features, dress, equipments and horses and everything else, exhibiting their wild notions of elegance and propriety.

They came out this morning not armed nor painted for war, but decked out in all their best regalia, pomp, paint and display of peace. The chiefs and braves were dressed with punctilious attention to imposing effect. The "bucks" (young men) were out on horse or afoot, in all the foppery and display of prairie dandies. In their efforts to be elegant, fashionable and exquisite, it must be confessed that the Prairie Dandy, after his manner, displays quite as much sense and taste as his city prototype, with this advantage. The Indian does not conceal his features with a superabundance of hair. [Brown, it should be noted, wrote in a day of beards, sideburns and mustachios.] In their bearings and efforts to show pride of dress and tinsel they are on a par.

Matrons, maids, and little children were also togged in their finest, the richness and taste of their garments giving evidence of the station or wealth of their husbands and fathers. A general sense of decorum prevailed, and exemplary beyond words was the conduct of the children. No paleface youngsters endeavoring on the last days before Christmas to merit the attention of Santa Claus could have shown such perfect behavior. Though the belles, with primitive coquetry, "flaunted, tittered, talked and made efforts to show off" before the young men, they subsided as the assembly was called to order, when "everything was as quiet as in a church."

The council ground was a circle, along two-thirds of which had been set up open lodges, skin-covered, while the remaining third was left open. In the arbor at the center was seated Colonel Mitchell and Major Fitzpatrick, Reporter Brown (who also acted as assistant secretary of the council), the military officers, the interpreters, and the white visitors. As the crowd gathered, announcement was made that only the head men of the various nations were expected to take seats within the circle. The other braves took places at the rear, as a rule behind their chiefs, and still farther back were placed the women and children. The north and west of the open space was assigned to the Sioux, with the Cheyennes next, and the other tribes ranging around to the farther end of the circle. Representatives of seven tribes were present and others were still on the way.

The Superintendent opened the meeting with a message of good will, interpreters one after one translating his words as he spoke. He was there on important business, and he wanted everything done in good faith. As evidence of sincerity, he continued, they would smoke the pipe of peace, but only those whose hearts were free from deceit should touch the pipe. A large calumet, of red pipestone, with a three-foot stem, and ornamented with bright-colored beads and hair, was brought forth. The proper mixture of tobacco and kinnikinnick (the inner bark of the red willow) was put in the bowl. The interpreter for the Sioux then lighted the pipe and handed it to Colonel Mitchell, who took a few puffs and passed it to Major Fitzpatrick, by whom it was passed on to the Sioux chiefs and by them to the chiefs next in the circle. Ceremonial modes varied with the individual. The commonest form was that of extending the pipe to each of the four points of the compass, then up toward the Great Spirit and down to the Bad. Most of the Indians added, for this occasion, a significant gesture — that of drawing the right hand slowly along the stem from the bowl to the throat — a symbolic act that pledged the utmost degree of sincerity and truthfulness. The whole proceeding took up a great deal of time, but the whites were patient, for its deep solemnity was reassuring.

Superintendent Mitchell then again addressed the council. He and his "white-haired brother," Broken Hand, had been sent by the Great Father at Washington to make peace with the assembled tribes. It was true that the buffalo were becoming scarce and that the emigrants' horses and cattle were eating up the grass.. For these injuries the Great Father expected to make compensation. The white men wanted unmolested passage over the roads leading to the West; they wanted the right to build military posts for their protection. The limits of the territory of each tribe should be defined, and a lasting peace established. The Great Father wanted each nation to choose a chief who would have control over his people and be responsible for their conduct. If the nations would agree to these terms he would give them an annuity of $50,000 in goods for fifty years. He was eager for a visit from representatives of each of the nations, and he wanted chiefs chosen to accompany Broken Hand to the Great Father's capital city. He regretted that the train of ox-wagons with supplies had been so greatly delayed; but it was on its way and ought soon to arrive.

Fitzpatrick then spoke briefly:

Colonel Mitchell has told you what the Government wants. Now I advise you to go and talk the matter over among yourselves — mingle with each other — be friendly now and hereafter. See that you understand the subject properly and that there be no hostilities between you.

Several of the chiefs followed with brief addresses in which they expressed their pleasure at the manifestation of peace and friendliness. The council then adjourned until Wednesday, and the interrupted run of feasts and dances was resumed.

On Tuesday the tribes held councils of their own to consider the proposals of the Commissioners. In the afternoon a band of about one hundred mounted Cheyenne warriors gave an exhibition of military maneuvers. They were painted, dressed in war costume, and were armed with guns, lances, or bows and arrows. The mane and tail of each mount were colored and its sides painted with symbols of the owner's *coups* — his record of enemies slain, of scalps taken, and of horses stolen. In the maneuvers the braves would fire their guns, shoot their arrows, give a yell and charge, while women and children at a distance kept up a succession of songs and wailings. At times the twisting, turning, and mingling of the horsemen appeared likely to trample the spectators, yet not an accident occurred, and the white onlookers were amazed at the precision of the drill. The maneuvers over, songs and dances followed, and then came a ceremonial counting of *coups*. The braves formed in a semicircle, whereupon one after one took the center and dramatically recounted all the outstanding feats of his career, while the tomtoms emphasized each feat with a resounding whack.

At 9 o'clock on September 10 the booming of the cannon and the raising of the flag announced the opening of the second session. And then came another exciting moment, for a delegation of Crows, enemies to all the assembled tribes, was seen approaching. Conducted by their interpreter, Robert Meldrum, and escorted by a party that had gone out to meet them, the Crows marched down the plain in a solid column, the two principal chiefs each carrying a highly ornamented pipe, and all singing their national songs. Though among bitter foes, they seemed not the least disturbed; and the vast throng, forgetful for the time of the blood-feud, gave them welcome. Reporter Brown was greatly impressed. "The finest delegation of Indians we have yet seen," he writes, for they "made a most splendid appearance." They had beautiful mounts, they rode better, held their seats more gracefully and dressed more lavishly, yet with finer taste, than any of the others. None of the tribe, he wrote, "had ever before been so far east of their own grounds." This of the Crows, those tireless wanderers who ranged as far east as the Mandans, as far south as the Canadian River, through a great part of the West, and as far north as their implacable enemies, the Blackfeet, would let them! Good reporter that he was, the Indian country was new to him, and some things he missed. He might also have expressed less wonder at the beauty of the mounts ridden by the Crows had he known that these freebooters were the most expert appropriators of other people's horseflesh in all the West, and that they thus had the best from which to make selection.

Colonel Mitchell met and formally greeted them. The chiefs dismounted and made short speeches in response. The calumet was passed around, a camp ground near the Colonel's was given them, and places within the council ring were assigned to the chiefs and head men. After they were seated another ceremonial smoke followed, this time with the chiefs of the other tribes, and they were at last ready to participate in the council.

This was the day for responses to the Commissioners' proposals. Many chiefs spoke, and their expressions were in the main favorable. They rejoiced, they said, at the prospect of an all-inclusive peace, and they wanted to obey the word of the Great Father. Nevertheless a note of misgiving for the future ran through all the talks. The chiefs lamented the poverty of their people and the passing of the buffalo; about this thing of farming, which the white man was always suggesting to them, they protested that they knew nothing, and they wondered how they should support themselves in the days to come. Finally, they hoped that the provisions and presents — a subject that seems not to have faded from their consciousness for a moment — would soon arrive. With the last of the Indian addresses the council closed for the day.

On September 11 a council with the Crows was the chief feature. Toward evening Colonel Alexander Culbertson, Indian Agent at the trading post of Fort Union, near the mouth of the Yellowstone, arrived in the company of Father De Smet and a delegation of thirty-two Assiniboine, Crow, Minnetaree (Hidatsa), and Arikara chiefs and head men.

De Smet, because of his great influence with the tribes, had been invited to attend the council, and his coming was eagerly awaited. From St. Louis he had voyaged by steamboat up the Missouri to Fort Union, where he was joined by Culbertson and the Indians. By a roundabout course they had journeyed overland far to the west of Fort Laramie — almost to Independence Rock — and had then turned east by way of the Oregon Trail. In this unique gathering he received a tumultuous welcome, and with the greatest pleasure he found himself again in the company of his old-time friends, Fitzpatrick, Campbell, and Bridger.

September 12 was devoted largely to a discussion of tribal boundaries. It was a difficult subject. All the tribes claimed more than their neighbors would allow; much of the inter-tribal warfare originated in forays into disputed territory; and as the dominant industry of the tribes — horse-stealing — could be performed only by such forays, there was little sentiment for fixed boundaries. Nevertheless the job of determining limits was vigorously tackled; and the three geographical experts — Fitzpatrick, Campbell, and Bridger — who knew every stream, mountain, and pathway in that vast region, were finally enabled to map out a territorial scheme to which the tribes gave assent.

So the talks and the feasts and the dances went on, with every day some nearer approach to a comprehensive agreement, though the wagon train — the final proof of the white man's sincerity — still failed to arrive. But there was one important matter that so far had remained unsettled. It was the grievance of the Shoshones against the Cheyennes for the killing and scalping of two of their warriors. The Shoshones had accepted and observed the truce, but a truce was not a reconciliation. There must be expiation of the offense, a symbolic "covering of the bodies" by the gift of blankets or of other presents equal in value, before even the peace pipe could be smoked. In this delicate affair the Cheyennes took the initiative. They gave a feast to the Shoshones, and the food was not dogmeat (which the Shoshones detested), but crushed and boiled corn. Speeches were made, the Cheyennes expressed the deepest regret for the offense, the expiatory presents were made, the peace pipe was smoked, and reconciliation was declared complete.

Sunday, September 14, was a holiday, and De Smet made effective use of it. Some lodges of buffalo hides, arranged and ornamented as a sanctuary, were set up near the circle, and here, in his own words, he "had the happiness of offering the holy sacrifice, in presence of all the gentlemen assisting at the council, of all half-bloods and whites and of a great concourse of Indians."[4] Already, on September 12, in what seems to have been a special ceremony, he had baptized the infant Andrew Jackson Fitzpatrick.[5] After this day's more elaborate ceremony eight half-breed children and five adults were baptized. To this energetic proselytizer the gathering presented a rare opportunity; and he was to continue his missionary efforts, with what seemed to him extraordinary success, until the break-up of the council.

The great treaty was completed on the night of September 16 and on the following day was presented for signature. It provided for a lasting peace among the signatory

---

[4] H. M. Chittenden and A. T. Richardson, *Life, Letters and Travels of Father Pierre-Jean De Smet, S.J.* (New York, 1905), 679.

[5] Data furnished by the Rev. G. J. Garraghan, S.J., of St. Louis University, from the original De Smet Baptismal Record.

tribes and with the whites; recognized the right of the United States to establish roads and military posts in the Indian country; made depredations by Indians or whites punishable and restitution obligatory; fixed the boundaries of the tribes, but left all the Indian country open to any tribe for fishing and hunting; provided for the payment by the Government of an annuity of $50,000 in goods for fifty years, and penalized violations of the treaty by withholding from the offender a part or all of the annuity.[6]

The treaty had been fully discussed, and all its provisions were understood. It was now again read, sentence by sentence, and explained in detail. Then Mitchell and Fitzpatrick signed it, whereupon the chiefs made crosses opposite their names (which had been written in by the secretary), and the white witnesses attached their signatures. The council was ended.

And still the wagons did not appear. The grazing grounds had become a barren plain, swept with every breeze by clouds of dust. Refuse and filth were everywhere, and the stench was almost unbearable. To escape the scene the soldiers moved two miles down the river. But the Commissioners decided to hold fast, and the Indians waited hopefully. Their feasts continued, for they still had dogs. "No epoch in Indian annals," writes De Smet, "probably shows a greater massacre of the canine race."

The eighteenth dragged along, and the nineteenth, and then, on the twentieth, the long suspense was joyfully broken, for the supply train pulled into camp and formed a corral. The Indians massed thickly about the wagons.

---

[6] C. J. Kappler, *Indian Affairs. Laws and Treaties*, Vol. II, pp. 594–96.

A $50,000 pile of merchandise and a throng of 10,000 Indians! But another day they must wait, for the distribution was not to begin until the morrow.

The morning came, and the Commissioners and their staff were ready. First the chiefs and the sub-chiefs must be presented with military uniforms. The list of dignitaries, graded by rank, had been made up only after much labor and discriminating care, for the matter of rank was a complex one not easily mastered by the paleface. Major generals of course came first, and then brigadiers and colonels. To each was given a coat and pantaloons, with sword and medal. The new toggery was at once donned, and with moccasioned feet, painted faces, and flowing locks, the chiefs stepped forth in the full splendor of their gorgeously colored and epauletted uniforms. It was a sight at once ludicrous and pathetic. But the Indians bore themselves with serene gravity, and the whites, for the best of reasons, forbore to laugh.

Then the goods were distributed, the head men of each tribe assisting in the work. The behavior of the crowd was excellent, and all the recipients appeared pleased. Throughout the day the distribution continued, and until the middle of the next day. Then the villages began to move away, and the whites were left to themselves.

It must have been with a feeling of quiet elation that Fitzpatrick witnessed the closing scenes of this tremendous drama. On the surface all that he had hoped and struggled for had been accomplished, and there was apparent promise of a lasting peace. Could he have read the future for even so much as a year, however, he would have been less satisfied. The august Senate of the United States was to tamper with the treaty, reducing the term of years of the annuity from fifty to a possible fifteen years; and the Indians, after a time, were to forget their good resolutions and to trouble one another, and later to make savage war upon the whites. By a strange irony of events, Fitzpatrick was himself to be forced to the humiliating task of seeking from the Indians ratifications to a treaty altered from the one they had supposed definite and settled. It was a great work that he had done, but by reason of factors he could not control it might bring no lasting benefits.

Chapter 16

The Closing Years

THE WHITES, with the Indian delegation, set out from the council grounds on September 23. Eleven chiefs and sub-chiefs were to go with Fitzpatrick to Washington. Of the Cheyennes there were White Antelope, Red Skin, and Rides on the Clouds; of the Arapahoes, Friday, Eagle's Head, and Tempest; and of the Sioux, One Horn, Little Chief, Shellman, Watchful Elk, and Goose.[1]

They followed the Oregon Trail. At the junction of Ash Hollow and the South Platte they came upon Prince Paul Wilhelm of Württemburg, traveling with Baldwin Möll-hausen in an open wagon toward the Wind River Mountains, where the two meant to have a season of hunting. This adventurous prince had first visited the frontier in the years 1822–24. At the mouth of the Kansas he had come upon young Jean Baptiste Charbonneau, who as an infant

---

[1] De Smet, *op. cit.*, 688. De Smet gives the Indian names of these delegates as well as the English equivalents.

had been carried by his mother, Sacagawea, the Bird Woman, with the Lewis and Clark Expedition all the way to the Pacific and back again. Greatly pleased with the lad, then about seventeen years old, the Prince had taken him to Stuttgart.[2]

On again coming to America, in 1829, he had brought the youth back with him; since about this time the name of young Charbonneau begins to appear in Western annals. Now, in his sixty-seventh year, the Prince was making his farewell visit, and with a naïve disregard of danger was traveling into the heart of the Indian country with but a single companion.

Prince Paul, upon meeting Fitzpatrick and his Washington-bound delegations, wrote in his diary: "There were a number of Indians whom he was taking to Washington. An old acquaintance of mine, a man of great renown throughout the West, accompanied them. This was the Indian scout Fitz-Patrick. I was overjoyed to see this lovable old huntsman of the Rocky Mountains again."[3]

At Fort Kearny the Commissioners held a council with

---

[2] See Prince Paul Wilhelm's book *Erste Reise nach dem Nordlichen America in den Jahre 1822 bis 1824* (Stuttgart, 1835).

[3] Prince Paul's account of his 1851 trip up the Platte River, translated by Louis C. Butscher (of the University of Wyoming), in the *New Mexico Historical Review*, XVII (July, 1942), 181–225.

Mr. Möllhausen, the sole companion of Prince Paul on the tour of 1851, was himself a famous character and the author of many books. In 1853 he was with Lieut. Whipple's company of the Pacific Railway Surveys. Möllhausen wrote an account of the expedition — *Diary of a Journey from the Mississippi to the Coasts of the Pacific with a United States Government Expedition*, translated by Mrs. Percy Sinnett (London, 1858). He tells of Whipple's employment at Albuquerque, New Mexico, of Antoine Leroux as guide to the Expedition, and on page 25, volume II, writes: "The three oldest backwoodsmen in existence are — this man [Leroux] and two others named Fitzpatrick and Kit Carson. Fitzpatrick has spent half a century in the steppes and wilderness of North America and all three are grey-headed old fellows whom one cannot avoid looking at with a certain feeling of respect and admiration." Then he tells the story of Fitzpartick being captured by Indians and saving the Pawnees. Then the party divided, Mitchell and others proceeding to the mouth of the Platte, while Fitzpatrick, De Smet, and the Indian delegates continued along the Trail. Fitzpatrick chose this course in order to show the delegates the progress in agriculture that had been made by the Potawatomies, the Delawares, the Kaws, and the Shawnees. At St. Mary's Mission, in the present Pottawatomie County, Kansas, Bishop Miege gave a banquet at which were served Indian-grown potatoes, carrots, turnips, squashes, parsnips, melons, apples, and peaches. The warrior delegates were greatly impressed with the quantity and excellence of the food, but if the exhibit made any converts to the cause of agriculture the fact is unrecorded.

The party arrived in Westport on October 16 and took

---

himself by a trick. This story is also published in the *New Orleans Delta* of January 2, 1859, as follows:

"Many years ago, when the white men who had seen the Rocky Mountains might still have been counted, and only very few of the prairie Indians knew the use of fire-arms, Fitzpatrick had one day got separated from his companions, and was pursuing his game alone in the wilderness. As ill luck would have it, he was seen by a party of Indians, who immediately prepared to give chase. There was not the smallest chance of escape for him, but the young hunter made a feint of running away, in order, if possible, to gain time. He happened to know that these savages, who, as yet, were little acquainted with the use of fire-arms, had, several times, when they had taken white hunters prisoners, put the muzzle of their rifle close to their breast, and fired them by way of experiment, to see what would come of it. He, therefore, thought it prudent to extract the bullet from his, and then continued his flight.

"The Indians followed, and very soon overtook him, and then they disarmed him and tied him to a tree. One of the warriors, who, it appeared, understood how to pull the trigger, then seized the rifle, placed himself a few feet in front of the owner of it, took aim at his breast and fired; but when the Indians looked eagerly through the smoke toward Fitzpatrick, they saw that he was standing safe and sound in his place and he quietly took out of his pocket the bullet he had previously placed there, and tossed it to his enemies, who were all amazement. They declared that he had arrested the bullet in its flight, was invulnerable, and a wonderful conjurer, and what was more, that some great misfortune would likely befall the tribe if they did not set him free immediately; and they therefore cut his bonds and made off as fast as possibe, leaving Fitzpatrick free to go where he pleased."

The story was also published in the *Semi-Weekly Vineyard* of Los Angeles, Feb. 4, 1859; and probably elsewhere.

the steamboat *Clara* for St. Louis. It was now that Friday, who seems so far to have been very much in the background began to emerge. His engaging manner, his command of English speech, and the interest awakened by some knowledge of his romantic history, caused him to be lionized by the paleface passengers. Two Oto chiefs, with three women, had been picked up somewhere along the route, and at one of the Missouri River landings two Iowa warriors, with one woman, who had been left stranded by a party of whites with whom they had been traveling, had been added. A Crow sub-chief, evidently a volunteer, had come all the way from the council, but at Brunswick, Chariton County, he became frightened or homesick, and escaped from the boat. Efforts to find him were for the time futile, and the boat went on. Four or five days later his dead body, partly eaten by hogs, was discovered near the town, but as to how he came to his death there is no word.[4]

At St. Louis Fitzpatrick escorted his charges about the streets, explaining to them the marvels of the city. Officials and leading merchants were visited, and the Catholic University gave the delegates a banquet. Then the party went on toward Washington. Whether or not Friday accompanied it cannot be said. He may have preferred the known delights of St. Louis to the uncertain experiences to be met in the east, and so have remained in the city. The Washington reporters do not mention his name nor any circumstances by which he can be identified. The only "educated Indian" singled out for notice is Black Elk, an Iowa.

The party, now composed of fifteen Indian men and four

---

[4] Data from files in the Indian Bureau Office, Washington.

women, two interpreters (John S. Smith and Joseph Tesson Honoré) and the conductor, Thomas Fitzpatrick, arrived in the capital during the last week of November and put up at Maher's Hotel. Here, a few days later, a reporter of *The National Intelligencer* saw the aborigenes and found them gradually recovering from the indisposition caused by their long and unaccustomed journey. During their stay in the city they attracted great attention. On December 4 they were taken through the Central Market, where they were amazed at the quantity of domestic and wild fowl for sale, and where one of the chiefs replenished his headdress with the wing feathers of a large turkey. On the invitation of the Secretary of War they visited some of the forts, and on that of the Secretary of the Navy they inspected the Navy Yard.

Colonel Mitchell arrived in the city about December 25, and on January 6, 1852, Commissioner of Indian Affairs Luke Lea, with Mitchell, Fitzpatrick, and the two interpreters, brought the visitors, "fully habited in Indian costume," to President Fillmore, in one of the parlors of the White House. The President, with his wife and daughter, and a number of invited guests, including Madame Louis Kossuth, wife of the Hungarian revolutionist, occupied a space in the center of the room, while the Indians squatted about on the carpet. The chiefs expected the proceedings to be opened by a peace pipe ceremony, but on being told that smoking in the presence of ladies was highly improper, readily accepted the situation.

The President gave a brief address, expressing his pleasure at meeting the delegates and his hope of a lasting peace. He urged them to turn their attention to agriculture

instead of the chase and warned them against any inter-
ference with the emigrants on the Oregon Trail. Responses
were made by several of the chiefs, who said that they were
glad to have made the long journey and to have met the
Great Father. One of them gently hinted that the present
of a horse would be highly acceptable, and another inti-
mated that horses for all and a bit of money would greatly
increase their pleasure. The President, in reply, said that
Agent Fitzpatrick had been allowed sufficient funds to pay
all their expenses, and that the iron horse of the whites was
a far more speedy and convenient way of returning them
to the frontier. Then he presented silver medals and also
flags, which Fitzpatrick distributed; good-byes were said,
and the ceremony was over.

Two days later, on the invitation of Kossuth, they visited him at Brown's Hotel, and each received from him a
medal. About the eleventh, led by Fitzpatrick, they started
on their return.[5]

There is, for the remainder of the year, no further word
about Fitzpatrick except that he returned to his agency
with $30,000 worth of goods to be distributed.[6] If he wrote
a report for the year 1852 it has not been found.

But with the spring of 1853 we have him in clear light
again, and are enabled to keep him so to the end. Early
in April he was ordered by Mitchell to proceed to Washington to give information regarding the affairs of his

---

[5] *The Republic* (Washington), Dec. 5 and 13, 1851; Jan. 7, 1852, and *National Intelligencer,* Dec. 1, 1851. These sources were found by W. J. Ghent,
and summarized in this part of the narrative.

[6] On Aug. 3, 1852, Supt. Mitchell telegraphed Commissioner Lea that $30,000
worth of goods had been taken out by Fitzpatrick for the Indians of his agency.
The goods were bought from R. and W. Campbell. — Central Agency File,
Indian Bureau, Washington.

agency. While there, on May 5, he was appointed sole Commissioner to negotiate a treaty with the Comanches, Kiowas, and other tribes south of the upper Arkansas. He was also instructed to visit the Indians who had participated in the Fort Laramie treaty and obtain ratifications of the Senate amendments reducing the term of the annuity to fifteen years. He now returned to the Missouri to prepare for his long journeys.

He was not well, and for a time it was feared that he would not be able to perform the duties assigned him. On May 18 Superintendent Alfred Cumming, who had replaced Mitchell, telegraphed Commissioner of Indian Affairs Manypenny that Fitzpatrick was ill and asked for authorization to appoint an assistant. It is not known that an assistant was appointed. But the veteran rallied and resolutely went about his business. Opportunity challenged him, and he was determined to meet it. For years the Comanches and Kiowas had pillaged the white man's caravans and committed many atrocities. The Government had been niggardly in furnishing troops, and the hostiles had not been adequately punished. There was little hope that the Government would do any better in the future, and it was therefore time to try another policy. If a sufficient annuity could be guaranteed, perhaps the hostiles would pledge themselves to stop their depredations. Arranging for the transportation of the goods, he made ready to start.

On June 20, at St. Louis, he made his will.[7] It bequeathed a third of all his property to his wife and the remainder

---

[7] Papers in the Indian Office files indicated the existence of a will, and it was found among the court records in St. Louis by Miss Stella Drumm of the Missouri Historical Society. It is reproduced in the Appendix.

to his son, with the provision that if another child should be born before his death or within nine months thereafter, the property other than the widow's third should be divided equally. Robert Campbell and Albert G. Boone, the latter a grandson of Daniel Boone, were named as executors, and B. Gratz Brown was one of the two witnesses. Westport had become Fitzpatrick's home, and is so designated in the will.

Messengers had been sent ahead to summon the Comanches, the Kiowas, and the plains Apaches to assemble at Fort Atkinson. Late in June, after seeing his goods started, Fitzpatrick set out from Westport. On his arrival at the fort he found the tribesmen there in force, with the Comanches the most numerous. For a time, however, the prospect of making a treaty seemed almost hopeless.

At first [writes Fitzpatrick] almost insurmountable difficulties presented themselves, in the distant and suspicious bearing of the chiefs, and the utter impossibility of obtaining any interpreters who understood their intricate languages. But little intercourse had ever existed between them and the white race, and that usually of the most unfriendly character. Whenever and wherever a meeting had occurred upon the vast plains they inhabit, it had been one not of traffic, but of plunder and bloodshed, or else of defeat and animosity.[8]

Strange, some may say, that the sign language could not have been profitably employed. There are those who in recent times have pictured this language as a medium so highly developed that it would express abstract ideas as well as things that could be seen, felt, and handled. The experienced Fitzpatrick did not find it so.

There were no trappers or traders amongst them [he continues] who could facilitate an interview; no one who could speak a syllable

---

[8] Fitzpatrick's Annual Report, included in the *Annual Report of the Commissioner of Indian Affairs, 1853*, 120.

of the English tongue; none present in whom mutual confidence could be reposed; and the "sign language," that common to all the wild tribes of the West, while it might answer the purpose of barter, could not be relied upon in matters of so much importance and delicacy.

But a way was at last found. The Indians were induced to bring forth some of their Mexican prisoners, and through the medium of the Spanish language communication was established. As a check for accuracy, interpretations were repeated by different persons. Additional help was given by an Arapaho Indian who had long dwelt with the Comanches; when words failed, the sign language was employed, and thus by a variety of means the conferees reached a satisfactory understanding.

Fitzpatrick comments upon the keen intelligence with which these desert warriors replied to propositions submitted to them. A right-of-way through their territory — which so far the whites had maintained only at great cost of blood and treasure — was readily granted; but vigorous opposition developed to the establishment of military posts, the reservation of land adjacent to the posts or the highways, and the cessation of hostilities against Mexico.

The treaty as finally agreed upon bound the three tribes to maintain peace among themselves and with the citizens of the United States. It recognized the right of the United States to lay out roads through the region, make reservations of land adjacent to them, locate depots for railroad purposes and establish military posts. The Indians agreed to make restitution for any injuries done the whites and to deliver up offenders, and the Government obligated itself to make an annual payment of $18,000 worth of goods for ten years, subject to an extension of five years, with the provision that the amount might be reduced or withheld in case of Indian violation of the treaty.[9]

The provision for establishing military posts was included in the treaty by Fitzpatrick with a view to future possibilities rather than from a belief in their efficiency under the existing circumstances. He had come to see that the forts should either be better garrisoned or else abandoned.

The policy [he wrote in his report] must be either an army or an annuity. Either an inducement must be offered to them [the Indians] greater than the gains of plunder, or a force must be at hand able to restrain and check their depredation. Any compromise between the two systems will be only productive of mischief, and liable to all the miseries of failure. It will beget confidence, without providing safety; it will neither create fear nor satisfy avarice; and adding nothing to the protection of trade and emigration will add everything to the responsibilities of the Government.

In the demand for the return of the Mexican captives Fitzpatrick struck a stone wall. For years these wild tribes had made incursions into Mexico to replenish their *caballadas* of horses and to obtain prisoners. As far as the interior of Chihuahua and Durango, even in the villages and towns, their names had become bywords of terror. The captives were readily adopted into the tribes; many of them married and soon became habituated to savage life, and had no desire to return to civilzation. These Mexicans were the husbands of their daughters or the mothers of their children, said the red spokesmen, and never would consent to a separation be given. All Fitzpatrick could win from the warriors on this point was the promise — probably soon violated — that they would desist from taking captives.

When the negotiations were finished, and the chiefs had

---

[9] Kappler, *Indian Affairs, Laws and Treaties*, II, 600–602.

made their respective crosses on the document, the white-haired Fitzpatrick, in the role of Santa Claus, distributed the goods of the first annuity. There was $18,000 worth, and the Indians were therefore enabled to get a sufficient idea of their annual income from the Government. It happened that Major Clifton, with Troop B of the First Dragoons, was present, and with him was still his faithful trooper, Corporal Percival G. Lowe, who had proved so good a reporter of certain episodes at the Fort Laramie Council.

In a smaller way [writes Lowe] this was as important a distribution of presents to the Indians as was that in 1851 at the mouth of Horse Creek. If it had any newspaper record I never heard of it. The big ox-train came in, the wily Apaches (called Prairie Apaches to distinguish them from those ranging in southern New Mexico and Arizona), the Kiowas and Comanches having assembled in full force, the goods were unloaded, boxes and bales opened, the nabobs of the tribes decorated in brilliant uniforms, medals and certificates issued, goods parceled out, winding up with plenty to eat, feasting, sham battles, etc. The Apaches were off their home grounds and anxious to return. Major Fitzpatrick seemed equally anxious to have the job over with and kept his little working force and a couple of clerks pushing things. The long drawn out dignity of the Horse Creek treaty was lacking.[10]

With everything completed, Fitzpatrick, on August 2, set out from Fort Atkinson for the farther West and North. He must visit the Cheyennes and the Arapahoes on the South Platte, and the Sioux at Fort Laramie, give them their annuities and obtain their consent to the Senate amendments to the Horse Creek treaty. As he journeyed up the Arkansas he appears to have been more deeply impressed than ever before with the good soil and rich vege-

---

[10] Lowe, *Five Years a Dragoon*, 135.

tation along the stream. In several respects he was the advance agent of a new day for this region. In the heart of the area that Major Long, more than thirty years before, had labeled the "Great American Desert," he saw vast possibilities. "My course," he writes, "led through rich alluvial bottom lands, rank with vegetation, and skirted heavily with cottonwood, near the margin of the stream. Fine soils prevail in these low grounds; and on the high table lands a short but nutritious grass affords excellent grazing, and will cause this country to be some day much prized for pastoral purposes." Thus he foresaw the great cattle herds that but two decades later were to roam the plains, even though he may not have envisioned the day of the cantaloupe and the sugar beet.

He reached the Pueblo and then turned northward up Fountain Creek and crossed the divide to the South Platte drainage. Again the gray-haired pioneer peered into the future. "The topography of this region," he writes, "presented many interesting features. Sheltered valleys, mild temperatures, large growths of timber and an immense water power may be numbered amongst its advantages. . . . Indications of mineral wealth likewise abound in the sands of the water courses and the gorges and canyons from which they issue; and should public attention ever be strongly directed to this section of our territory, and free access be obtained, the inducements which it holds out will soon people it with thousands of citizens and cause it to rise speedily into a flourishing mountain State."

He could not have imagined how soon his prediction was to be verified. Following the same track, only five years later, came the noted Russell party of prospectors who panned gold from these streams — a discovery that caused the great "Pike's Peak or Bust" stampede of 1859 and the beginnings of settlement. Here also was speedily to rise the "mountain State" he visioned, first assuming the name of Jefferson and later that of Colorado.

On the South Platte, in the vicinity of Fort St. Vrain, he found large camps of the Cheyennes and the Arapahoes. But as many bands were still out, and as he wanted the largest possible representation to consider the ratification of the Senate amendments, he had runners sent to bring in the absentees. After a wait of ten days a large majority of both nations was assembled. Fitzpatrick then explained the amendments, which were at once ratified. Then the goods, provisions, and ammunition were distributed, and almost as by magic the lodges disappeared, and the Indians scattered to other fields.

He reached Fort Laramie about September 10 and found the Sioux in great numbers. They were, however, in a bad temper. There had been a little brush between the troops and the warriors of one of the villages, and several Indians had been killed. Fitzpatrick called a council, but its proceedings were frequently interrupted by denunciations of the troops and demands for redress. The Indians "stoutly insisted," he writes, "upon the immediate removal of the post from amongst them, saying that, when first placed there they were told it was for their protection, but now the soldiers of the Great Father are the first to make the ground bloody." After some turmoil he called upon Captain Richard B. Garnett, the commander of the fort (ten years later to be killed in Pickett's charge at Gettysburg), to give an explanation of the affair. That given, the Indians, somewhat pacified, readily assented to the treaty amendments. The annuities were then distributed, and with good feeling restored the assembly dispersed.[11]

Fitzpatrick had now accomplished the full purpose of his mission. After attending to some further agency matters at the fort he started eastward, never again to see the mountains and the plains that for thirty years had been his home. He had come into the Far West in the vigor of young manhood, and here he had developed into a rich maturity. In his time the populous villages of the beaver had virtually disappeared, and the countless herds of the buffalo had begun to dwindle. He had seen the beginning and the end of the rendezvous and the growth of the private trading post. He had been ten years in the mountains before Fort Laramie was established; he had been for a time one of its owners, and he had seen it pass through its long career as a trading post to become a military fort of the Government.

His trapper companions no longer followed the streams of the wilderness. Some had fallen in pitched battle, and others on solitary trails. The survivors had sought the new communities of the farther West, or else had returned to their eastern homes — all of them with the rich heritage of memories of a life lived to the full and now content to settle down to a humdrum existence. The trails they had blazed had become highways along which flowed an ever-increasing tide of emigration to the Pacific. The nearer lands also were soon to be peopled; for the pressure of population against the boundaries of the Indian country was becoming restless, and within a few months Kansas

---

11 *Annual Report of the Commissioner of Indian Affairs, 1853* (Washington, 1853), 127.

and Nebraska were to be thrown open to settlement. Keenly aware of the momentous changes that were working themselves out in the West, Fitzpatrick was endeavoring to make smooth and bloodless the inevitable course of progress.

At St. Louis, in November, he penned the last account of his labors. "In concluding this report," he writes, in what seems a mood of valedictory, "I cannot refrain from touching upon one or two topics nearly connected with the present conditions of those Indians and with the future development of the widely extended country they inhabit. What may be their destiny and what may be its eventual growth in power and wealth, are problems which human foresight can now scarcely solve." He then recalled the former policy of the removal of tribes and the contraction of their territory and pointed to its evil effects. "Penned up in small secluded colonies they become hospital wards of cholera and smallpox," he declared, "and must be supported at an immense annual cost to the Government." Further on he asserted: "It is the legalized murder of a whole nation." The policy that had been pursued with the eastern tribes was not applicable here. The wild tribes were already desitute of food. "The lapse of a few years," he writes, "presents only the prospect of a gradual famine."

After mature reflection, therefore, upon the difficulties which must embarrass any line of policy that can be traced out [he concludes], having the improvement of the Indians in view, and judging from the experience of many years passed amongst them, I am constrained to think that but one course remains which promises any permanent relief to them, or any lasting benefit to the country in which they dwell. That is, simply to make such modifications in the "intercourse laws" as will invite the residence of traders amongst them, and *open the whole Indian territory to settlement.*

In this manner will be introduced amongst them those who will set the example of developing the resources of the soil, of which the Indians have not now the most distant idea; who will afford to them employment in pursuits congenial to their nature; and who will accustom them imperceptibly, to those modes of life which can alone secure them from the miseries of penury. Trade is the only civilizer of the Indian. It has been the precursor of all civilizations heretofore, and it will be of all hereafter. It teaches the Indian the value of other things besides the spoils of the chase and offers to him other pursuits and excitement than those of war. All obstructions to its freedom, therefore, only operate injuriously. . . . it seems unwise to subject these tribes to the vices without introducing the virtues and advantages we ourselves enjoy.[12]

In December Fitzpatrick was called to Washington for a discussion of the treaty he had signed with the Comanches, the Kiowas, and the Apaches. He journeyed by way of New York City and was probably accompanied by Robert Campbell. According to his grandniece, Mrs. H. G. McCarthy, of Washington, D.C., a newspaper announcement of his arrival at a New York hotel was noticed by Mrs. Mary Fitzpatrick Leonard, her grandmother. An infant when Thomas Fitzpatrick left Ireland, she had grown up in the belief that somewhere in the wilds of North America she had a brother. After her marriage she had emigrated, with her husband and children, to the United States. On seeing the name she at once surmised that the man was her brother. Her daughter called at the hotel, only to find that he had left the city; but she left a note for him, which was forwarded. He returned, and brother and sister had a happy reunion. Learning that she was living in rather straitened circumstances, he gave her a thousand dollars with which to start her sons in business. The next word she had concerning him was of his death.

---

[12] *Ibid.*, 129.

Fitzpatrick arrived in Washington on January 4, 1854, and registered at the nationally-known Brown's Hotel, on Pennsylvania Avenue. Business with the Indian Bureau must have occupied most of his time for the next two or three weeks, and a journey to New York and back may have followed. Late in the month or early in February he took a severe cold, which resulted in pneumonia. His illness was brief. On the morning of February 7 he passed away. The adventurous wanderer who had braved every peril of the wilderness, whose nightly couch had been a bundle of pine boughs or the naked earth, and whose roof the canopy of the stars, was fated to die peacefully in bed in a metropolitan hotel. "It would have been a fitter end for him," as Frémont so feelingly said of Jean Nicollet, "to have died under the open sky, and been buried rolled up in a blanket, by the side of some stream in the mountains."

Robert Campbell, whom by his will Fitzpatrick had made his executor, was in the city and took charge of his affairs. The funeral was held on the morning of the eighth, and burial was in the Congressional cemetery. "We understand that nearly all connected with the Indian Bureau attended his funeral this morning," said the *Daily Globe*, which gave a brief but highly laudatory tribue to his memory. The *National Intelligencer* and the *Daily National Era* also briefly noticed his death and his long and worthy career; and so, a little later (Feb. 13, 1854), did the *Missouri Republican* of St. Louis. His white hair and the wearing effects of recent illness had given him the appearance of advanced age. "We presume his age must have been

---

[13] These data were obtained from Mrs. McCarthy. See Ghent's letter to me of Sept. 15, 1928, and her letter to me of March 14, 1929; in my personal file.

approaching seventy years," said the *National Intelligencer*.[14] He was actually but fifty-five. For many years he rested in an unmarked grave.[15]

His will was probated in St. Louis on February 20. The estate consisted of $10,056.15 in cash on deposit with Robert Campbell (reduced by various deductions to about $8,500), and two lots and two small houses, presumably in Westport. Campbell was made curator for the son, as also later for a posthumous daughter, Virginia Thomasine, born on May 13, who shared equally with her brother in the estate.[16]

At some time before April 1856, Mrs. Fitzpatrick married Lucius J. Wilmott (or Wilmot), evidently of Westport. Little is known of her later life except that in the Little Arkansas Treaty Council, held in 1865, she served as Government interpreter for the Arapahoes.[17] In the treaty the Government granted to her and to her children, Andrew Jackson and Virginia, 640 acres of land to each.[18] Margaret is said to have died, probably by violence, at the age of about forty years. The son was killed by a train in California in 1880. Virginia was educated at St. Mary's Academy, in Leavenworth, and on January 9, 1873, was married to John Meagher. By this union she had a son and a daughter. The son, Henry, served in the Spanish-American War

---

[14] *Daily National Intelligencer*, Feb. 8, 1854.

[15] The United States Government in 1940 placed a marble headstone over the grave. This information was supplied to me by William Strahl of Washington, D.C., in a letter of Oct. 7, 1940. Mrs. Strahl's grandmother was a younger sister of Thomas Fitzpatrick. I visited the grave in 1953 and took a photograph of the marker.

[16] See the will and estate papers in the Appendix to this volume.

[17] *H. Ex. Doc.* 1, 39th Cong., 1st Sess., 701.

[18] Kappler, *op. cit.*, II, 889.

as a member of Roosevelt's Rough Riders. Virginia, or, as she was more familiarly known, Jennie, separated from Meagher about 1879 and was subsequently divorced from him. She became matron of the Arapaho school at Darlington, Oklahoma, and later was employed in the Seger school at Colony and in the school at Grand Junction, Colorado. On December 21, 1891, in Kansas City, she was married to Frank Mason, who eighteen months later deserted her. She was a third time married on September 23, 1897. Her husband, Dr. Allson H. Jackson, of El Reno, died on Noverber 29, 1928. A year later (Dec. 2, 1929,) Virginia passed away.[19] She was an accomplished horsewoman, who took part in many races. Her educational work was notable, and she was widely known for her generous helpfulness, her charm of manner and her lively and adventurous dispositon.

The outstanding figure among the "mountain men" of the trapper and early emigrant periods, especially after the death of Jedediah Smith, was Thomas Fitzpatrick. Trapper, explorer, Indian fighter, guide, Government agent, and negotiator of treaties with the Indians, he bore a leading part in the early history of the great Central Plateau. His praise is written large by Senator Benton, Father De Smet, Lieutenant Frémont, General Kearny, Lieutenant Abert, Superintendent Harvey, John Bidwell, Percival Lowe, and others; and the good name he won among the Indians is still a tradition among the tribes he served. They found him, despite his generally unfavorable view of the red man, an honest agent and a true friend. What had been appreciation of

---

[19] I have two letters Virginia wrote to me from El Reno, Okla., on July 7, 1928, and Sept. 24, 1928. She knew nothing about her family's background.

his honesty and friendliness came in later days, after they had experienced fraud and deception, to be a profound veneration for his memory. The Arapahoes, said Chief Little Raven, in 1865, had had "but one fair agent; that was Major Fitzpatrick." "Major Fitzpatrick was a good man," said Chief Black Kettle, of the Cheyenne, on the same occasion. "He has gone ahead of us, and he told us that when he was gone we would have trouble, and it has proved true. We are sorry."[20]

"Fitzpatrick was greatly esteemed by the Indians, and among the white men since is reputed to have been the best agent these tribes ever had," wrote C. W. Bowman in Baskin's *History of the Arkansas Valley, Colorado* (1881) (p. 833). Percival Lowe, the Dragoon, who, it will be remembered, met Fitzpatrick at the South Platte crossing, later at the Great Council of 1851, and again at the council with the Comanches, the Kiowas, and the Apaches in 1853, gives similar testimony. In an address before the Kansas State Historical Society in 1890, he said: "Major Fitzpatrick ('Three Fingers,' as the Indians called him), a man of great experience with all the tribes and in whom they all had confidence, acted for the Government. They claimed that Major Fitzpatrick had never lied to them in the twenty years they had known him as trader and agent. It was a certificate of character that few agents could get."[21]

This conclusion by W. J. Ghent and me was written in the first biography of Broken Hand (1931):

The two men with whom he is most likely to be com-

---

[20] At the council negotiating the treaty of 1865. *H. Ex. Doc.* 1, 39th Cong., 1st Sess., 703, 705, 708, 709.

[21] Kansas Historical Society *Transactions*, IV, 365. This was subsequently reproduced with some changes in his *Five Years a Dragoon*.

pared are Carson and Bridger. The three were close friends, and in many a daring adventure they were comrades. It takes nothing from the well-won renown of Carson and Bridger to award him higher rank — a rank they would themselves, during his lifetime, have freely acknowledged. Older by ten years than Carson and by five than Bridger, he was a leader when they were subordinates; and he died when Carson had yet fourteen years before him and Bridger twenty-seven. In some respects their histories are closely parallel; but though they had much in common they were strongly marked with individuality. All three had the photographic mind — the ability to register a scene once viewed and to describe it in terms of amazing exactness. Equals in courage, Carson was the most impetuous, Bridger the most wary, Fitzpatrick the most cool and balanced in judgment. In native ability to outguess his savage foes or to surmise where danger most threatened, it may be that Bridger somewhat excelled the two others. Of the three, Carson, it seems, had the most appealing personality. Carson won the affection of men, Bridger their interest, Fitzpatrick their admiration and regard.

In all-around capabilities, however, Fitzpatrick was much the superior of the other two. He had most that they had, and much more besides. The men of his day gave him this distinction, and by the facts it is amply sustained. He was the best fitted to command, and in time of war might have risen to high rank. He had, in the highest degree, what was perhaps the most essential quality of a successful "mountain man"—the ability to avoid an unnecessary fight. "It was a maxim of one of the oldest scouts of the frontier," said Edward H. Allison, himself a scout, as well as an interpreter and a master of the Sioux language, "that the best Indian fighter was the one who had the fewest fights. I would revise that a little and say that the best Indian fighter is the one [who] makes the best use of his brains." None of the "mountain men," in dealing with the savages, made better use of his faculties than Fitzpatrick.

And then he had education, which his two comrades had not. Bridger was illiterate all his life, and Carson was to attain a degree of semi-literacy only during his last years; but Fitzpatrick, though he left school at sixteen, was one who read and reflected, who knew something of history and statecraft, whose letters and reports in the Indian Office show a mind of native strength and capacity, well stored and disciplined. He wrote English not as a frontiersman, but as a scholar; what he had to say he set down with force and clearness, and with a happy sense for the right word in the right place.

An attempt at comparison with Carson and Bridger is inevitable; but a more fitting attempt would be with men of a broader range and a more commanding personality — with men such as John C. Frémont, William Henry Ashley, Jedediah Smith, Joshua Pilcher, and William L. Sublette. Yet here, by reason of the difference of circumstances, the effort must necessarily fail. Though fate gave Fitzpatrick a pioneer task of first importance in the handling of Indian affairs on the plains, it denied him the material means that enabled Ashley to become the *entrepreneur* of exploration; it denied him no less the free rein that enabled Smith to press forward into so many unknown regions, and it gave to Frémont, that petted child of Fortune, the honors of an expedition that might have been his own.

Lovers of the early western scene, with its heroic actors, have craved a fuller knowledge of this mysterious figure — at times in view, at other times unaccountably obscured — only to be baffled in their search. Now that his life story is known, he may be fitly judged against the background of his time and environment. It can hardly be doubted that as the years pass he will more clearly emerge as a character of the first consequence on the frontier and in the wilderness — an epic figure, unique and incomparable.

Appendix A
Friday, the Arapaho[1]

A LITTLE ARAPAHO BOY who strayed from a moving village of his tribe near the Cimarron River and the Santa Fe Trail became lost. His efforts to find his people and the searching by his parents proved futile. One day passed, and then another, and another. The nights, in late May, were cold, and the thinly clad wanderer curled up in the shelter of bushes to sleep through the darkness. There was no food. The hungry, bewildered boy became weak and his mind wandered. He saw himself at the village feast, amid kettles of steaming soup and piles of boiled and roasted meat. After about a week — he had not counted the days — he looked out from the underbrush in which he had taken refuge, and saw men and animals approaching.

At first he thought the men were his people, but soon realized that they were not Arapahoes but palefaces. He was too weak to escape. A tall man came near, saw him,

---

1 Much of the information for this story is from Rufus B. Sage, reprinted in LeRoy R. and Ann W. Hafen, eds., *Rufus B. Sage; His Letters and Papers. . . . Scenes in the Rocky Mountains* (Glendale, Calif., 1956), II, 300–308.

tenderly took him up and carried him to one of the wagons, where food and drink were given him. The kind man was Thomas Fitzpatrick, and from that moment the boy was bound to him by the closest ties of grateful affection. Friday was the day, and "Friday" was accordingly the name given to the rescued lad.

The caravan that so fortunately for the boy had come along the Trail to the Cimarron was that of Smith, Jackson, and Sublette, bound for Santa Fe in 1831. Fitzpatrick, then head of the Rocky Mountain Fur Company, was traveling with the caravan.

The boy was then, according to Arapaho tradition, near nine years old, but he was probably younger.[2] Under the good care given him he quickly recovered. So bright a boy soon picked up enough English to tell his story.

After making up his pack train of supplies at Santa Fe for his mountain trappers, Fitzpatrick journeyed northward, taking his Indian boy along. On the North Platte he turned over the goods to his partner and then he and Friday returned in the fall to St. Louis. Here he put Friday in school. Usually Indian boys fretted at such restraint, but Friday appears to have liked his lessons and came to love the whites. How long he stayed in school is not known, but long enough at least to learn to speak good English.

Charles Larpenteur, trapper and trader, makes mention of seeing him in charge of Fitzpatrick's friend, Robert Campbell, westward bound from St. Louis in the spring of 1833.[3] The next year William M. Anderson traveled with Friday and his guardian Fitzpatrick from the Rocky Mountains back to Missouri and writes of the Indian boy:

We have a little Indian foundling, belonging to Mr Fitzpatrick,

---

[2] Letter from Jesse Rowlodge, Corresponding Secretary of the Cheyenne-Arapaho Tribal Council, Geary, Oklahoma, Jan. 14, 1930. See also the source cited below in footnote 4.

[3] Elliott Coues (ed.), *Forty Years a Fur Trader, . . . Charles Larpenteur* (New York, 1899), 12.

named from the day of his discovery, Friday, — he is a very interesting object to me, growing more so each day that passes — His astonishing memory, his minute observation, and his amusing inquiries — make an extremely entertaining companion — He still remembers his name, his sisters and many of his tribes fireside anecdotes, tho he has been absent 4 to 5 years [three years] and was not over six years old when found almost starved in the prairie — He is of the Arapahoe tribe — his Indian name was "Warshinun" or Black-spot.[4]

Friday was not, however, to remain among the palefaces. His parents heard of the rescue of an Arapaho boy, who, they felt sure, was their own, and made every effort to regain him. When the boy was first told about them he would hardly listen, for he wanted to stay with the whites. In time, however, he was persuaded to visit his parents. Reluctantly he made the journey, and at last became reconciled to the Indian life and thereafter lived with his people, though occasionally he returned to see his friends in St. Louis.

Talbot, of Frémont's second expedition, tells of his first meeting with Friday, then about nineteen years old. It was on July 13, 1843, somewhere on the upper South Platte:

We were accompanied [he writes] by many Indians in our travel today. Among others a handsome young Indian came dashing up to Fitz, and cordially shaking his hand expressed in the best English terms the great delight it gave him to meet Fitz, with a thousand kind interrogatories, as to his health, purposes, & &c. We were much surprised at this unusual Indian salutation, until we heard its cause explained.[5]

Fitzpatrick told Talbot of the finding of the boy. He must also have related the story — mentioned only by Talbot — of Friday's unhappy romance. He fell in love with an attractive young girl living near St. Louis. But the maiden

---

[4] Dale L. Morgan and Eleanor T. Harris (eds.), *The Rocky Mountain Journals of William Marshall Anderson* (San Marino, Calif., 1967), 223.

[5] C. H. Carey (ed.), *The Journals of Theodore Talbot, 1843 and 1849–52* (Portland, Oregon, 1931), 20.

rejected him, doubtless because he was an Indian; and it was this episode, according to Talbot, that caused him to forsake the career Fitzpatrick had planned for him and to return permanently to the wilds.

Three days after the meeting with Fitzpatrick Friday came in to bid his benefactor an affectionate good-bye. He was starting out with a war party of his tribesmen to settle a little matter with the hereditary enemies of the Arapahoes, the Utes, and Talbot saw him no more.

It was on one of Friday's journeys to St. Louis, in the summer of 1844, that the traveler, Rufus B. Sage, met the young Arapaho. Somewhere on the Arkansas, between the Big Timbers and the Cimarron crossing, he joined Sage's party returning to the settlements, and the chronicler was at once strongly attracted to him.

I find him agreeable and interesting [he writes]. I am indebted to him for much valuable information relative to the habits and peculiarities of his own and various other Indian tribes, while his vast fund of ready anecdotes and amusing stories serves to beguile the weariness of camp hours. . . . His character for honesty, integrity and sobriety, has as yet stood unimpeached. A chief by birth, he might assert a more prominent station among his people; but he declines it, with the noble resolve: — "Until by my own achievements I have earned that honor, I shall never consent to become a *chief;* for certainly then my people will listen to me!"[6]

Sage praises highly the skill of Friday as a buffalo hunter, and as well his prowess in arms, for already he had become known as a warrior. At Walnut Creek the two men parted from the caravan and started forward alone. They rode all the way to Council Grove, in the present Kansas, whence Sage struck off for Van Buren, Arkansas, while Friday proceeded on to Independence and then to St. Louis.

He next appears in a meeting with Fitzpatrick on July 18, of the following year (1845). Colonel (afterwards General) Philip St. George Cooke tells the incident. Kearny's expe-

---

[6] Sage, *op. cit.,* II, 304.

FRIDAY, THE ARAPAHO
(Photograph taken by W. H. Jackson in about 1874)

dition to South Pass, guided by Fitzpatrick, was returning by way of Fort Laramie and Bent's Fort. On the upper waters of Lodge Pole Creek in southeastern Wyoming, the expedition met a small band of Arapahoes. Friday, who was one of them, instantly recognized Fitzpatrick, and the soldiers were astounded at the sight of their stern, impassive guide greeting, with sincerest demonstration of affection, an Indian warrior.[7]

In 1851 Friday was one of the Arapaho delegation to

[7] Philip St. George Cooke, *Scenes and Adventures in the Army* (Philadelphia, 1859), 401.

the great Indian council held on Horse Creek, near Fort Laramie. Here he had ample opportunity for long talks with Fitzpatrick, who was one of the United States Commissioners. Friday was selected as one of the three delegates from his tribe to visit Washington under the guidance of Fitzpatrick, and it is in the account of this episode that his Arapaho name of Vash first appears. On the steamboat *Clara*, which brought the delegation from Westport down the Missouri, he was the object of extraordinary interest among the white passengers and was lionized. Whether or not he went on to Washington is uncertain.

We lose sight of him for a time, but he again appears in 1858. His kindly benefactor, Fitzpatrick, was no more, and Friday had drifted farther away from the white man's mode of life. He was now a man of family, with a promising warrior son whom he had named Bill. Also he was the leader of an independent band of Arapahoes, numbering some 250 braves, who roamed about the upper waters of the Cache la Poudre and the Big Thompson, in the present Larimer County, Colorado. In the fall of that year, on the ridge north of the present headgates of the Larimer County canal, he had a stubborn and sanguinary fight with a band of his old-time enemies, the Pawnees. The Arapahoes pursued their foes to the top of the ridge, closely besieging them there, but on the night of the third day, in the midst of a great thunderstorm, the Pawnees effected their escape. Both sides suffered heavy losses.[8]

The range of Friday's wanderings were extensive. On September 21, 1859, General W. F. Raynolds, at the head of a small exploring party, met the chief, in company with Chief Owl (whom Raynolds calls Little Owl) and four other Arapahoes, near the North Fork of the Powder in the central part of what is now Wyoming. He "speaks English

---

[8] Ansel Watrous, *History of Larimer County, Colorado* (Fort Collins, Colo., 1911), 83–84.

quite well," writes the soldier, "having spent some time while a boy in St. Louis." Biscuit and coffee were served, and the Indians, well satisfied with their visit, returned to their nearby village, which consisted of some 180 lodges.[9]

At the Deer Creek camp, near the present Glenrock, Wyoming, where Raynolds' party spent the winter of 1859–60, Friday appears to have been a frequent visitor. Dr. F. V. Hayden, the naturalist and surgeon of the expedition, writes of him as "an intelligent Indian, . . . now the most influential person" in his tribe, and gives a brief and somewhat faulty account of his rescue by Fitzpatrick.[10]

The Civil War came on, bringing unrest among the tribes of the plains, and finally open conflict. Through all this turmoil Friday remained a constant friend of the Union. He was, however, at times a source of trouble. By the treaty of Fort Wise, February 18, 1861, the Cheyennes and the Arapahoes had ceded all of the lands given them by the treaty of 1851 except a reservation along the Arkansas. Friday, however, preferred the Cache la Poudre country, and with Owl, and sometimes with Many Whips, and their small bands, insisted on remaining there despite repeated efforts of the citizens and the authorities to induce him to move. Colonel Albert Gallatin Boone, a grandson of Daniel Boone, and at the time agent for the Upper Arkansas, became provoked over his display of obstinacy and evidently wanted something done about it. In a letter of November 16, 1861, to the United States Commissioner of Indian Affairs, Boone gave his estimate of the chief — a decidedly unfavorable one — though admitting that Major Cota, of the adjoining agency, thought him and his fellow-chief, Owl, "two of the greatest Indians alive."[11]

---

[9] W. F. Raynolds, *Report of the Exploration of the Yellowstone River* (1868), 64.

[10] F. V. Hayden, *Contributions to the Ethnography and Philology of the Indian Tribes of the Missouri Valley* (1862), 322–23.

[11] Files of the Indian Office, from which, unless otherwise noted, the data for the period 1861–81 are taken.

He was frequently in the new settlement of Denver, metropolis of the recently created Territory of Colorado, and was always well received. On July 2, 1863, he visited Governor John Evans to assure that official of his friendship. It was a welcome visit, for at this time the plains Sioux, the Cheyennes and most of the Arapahoes were eager to take to the warpath, and they vainly solicited Friday to join them. Minor depredations occurred from time to time, and on June 12, 1864, the Cheyennes, aided by small bands of other tribes, began a series of massacres. The war fever rapidly spread among the savages and the white settlers, in terror, sought refuge in the forts or in Denver.

It was about this time that some of the hostile Cheyennes set up their tepees along the Cache la Poudre. Incensed at the refusal of Friday and his followers to make war on the whites, the Cheyennes taunted them with being squaw men and cowards. One of them went so far as to ask Friday, in a sneering tone, if he had a single fighting man in his band. The taunt enraged young Bill Friday, who shot the Cheyenne dead, and then fearing that his act would get his father into trouble, fled north with his three squaws. Later, in the hope that the episode had been forgotten, he started to return, but was overtaken by the Pawnees, who killed him, cut off his head and set it up on a pole.[12]

Friday, with his small following, was usually, during these turbulent times, about Fort Collins. At Latham, a transient town and station on Ben Holladay's stage line, he became acquainted with the station-keeper, Frank A. Root, later the co-author, with William E. Connelley, of *The Overland Stage*. They had several long talks. Friday was "a remarkably quiet and evidently an intelligent Indian," says Root, and he appeared devotedly attached to the whites. His English may have deteriorated in the twenty years

---

12 Watrous, 91.

since Sage and Talbot talked with him, for Root concedes no more than that "he could speak the English language so as to be quite easily understood." As to his character there is nothing but praise. "I regarded [him]," writes Root, "as one of the best and most trustworthy Indians I ever became acquainted with."[13]

In midwinter the plains Sioux began a series of bloody raids, and for a time, despite the untiring efforts of the military, the frontier was again ravaged. Friday maintained his unflinching loyalty to the whites, and though his influence among his people had greatly declined, his friendship was gratefully recognized. He was in Denver in the midsummer of 1865, and in the *Rocky Mountain News* of July 8 appears this tribute:

Friday declares that he knows the whites mean to be friendly with all Indians who behave themselves and not be fools, and after their kindness to him he will never join their enemies. Friday's loyalty is thus in the trying hour proved beyond question. For his services in times past he deserves the grateful acknowledgments of the people of Colorado and of the Government.

The fall of the year found most of the plains Sioux, the Northern Cheyennes and the Northern Arapahoes pushed back into the upper part of what is now Wyoming. Friday, with a small band, lingered about the Cache la Poudre. By May 1869, however, he had thrown in his lot with the Northern Arapahoes, under Medicine Man, who is said to have had a following of some 900 warriors. His position from then on was one of extreme difficulty, for his tribe, though professing peace, kept up an intermittent warfare on the whites for the next six or seven years. All that we learn of Friday indicates that he steadfastly counseled peace with the whites and that he never took part in any of his tribesmen's depredations. On October 8, 1869, he

---

[13] F. A. Root and W. E. Connelley, *The Overland Stage to California* (Topeka, 1901), 347–48.

was one of several Arapaho chiefs who visited Governor J. A. Campbell, of the newly created Territory of Wyoming, with the proposal that his tribe be settled on the Wind River reservation, which had recently been established for the Shoshones. The Governor favored the plan, but when it was submitted to Washakie, the noble-hearted chief of that tribe, it met with a stern disapproval. Friday was a good man, said Washakie, whom he remembered as a friend of his youth, but the Arapahoes as a whole were an untruthful, a treacherous, and a trouble-making people, and he did not want them around.

Nevertheless, the negotiations continued, and by the last of January 1870, Washakie had given a reluctant consent to a temporary occupation of a part of his reservation. The Arapahoes at once moved in. They had committed a number of depredations in the previous summer, and were no sooner settled than they started in again. Friday strove to keep them at peace, but in vain. He was in their main camp on the Wind River on the night of March 30, 1870, when it was visited by Captain Henry G. Nickerson, intent upon learning the Indians' plans. Most of the warriors had already left on a fresh raid, which was to result in further massacres on the following day, and those in the camp received Nickerson with angry denunciations and threats to kill him. "It was only," he wrote twelve years later, "through the untiring and strategic efforts of Friday, a sub-chief . . . whom I had befriended while in Miner's Delight when he had lost his horse and frozen his feet, that I made my escape."[14]

After these massacres they left the reservation and camped about the country north of Fort Casper, on the North Platte. Friday, who seems to have been a restless traveler, then took a jaunt into what is now northeastern Montana, doubtless to visit those turbulent cousins of the

---

[14] *Collections of the Wyoming Historical Society*, I, 181–82.

Arapahoes, the Gros Ventres. Peter Koch, the Montana pioneer, tells of talking with him in August 1870, at Fort Musselshell, on the upper Missouri. He had with him a party of twenty-four Arapaho men and nine women. Koch writes of him as a chief and says that he "spoke English well." Two weeks later the party was again at the fort, on its way home.[15] The Arapahoes, under their bellicose head-chief, Black Coal, from time to time continued their depredations, in spite of the settlers and the military; and it was not until what is known as the Bates Battle of July 4, 1874, in the Owl Creek Mountains, at the head of the Powder River, that they were sufficiently humbled to realize the advantages of peace.

Some of them took part in the Indian War of 1876. The war ended with the main part of the tribesmen gathered at the Red Cloud Agency near Fort Robinson, Nebraska. In October 1877, the Government obtained permission of Washakie to settle them temporarily near the Wind River reservation, whereupon they were at once taken by military escort to one of their old camping grounds north of Fort Casper. Friday was among them. Major Henry W. Daly, who accompanied the expedition and had several talks with him, writes that he talked English "like a college student."[16] By April 1878, most of the tribe had, in accordance with the Government's wishes but against the will of Washakie, entered the reservation. The others followed, and there the tribe has remained to this day. For what is deemed an unwarranted intrusion the Shoshones demanded of the Government several millions of dollars.

Friday, who for some years had been a Government interpreter, continued to make his home with them and to serve in that capacity. Though a warrior chief, he was never to be the head chieftain. His independent tribe had long

---

[15] *The Frontier* (Missoula, Mont.), January 1929, 156–57.
[16] Henry W. Daly, in *The American Legion Monthly,* April 1927.

before been merged into the tribe led by Medicine Man. Black Coal had followed, with Sharp Nose as his chief lieutenant. Among a people so generally hostile Friday's friendship for the whites must have been an insurmountable obstacle to the attainment of the supreme honor.

It is not a pleasing picture of Friday that is given by Lieutenant H. R. Lemly, who visited the Arapahoes, probably in 1878. "At fifty," writes Lemly, "he had relapsed into barbarism. He had forgotten how to read and write, possessed as many squaws as fingers and was a pander of the vilest description. His knowledge of English facilitated the practice of this vocation at the agency and military posts, and procured him employment as official interpreter, in which capacity he accompanied me."[17] As to part of the characterization, at least, Lemly was doubtless wrong, for the report of Agent Charles Hatton, in announcing the death of Friday, only three years later, mentions but a single widow and speaks of him with respect as one who had rendered almost invaluable aid in the many activities of the agency. Friday, as we know, was a full-blooded Indian. Except that he would take no part in any act of violence against the whites, he had an Indian's standards of morality, and is to be so judged. And the Arapahoes did not have the reputation for chastity that the Cheyennes enjoyed. If it be true that he was a pander — an assertion nowhere confirmed — those who paid him for the service must have been white men — and between agent and employer in such a transaction there can be little distinction of guilt.

Friday died of heart disease, after a few days' illness, on May 13, 1881, at the probable age of 56 years. His loss was deeply felt at the agency, for he was the most useful Arapaho on the reservation. He was the only one who could speak English, and there was at hand no other English-

---

[17] H. R. Lemly, in *Harper's Magazine*, March 1880, 494.

speaking person who could speak Arapaho. In his long career he had borne a man's part in endeavoring to preserve peace between red men and white. The kindness of Thomas Fitzpatrick in rescuing and caring for a forlorn waif had been repaid by a lifetime of loyalty to the whites, maintained at times amid infinite difficulties and at the cost of an honor no Indian warrior ever disdained — the supreme headship of his people.

Appendix B

MAJOR FITZPATRICK
The Discoverer of the South Pass!

By SOLITAIRE[18]

THE GROWING IMPORTANCE of that great highway to the Pacific, the South Pass, has naturally led to the inquiry, who was the white man whose footsteps first awoke an echo on this dividing ridge of the American continent? The credit of its discovery has been claimed — in a quiet way — by several, and of late, in a lecture delivered in this city, has been attributed to Gen. Ashley, a deceased citizen of St. Louis. The gentleman who named Gen. A. has been wrongly informed; to none of those heretofore publicly named does this honor belong — and, for the guidance of the future historian of the west, we deem it but justice to state, while the witnesses are still living to confirm the assertion, that Major Fitzpatrick, in the year 1824, led through the South Pass the first band of white men who ever crossed that route to the Pacific slope. We do not consider our assertion at all questionable, for witnesses of the fact are at present living a few miles from Saint Louis; and

---

[18] "Solitaire" was the pseudonym of John S. Robb. This article was published in the *Weekly Reveille* of St. Louis on March 1, 1847.

in the mountains, among the traders and trappers, the Major's celebrated expedition to the Crow country in the year above named, his subsequent discovery of the pass, and the trapping grounds of Green River, are matters of notoriety.

After the disastrous expedition under Gen. Ashley, in 1823, when his trapping party was attacked by the Rickarees, Maj. Fitzpatrick and his partner, Jedediah S. Smith, who was afterwards killed on the Cimarone, procured an outfit of goods from the General, and started with sixteen men on a trapping and trading expedition to the Crow country. William L. Sublette, formerly of this ctiy, who recently died while on way on business to Washington city was one of the party. While on their route, upon one of the tributaries of Powder river, Mr. Smith was attacked and seriously injured by a grizzly bear, and the company was forced to leave him behind, in the care of two men, in a very hostile country. In a few days after their departure, Col. Keemle, the senior editor of this paper, then acting agent of the Missouri Fur Company, at the head of another trapping party, fell in with Smith and his companions, and accompanied them to the village of a roving band of Cheyennes, where Fitzpatrick's company again joined Smith, and, taking him along, they proceeded to the Big Horn, thence on to the waters of the Yellow Stone, where they wintered with the Crow nation. While among the Crows the Major learned from a chief that a pass existed in the Wind river mountains, through which he could easily take his whole band upon streams on the other side. He also represented beaver so abundant upon these rivers that traps were unnecessary to catch them — they could club as many as they desired. Having ascertained its locality, as near as the Indian chief could describe it, he started with the greater portion of his band, leaving behind him in the Crow country, upon Wind river, his worn down horses and mules, in the care of Smith and a few hands, and with the best of pack animals moved forward on this expedition of discovery. After laborious travel and hardship through the winter snows of that elevated region, they were gratified by reaching this important highway, through which the Major led his troop of pioneers down upon the Big Sandy, and thence to Green river — thus marshalling the way for that tide of emigration which now is treading towards a new land once thought unapproachable from this side of the Rocky Mountains.

Their visit to Green river and its tributaries was attended with marked success; beaver were plenty, and they were soon rewarded for their toil. One night, while engaged upon these streams trapping, a party of Snake Indians ran off every horse and mule belonging to their party. This, at such a distance from headquarters, was a great calamity; but they, nevertheless, continued their labors until a sufficient quantity of furs had been realized to warrant a trip home, when Fitzpatrick concluded it was time to hunt their animals. After an expedition — one of the most daring ever attempted in the mountains — they recovered their animals from the Indians, and, travelling night and day to get beyond pursuit, they reached their trapping grounds, packed their beaver, and started homeward through the Pass.

At a rendezvous upon the Sweet Water, agreed upon before setting out, they met Smith, and here the Major had skin boats constructed, in which he descended that stream. He was the first white man who ever navigated its waters. Entering the Platte they ran into the Canon, between the Sweet Water and Goat Island; and at the same spot where Capt. Fremont lost his instruments by the upsetting of his Indian rubber boat, Fitzpatrick, after all his hardship and adventure, lost the greater part of his furs. By great exertions in swimming and diving in the stream, they recovered sufficient to pay off their liabilities to Gen. Ashley for the

THOMAS FITZPATRICK GRAVE MARKER
In the Congressional Cemetery, Washington, D.C.

outfit purchased from him. The Major cached the furs he saved near where he encountered the disaster, and, proceeding from thence to Council Bluffs procured horses, returned, and brought in his stock of beaver.

Gen. Ashley, at this period, was in St. Louis, where he received a letter from Fitzpatrick, relating to him the discovery of the South Pass, their successes in trapping on the newly found streams, and their disasters. In that letter the Major stated that the new route would easily admit of the passage of wagons; but little did he dream then that he himself, twenty years after, would encamp in that same passage with the first train of American emigrants destined to the new land beyond, and who were not only carrying along their wagons, but all the household necessaries for furnishing their new homes! Such, however, in the course

341

of human events, became also a portion of western history.

Gen Ashley realized a fortune through Major Fitzpatrick's discoveries, for it opened to him one of the most valuable sources for obtaining furs ever discovered in that region. We wish we could say as much for the discoverer — at least, we will not passively see him lose the credit of what, at this day, is rightly considered a great achievement. Many of the streams and remarkable places through that portion of the country owe the preservation of their Indian names to the Major; for on his expeditions he always persisted in retaining them in preference to new titles, and by those names they are now known. Some of them have been translated into English, but the Indian meaning is still retained.

The natural diffidence and modesty of this veteran mountaineer has permitted many erroneous statements in regard to that country to remain uncontradicted; and, indeed, except as matters of information to his friends, he has attached but little importance to his discoveries; but no misstatement should be allowed to remain uncontradicted which appropriates to another the hard-earned laurels of this old Pioneer!

Appendix C

Will of Thomas Fitzpatrick

IN THE NAME OF GOD AMEN. I Thomas Fitzpatrick of the State of Missouri and the town of Westport being of sound and disposing mind and considering the uncertainty of death do make and constitute this my last Will and Testament, hereby revoking all former Wills or codicils — and dispose of my property as follows towit. First I will and bequeath to my wife Margaret Fitzpatrick the one third part of all my estate real and personal after my lawful debts shall have been first paid, and also the one third part of any property that may come to me before my death of what kind soever. Second — To my child Andrew Jackson Fitzpatric I will and bequeath all the residue and balance of my estate, but upon this condition however that if my wife shall give birth to a child before my death or within nine months thereafter then the residue of my said estate shall be divided equally between said children that is to say between the said Andrew Jackson Fitzpatric and the child or children so born.

In Testimony Whereof I have hereunto set my hand, and affixed my seal this twentieth day of June A.D. Eighteen Hundred and Fifty Three.

John Campbell ⎫ Witnesses   Thomas Fitzpatrick (Seal)
B. Gratz Brown ⎭

I do further make this codicil to my last will and testament that is to say I do hereby appoint Robert Campbell of the City of Saint

Louis & State of Missouri and Albert G. Boone of the town of Westport and the same state as Executors to this my will and request that
they will act in that capacity.

June 20, 1853

John Campbell } Witnesses   Thomas Fitzpatrick (Seal)
B. Gratz Brown

State of Missouri
County of St. Louis

Be it remembered that on this twentieth day of February in the
year of our Lord one thousand eight hundred and fifty four before
me Peter Ferguson Judge of the Probate of the County of Saint
Louis personally appeared Benjamin Gratz Brown, who being by
me duly sworn on his oath saith — I was present and saw Thomas
Fitzpatrick the testator subscribe his name to the foregoing instrument and the codicil thereto and heard him publish and declare
the same to be his last will and testament — I subscribed my name
as a witness thereto as did John Campbell in the presence of the
testator — the said John Campbell was also present at the time of
the publication of said will by said testator and at the time of publishing and executing said will he the testator was of sound and disposing mind to the best of my knowledge and belief.

B. Gratz Brown

Sworn to and subscribed before me this 20th
day of February 1854

Peter Ferguson
Judge of Probate

I Peter Ferguson Judge of Probate of the County of St. Louis having examined the preceding instrument in writing purporting to be
the last will and testament of Thomas Fitzpatrick and a codicil
thereto and the testimony of Benjamin Gratz Brown a subscribing
witness to the same consider, that said instruments are duly proved
to be the last will and testament of said Thomas Fitzpatrick deceased — In Testimony whereof I hereto set my hand at the County
aforesaid this twenty third day of February in the Year of our Lord
one thousand eight hundred and fifty four

Peter Ferguson Judge of Probate

(Probate Files 4151).

NOTES ON THE WILL

The inventory of Thomas Fitzpatrick's estate showed:

Cash on deposit with R. Campbell	$10,056.15
" owned by him at time of his decease,	15.85
Note of S. F. & R. Scott	212.73
" " " "	23.13
" Mrs. Digby	40.00
Two lots and too small houses	
1 Walnut wardrobe	
1 Liquor case	
	$10,347.86

James E. Yeatman and Kenneth Mackenzie were sureties on Robert Campbell's bond.

Robert Campbell was curator for Andrew Jackson and Virginia, son and daughter of Thomas Fitzpatrick.

Among the papers in the files are:

Bill from Albert G. Boone for "Expense of bringing two Ponies from Pottowattomie Mission to West Port by direction of R. Campbell, Executor	$ 5.00
For keeping same in West Port previous to sale	6.85
" Auctioneers fees selling two Ponies	2.00
" Magistrates fees in appraisement of furniture,	.50
" " " " " " ponies	.50
	14.85

Bill from Brown's Hotel, Washington, D.C.:

From Jany 4 to Feb 8, 1854. To Board 35 days $3.	105.
Sundries, Washing, fuel &c &c	24.50
	129.50

On June 21, 1854, at Westport, Margaret Fitzpatrick gave receipt for money received from Robert Campbell, also numerous other receipts until January 1856. On April 8, 1856, she signed herself Margaret Wilmott. L. J. Wilmott, her second husband, also signed.

Index